Ethnologia Europaea

Journal of European Ethnology

Volume 48:1
2018

Special issue: Practices of Resistance

Edited by Jutta Lauth Bacas and Marion Näser-Lather

GU00690713

MUSEUM TUSCULANUM PRESS

Copyright © 2018	Ethnologia Europaea, Copenhagen
Printed	in Sweden by Exakta Print AB, Malmö 2018
Cover and layout	Pernille Sys Hansen, Damp Design
Cover photo	"Solidarity in Athens" by Jutta Lauth Bacas
	ISBN 978 87 635 4626 3
	ISSN 0425 4597

This journal is published with the support of the Nordic Board
for Periodicals in the Humanities and Social Sciences.

Ethnologia Europaea is an official journal of Société Internationale
d'Ethnologie et de Folklore (SIEF).

sief

Museum Tusculanum Press
Dantes Plads 1
DK-1556 Copenhagen V
Denmark
www.mtp.dk

CONTENTS

PLURALITY OF RESISTANCE AND CHANGES IN THE MEDITERRANEAN REGION
An Introductory Discussion on Differences and Similarities of Protest Practices

Jutta Lauth Bacas, University of Malta
Marion Näser-Lather, University of Marburg

In the European countries next to the Mediterranean Sea, we presently observe not only the manifold effects of austerity policies but also significant political and social changes triggered by the (economic) crisis since 2008. In many of these countries, we perceive new forms of social practices of networking, leading to growing opposition and protest articulated by local communities or by social movements, which are based on common acts of solidarity, co-operation and the establishment of (close) personal relationships. Many of these forms of protest do not seem to be characterized by typical and well-known political ideologies or trade unions' demands (cf. Žižek 2012). Instead new practices develop, such as the (re)appropriation of public space, networking, alternative ways of protesting (such as in the case of Occupy or the Indignados[1]), and sharing, inspired by concepts of grassroots-democracy, solidarity, and anti-consumerism (see, e.g., Corredera 2012; Fernández-Savater 2012). These movements can be understood as newcomers in the political arena of many Southern European countries, since they see themselves in a distinct opposition to the established – often clientelistic – political structures of their societies.

The present special issue of *Ethnologia Europaea* focuses on these emerging collaborative protest practices in Mediterranean countries, which are related to or can be seen as effects of the ongoing economic crisis. Building on the assumption that the Mediterranean can be understood as a common frame of reference for comparative research and analysis (Kavanagh & Lauth Bacas 2011), six case studies are presented, which – based on in-depth fieldwork and participant observation – reflect collaborative interactions as practices of resistance and social or political change within new protest groups, solidarity initiatives and cultural projects related to specific local conflicts that have arisen in the wake of the crisis.

In this introduction to the special issue, we will first present the basic analytical concepts referred to in the title of this volume: a heuristic definition of the concept of *resistance* as well as our understanding of *the Mediterranean* as a comparative framework for anthropological study and analysis. Second, we introduce the six ethnological and anthropological case studies. Based on ethnographic research in France, Italy, Slovenia and Greece, they address the social practices of networking and close collaboration in the context of social change or political activism since 2008. In a third and fourth step, we investigate the differences and the similarities of these new Mediterranean protest movements alongside the following questions: First, which different visions and differing resistance practices are developed and collectively applied to accomplish political goals? And second, are there any similarities between the social movements and initiatives presented here, which can be related to "the Mediterranean" as a common frame of action and reference?

Concepts of Resistance and "the Mediterranean" – a Heuristic Approach

The Oxford English Dictionary defines "resistance" as the refusal to accept or to comply with something. This starting point allows for an understanding of resistance in relational arrangements of symbolic and social power relations, in which social actors oppose something they see as unjust or unfair. In contrast to social "protest", which is characterized by its being an event, by the collectivity of the actors (Thiele 1992), by its being public and by the existence of social or political causes, practices of resistance can be more continuous. They can also be expressed in symbolic acts or subcultural rituals (Hall & Jefferson 1976), or can be less visible and more hidden (Scott 1985, cf. below) and not necessarily connected with a political goal or concrete demands. At the same time, resistance is distinguished from protest in that it not only means the voicing of dissent, but also undertaking concrete actions for change. Finally, while public protest often becomes professionalized in the course of the development of a social movement (Rammstedt 1978), resistance is less likely to be. Of course, the distinction between the two concepts may be blurred when applied to concrete case studies.

Inspired by James Scott (1985), Stellan Vinthagen and Anna Johansson (2013) distinguish between the following types of resistance: first, publicly declared resistance (e.g. revolts, petitions, demonstrations, or invasions), which may appear amongst others in the form of counter-ideologies; second, disguised resistance which is characterized by its low profile, being held secret, or happening from within the accordant system. This disguised form can exist as everyday resistance (e.g. poaching, squatting, desertion, evasion), composed of direct resistance by disguised resisters, hidden expressions of anger or dissident subcultures. Everyday resistance thus is characterized by individual as well as collective actions that are not organized, formal or necessarily public or intentionally political. It is this latter type of everyday resistance that is of particular importance for the approach of this themed issue. Diverging from the original understanding of "civil resistance" as mass movements (see Ortner 1995: 174), for the analysis of our case studies we focus on small-scale or micro-level forms of resistance[2] by local actors, especially on concepts of everyday resistance such as brought into focus by James Scott (1985, 1989, 1990) and described, for example, by Gary Marx (2009). In a theoretical meta-analysis, Jocelyn Hollander and Rachel Einwohner (2004) have highlighted some kind of action and a sense of opposition as central for definitions of resistance. Action is in this case defined as active behaviour which opposes opponents or ideas perceived as being unjust or unfair. This distinction will be important for our argument in the following, as we discuss the contributions to this issue by comparing the *how* and *against whom*.

In a next step, we would like to reflect on the concept of "the Mediterranean" and its analytical relevance for our comparative approach. Stereotypes about the Mediterranean way of life are widespread, for example the *dolce far niente* (sweet doing nothing), and the Mediterranean, patriarchal man who is characterized by familism, sensuality, hospitality, but on the other hand also by his unpredictability and violent behaviour. Not only have they been produced by the tourism industry, the media and fictional products of pop culture such as films or TV-shows, but also by early anthropological Mediterranean Studies of the 1960s and 1970s (see for example Peristiany 1963; cf. Driessen 2001: 15, 21). The tendency was to conceptualize the area of the Mediterranean's littoral states as a more or less culturally homogeneous unit, imagined as persisting until the present (the 1960s) or at least as having existed until very recently. Georg Stauth and Marcus Otto (2008: 20) argue that this imagery of the Mediterranean's origins always have implied the notion of a lost unity.

However, since the 1980s, the supposed "unity of the Mediterranean area" has been increasingly contested, deconstructed and criticized as culturalist, orientalist and stereotypical (Herzfeld 1984; Llobera 1986; Pina-Cabral 1989; Giordano 1990). Although basic categories such as honour and shame have been questioned and deconstructed (Herzfeld 1984; Dir 2005: 8, 22), the term Mediterranean is nevertheless used in an on-going process of categorization, as Henk Driessen has pointed out (2001: 15). Within current Mediterranean Studies, the Mediterranean is clearly no longer understood as a homogeneous space of traditional ways of life or traditional attitudes. Today, ethnologists and social anthropologists working in the region are convinced that an unreflexive concept of a "Mediterranean culture area" merely reinforces stereotypes. Thus, another concept of "the Mediterraneans" (in the plural) has been introduced (Abulafia 2005; Greverus & Welz 2001), with the aim of departing from the theoretical perspective of the Circum-Mediterranean area as an all-encompassing entity and, in its place, referring to the multiple realities of the region. This acknowledgment of the de facto pluralization of cultural practices and discourses in Southern Europe is a relevant starting point for our comparative approach and analysis, too.

On the other hand, the unforeseen persistence of certain cultural patterns, to which Klaus Schönberger (2015) recently pointed, prompts anthropologists to reflect carefully on their analytical tools. Lidia Sciama (2013) and Paola Sacchi and Pier Paolo Viazzo (2014), for instance, have argued that a more reflexive understanding of honour and shame can prove valuable for empirical and historical research within different Mediterranean societies. Sciama (2013) stresses the complexity of the relationships between people in the Mediterranean, which makes it problematic to categorize the accordant countries as a unified cultural region, but she nevertheless finds overlapping regional realities. Goddard, Llobera and Shore propose to make the concept of "the Mediterranean" productive by widening the analysis beyond old terms and concepts: gender and kinship should be related to personhood and seen within the context of civil society; likewise, focus should be on Europe instead of being on the Mediterranean only (Goddard et al. 1994: 86).

William Kavanagh and Jutta Lauth Bacas (2011) also propose a non-essentialist research approach to the littoral countries of the Mediterranean, arguing that socio-cultural differentiations have to be taken into account. Thus, the Mediterranean space can be seen as a patchwork of interrelated regions and micro-regions as well as a relevant base of reference for regional comparisons. This understanding of the Mediterranean as a frame encompassing a patchwork of different regions and pluralized cultural practices opens up comparative approaches also presented in this special issue. Therefore, a reflexive reevaluation, a de-essentialization and a recontextualization of the basic categories of Mediterranean Studies – honour, patronage, familism[3] – can still be used as approaches for a better understanding of changing conditions within the multiple realities of the Mediterranean (Lauth Bacas 2013: 224). In the closing part of our introduction, we will discuss whether this reflexive concept of the Mediterranean can be applied on current protest movements, too. In comparing the protest movements, our aim in this special issue is to provide a deeper understanding of how protest and practices of resistance are contextualized, how they make use of localized social and cultural resources and achieve complexity in local response to austerity and neoliberal state politics.

Current Practices of Resistance and Social Change in the Mediterranean: Six Case Studies

The ethnological and anthropological case studies included in this special issue portray six different protest groups and their actors, their visions and goals and the forms of their social action and resistance practices as engaged responses to crisis situations in different countries next to the Mediterranean. The issue starts out with a new type of digital resistance developed in a harbour district of Marseille, moves on to urban gardening in Ljubljana as an everyday form of resistance, and continues with a spotlight on Genuino Clandestino, a network of small-scale farmers in Italy. Three vivid protest movements against austerity politics are presented, which are all staged in crisis-driven Greece: two case studies investigate solidarity networks in urban contexts (Athens and Volos), and one study investigates the urban-rural nexus and rural solidarity networks on the Peloponnese peninsula.

In his paper, the anthropologist Philip Cartelli describes a media-based protest against the commodification of the Panier, a historic harbour-district of Marseille, and against the orchestration of Marseille as a Mediterranean port city, through the web documentary project of the Tabasco video collective "Et le Panier dans tout ça?" (And what about the Panier?). The project functions as digital resistance, creating a counter-public and giving a voice to residents, the marginalized, ethnic minorities, and to working-class perspectives regarding the metamorphosis of their quarter. While the Tabasco video project was supported by the cultural institutions that undertook the urban renewal project of the Panier – the MuCEM and the Villa Méditerranée administration – it questions the positive role of these institutions, showing for example that the concept of the Mediterranean is quasi only employed by the institutions promoting it and contrasting this fact with the strong local identity of the quarter's inhabitants. The video documentary points to the eviction of citizens and marginalized groups in the course of the redevelopment of the Panier, such as people who publicly drink alcohol, recreational swimmers, and fishermen. The documentary also shows the emergence of practices of resistance, such as swimming there and climbing the representative buildings despite the presence of security guards. As Cartelli points out, in France there has not been a huge anti-austerity movement such as in Spain or Greece. In Marseille, a protest rather manifests itself in form of everyday discourse. In this context, Cartelli interprets the Tabasco video project and the accordant workshops as a form of political action. As Adriana de Souza e Silva (2006) has pointed out, the use of digital media can lead to a reconfiguration of social space facilitating networking and the exchange of information between social actors facing similar problems.[4]

Practices of everyday resistance are also the topic of Saša Poljak Istenič, a social anthropologist, in her analysis of urban gardening in Ljubljana, which she interprets as a practice opposing the growing neoliberal market economy. She points out to the ambiguity of these protest practices, which at the same time contribute to market and advertisement logics promoting the city as a "European Green Capital". Poljak Istenič shows that in the case of the Slovenian capital, urban gardening as a form of protest combines the nostalgic reinvocation of socialist ideas and neoliberal practices. Analysing two strategies of resistance – horizontal, leaderless anarchist initiatives with guerrilla tactics of occupying and squatting and creative communities of mainstream culture – Poljak Istenič comes to the conclusion that only the anarchist initiatives are not incorporated into mainstream discourse while the creative groups are. Using the example of the Zadruga Urbana, Poljak Istenič shows this group's aim to create a utopian non-hierarchic, non-commercial society of equality and solidarity on the basis of a shared economy. The initiative produces food sustainably, transforms places into collective gardens, conducts public dinners and organizes alternative non-profit markets. The gardens also serve as manifestations of critique against consumption as predominant practice and the capitalist management and commodification of urban places.

Poljak Istenič hints at ambiguities and ambivalences of the local protest movement Zadruga Urbana, which was not successful insofar as it did not lead to a changing of the rules of the city regarding the temporary use of gardens. However, the participation in ecological projects and alternative markets has strengthened participants, given them agency and a sense of community and connected them as equals, changing power relations. By producing food in a way that assumes other parameters – leaning on solidarity and reciprocity, undermining austerity economy and constructing relationships of personal trust in the intimate social environment – control over the participants' own lives is partially reestablished, which Poljak Istenič interprets as a potential of resistance. At the same time, grassroots activities fulfil gaps created by austerity measures, and the positive alternative futures that they create to protest against the neoliberal system (e.g. self-management of public spaces, participatory decision-making, horizontal cooperation, production of local food etc.) become incorporated into dominant urban policies.

The importance of personal trust is stressed by an initiative showing some similarities to Ljubljana's urban gardening movement: the network Genuino Clandestino in Italy, which has been researched by ethnologist Alexander Koensler. Genuino Clandestino is a network of small-scale farmers, who produce ecological food and oppose bureaucratic EU-regulations imposed on their production process in the name of transparency, food safety or environmental protection. According to the viewpoint of Genuino Clandestino members, the EU-regulations de facto erode informal personal relations and favour large industrial productions, thus fostering a continuous transformation of farming into global agribusiness. Genuino Clandestino sees its network as based not on impersonal rules of the Brussels bureaucracy, but on personal trust. Members sell their products on informal markets, in squatted social centres and during alternative festivals. The movement has established an alternative system of self-certification reinventing the modes to certify in more democratic and inclusive ways. In a first wave of experiments, producers would exhibit statements describing the way in which they produced their products. In a second wave, many groups of Genuino Clandestino considered the need to develop more sophisticated alternative certification principles, with evolving definitions ranging from "participatory self-certifications" to "participatory guarantees". Thus, the movement shows evolving modes of the governance of transparency and the possibilities for opposing and reinventing them, based on personal trust.

Trust is of special relevance in the context of the Greek crisis, as citizens' *distrust* in state institutions and in national politicians had risen to a peak level after the introduction of far-reaching austerity measures. To briefly recall their history: After the signing of the first Memorandum in 2010, the Greek government decided to implement a neoliberal readjustment programme by raising taxes and cutting wages, salaries and pensions. As a result, most private households in Greece had to pay the price of neoliberal reforms; they had to cope with less income and higher taxes as well as higher everyday expenses. Not surprisingly, next to strikes and demonstrations, a large number of local protest movements mushroomed all over the country, which also triggered the interest of researchers. Three pieces of this new research on recent Greek social movements are included in our special issue.

Starting with fieldwork in 2014, anthropologist Andreas Streinzer investigates a local solidarity network in Volos, a port city in Thessaly situated midway between Athens and Thessaloniki. To cope with declining cash income, a group of citizens in Volos developed a Local Exchange and Trading System (a so-called LETS). Its members exchange household services and goods for private consumption between each other, which are internally assessed and calculated in a complementary currency, the so-called TEM. By participating in this Volos-based exchange and trading system, its members intended to practically enact their resistance to austerity policies imposed by the Troika and to eurozone capitalism as a whole. By invoking notions of solidarity as a guiding principle for their actions, the LETS founders in Volos aim at building a new form of relational arrangement that would allow them to enact economic relations otherwise than how they are enacted under the prevailing (euro) economy. Resistance, in this case, is a feature of social practice that takes an oppositional stance towards hegemonic practices or groups. By now (five years after its inauguration), the Volos-based TEM has developed into the largest complementary currency in Greece in terms of membership and turnover.

Anthropologist Monia Cappuccini investigates the Greek capital of Athens as another relevant hub for developing strategies against austerity policies. Researching two social movements, the Syntagma Square movement and the Social Solidarity Network of Exarchia, Cappuccini studies the interactions and impacts of grassroots mobilizations as resistant practises in response to the economic crisis. Starting from an interest in the occupation of the Syntagma Square as a social protest in an urban public space, Cappuccini turns to the inner urban neighbourhood of Exarchia, attempting to portray how this "resistance identity" has developed and transformed into a more "everyday practice". As Cappuccini's data show, her interlocutors chose to take action against neoliberal strategies in small-scale and well-connected solidarity networks; its members became active in order to prevent that private households had their electricity supply cut off as a consequence for not paying the E.N.F.I.A, a newly established real-estate tax (referred to by many Greeks as "charatsi"). For their form of localized protest, a fast response based on close communication (via mobile phones) and mutual trust and reliability is essential; every time the state-owned Electricity Company DEI sends out its employees to cut off the electricity supply of a flat in Exarchia, Social Solidarity Network members set up a picket line in front of the house to prevent the personnel from cutting off the electricity. This model of protest is working – the solidarity movement has successfully prevented many power cuts since 2012.

Studying rural solidarity networks in Greece, James Verinis argues that because of or despite the lack of institutional support frameworks, local farmers affected by the Greek crisis have found ways and new forms of coping and collaborating on their own terms. In his research in the Laconia district of the Peloponnese peninsula, Verinis investigates newly emerging forms of solidarity between Greek farmers and non-Greeks (Albanians most notably) who have become landowning farmers in the past decade. As his ethnographic findings show, rural families and local business-owners in the periphery of Greece are presently extending their social networks and incorporating non-Greeks into their personal and professional lives by, for example, becoming godparents of immigrant children and also by selling local non-Greeks portions of their farmland – as opposed to absentee Greek landlords. By doing so, they aim at establishing sustainable face-to-face networks on local terms. These solidarity networks are based on local concepts, seen by the actors as forms of reliance on kin networks, neighbourhood, or the village. This reconfiguration of social relations between Greek farmers and Albanian immigrants through arrangements of reliance on "each other" is considered by Verinis as novel in the agricultural landscape of the Peloponnese peninsula with transformative potential in the context of an encompassing economic crisis.

The Plurality of Resistance Practices and Meanings

As stated above, in contrast to public protest as an event, practices of resistance are more continuous and more polymorphous in their appearance: taking place in a broad spectrum of everyday to more organized collective actions, expressing opposition in more symbolic or hidden to more direct or open ways, being more or less recognized by the powerful (see also Hollander & Einwohner 2004).

Starting from this recognition of the potential variety of acts of resistance, we now move on to a discussion of the six case studies included in this special issue, not to construct a typology, but to evaluate the examples from France, Slovenia, Italy and Greece as case studies providing different information in their own right. In comparing these cases through an anthropological lens, we recognize a number of differences between these protest movements and their localized practices of resistance, thus spelling out the many meanings of resistance and the plurality of resistance practices in varying Mediterranean contexts. The above-mentioned multiple realities of the Mediterranean region (cf. Greverus & Welz 2001) are characteristic for the social movements of the region, too: Social protest and practices of resistance are always related to their specific historical and regional contexts. They make use of contextualized social and cultural resources and achieve an impact by locally responding to austerity and neoliberal politics.

One might ask why the Slovenian case study should be seen as belonging to the Mediterranean region, given the fact that Slovenia only possesses some kilometres of coastline bordering the Mediterranean Sea. In the course of the preparation of this special issue, Saša Poljak Istenič herself reflected on this issue. In a note to the guest editors, Poljak Istenič argued that, while only a few Slovenian anthropologists have engaged in research reflecting "the Mediterranean" framework (cf. Brumen 2000; Baskar 2002), the city of Ljubljana, Slovenia's capital, in their public relations communication occasionally refer to "the Mediterranean".

We can see that within the researched movements, change is related mainly to modifying *local* life worlds and conditions through practices of empowerment and participation or mutual cooperation. With regard to the practices deployed to accomplish their goals, the cases demonstrate an impressive variety of offline- as well as online-practices of resistance by activists, which include on-the-spot actions like the formation of picket lines, middle-term actions like urban gardening and squatting – leading to long-term actions documenting and publishing oppositional world views, such as video activism. This categorization is made mainly for heuristic reasons: in reality, strategies and practices of resistance can have overlapping effects. For example, the activity of a group of citizens in Exarchia, Athens, who occupy the entrance of a flat and prevent state employees from cutting off the electricity supply has a short-term effect: the tenants staying there are able to use their electric devices despite their (due to austerity measures) unpaid bills. The middle-term effect is public protest articulated in media; the long-term effect can be seen in the punctual boycott of state measures introduced to the Greek public sector in accordance with the neoliberal demands of the Troika.

Klaus Schönberger and Ove Sutter have differentiated protest practices into actions which appeal, actions which mobilize, actions which inform and actions which provoke (Schönberger & Sutter 2009: 20–22). In contrast to such forms of protest striving above all for mobilization and third-party-effects, the practices of resistance observed in the case studies presented in this issue mostly aim for particular changes in the lives of the participants and can be, thus, related to everyday resistance. An exception is

Cartelli's example of video activism, which points to the creation of counter-spaces as resistance to commodification. In the case of the urban gardening practices in Ljubljana, activists do both: creating a counter-public and, at the same time, improving their living conditions by harvesting their own, organic food. According to Henri Lefebvre (1996), especially marginalized people construct counter-spaces in which they strive to maintain their attachment to particular localities and assert their right to determine the activities that go on in particular spaces. Counter-spaces, Lefebvre implies, are necessary spaces of concrete personal relations, as they are in part a protest against the abstraction imposed by authorities as part of their arsenal of social control. All examples of everyday resistance presented in this volume are at the same time situated locally and globally framed as collective practices responding to aspects of global changes and conditions such as neoliberalism and the crisis.

All of the cases point to the relevance of materiality and embodiment, of face-to-face interactions, as opposed to forms of protest that are based only on digital practices,[5] for even if in the case of the Tabasco video collective, the dissemination of information via the internet facilitated the emergence of a counter-public, the workshops, which were conducted in the form of face-to-face communication, were directly effective in raising consciousness and changing perceptions. As Judith Butler (2011) has stated: "For politics to take place, the body must appear."

In some of the cases, resistance *promoting* change is being pursued – rural solidarity networks, peasant activism and urban gardening being the examples – while in others, the goal is resistance *against* an unwanted change, as in the case of the Tabasco video project and the Exarchia solidarity networks. Some of the initiatives try to reestablish social life as it is envisioned as having been predominant in the past, characterized by close relationships, interactions in small-scale social networks, and personal trust.

However, the examples of the Tabasco video project as well as of the urban gardening initiatives described by Poljak Istenič also show the ambivalences of conducting protest from a position of being part of the neoliberal system, which is, at the same time, directed against the system. Thinking about governmentality (see Foucault 2004) and about the theory of empire by Michael Hardt and Antonio Negri (2002), one can ask: Is there an alternative to neoliberalism and techno-capitalism? Apart from those cases where a revolution intends to overthrow the societal order, activists more or less tend to run into danger of being absorbed or instrumentalized by hegemonic discourses. Movements are, like any other social actor, influenced by the cognitive, emotional, cultural and epistemic horizon of their society of origin (see Baumgarten & Ullrich 2012; Ullrich & Keller 2014). This embedding of protest practices in their societal context will be investigated in the next section in more detail.

Yet, as we can see from the examples of the six case studies presented, activists are successfully creating spaces of resistance and alternative forms of living, creating in their interactions little pockets of freedom in the sense of Hannah Arendt (1968: 326): spaces that enable participation and give people the freedom and warrant to enact relationships and practices that differ from those characterizing mainstream society, testing and demonstrating alternative possibilities. These small acts of resistance holding the potential for lasting change begin with vital issues directly affecting people's everyday lives, such as the reappropriation of control over life conditions, as it is represented in the form of food activism – a phenomenon currently on the rise in countries like Germany and the USA related to the perceived uncertainties and mounting mistrust regarding the industrialization of food production – and also, in resistance against the attempts to being cut off from electric power.

The Relevance of Mutual Trust in Mediterranean Protest Movements

How do the six different case studies presented here show similarities regarding the modes and forms of protest, which could be related to their common Mediterranean context? Based on a reflexive understanding of the Mediterranean, presented here as a fragmented reference frame (cf. Kavanagh & Lauth Bacas 2011: viii), how do these Mediterranean cases depart from other forms of protests? Or can the strategies and actions of the activists in France, Slovenia, Italy and Greece be seen as effects of the all-embracing worldwide crisis, of neoliberalism or post-democracy more generally (c.f. Crouch 2008)?

More broadly, and not only in the Mediterranean countries, the crisis has led to growing debt (cf. Wallerstein 2010: 137) and rising social inequities (Della Porta 2015: pos. 887f.). The overall situation in crisis-driven countries (in Europe and beyond) is characterized by rising unemployment, the stagnation of wages, the reduction of social services (Streeck 2014: 149), the privatization of public services and goods (Graefe 2004). Post-democracy, which is characterized by a feeling of impotence towards global developments and the power of companies and banks, can lead to a distance between institutions of the state and a strong localism. In this situation, in many European countries, protests, movements and initiatives emerge sharing certain structural similarities that exceed the different societies.

Describing social movements, which have developed in reaction to said crisis, Donatella Della Porta (2015) has coined the term anti-austerity movements. Those movements oppose austerity measures and can be read as a symptom of the crisis of neoliberalism and of political responsibility: institutions are (and are perceived to be) particularly closed towards citizens' demands. Members of such movements are mainly the precariat, as Della Porta argues, and young people who are often unemployed and have a high level of education. They are organized through direct democracy. They fight for an alternative to globalization as it exists and for social equality. Also, they are oriented towards the common good, consensus, equality, inclusion, and transparency. As examples for anti-austerity movements Della Porta names the Indignados, the J14 protesters occupying Rothschild Boulevard in the Israeli capital, Tunisia, the protests of Egypt, and Occupy (Della Porta 2015).

One could argue that the cases presented in this

special issue function as austerity movements; the reason for the protests is the crisis and the protesters are the so-called precarious – people who suffer most from the crisis. As we can see, however, this is only partly true. In the case of the Tabasco Video Project described by Cartelli, the reason for protest is rather the commodification of public places and thus, the protest can be linked to the right to the city movements (cf. Lefebvre 1996) – the right to the city meaning the right to centrality and to participation in public life and against gentrification. Furthermore, while the resistant voices in the videos belong to marginalized groups, the initiative took its starting point in collaboration between not entirely underprivileged film-makers and the municipal institutions. In the case of Genuino Clandestino, while the crisis may have fuelled incentives for establishing an alternative system of food production and its evaluation, the protest originated in resistance against EU regulations. Also, the activities of the peasants emerge from a decade-long activism on the margins of communist and anarchist ideologies; the activists themselves are mostly dropouts of all age groups belonging to the educated middle classes. Interestingly, Dieter Haller has pointed to the fact that the current movements in the Mediterranean have been sustained by the middle classes, their rage against the impositions of the neoliberal system and their mistrust towards political elites (Haller 2011: 10) – supporting the thesis of similarities between the initiatives, which can be related to their situatedness in the Mediterranean region.

To elaborate on this thesis, we can identify common features between the cases presented in this special issue; however, we are definitely not arguing for homogeneity in Mediterranean protest movements. Instead, we would like to develop a more complex understanding of the field under study by identifying some common underlying features in these clearly different yet related practices of protest.

Firstly, in all cases we see a political discourse being established in which the activists stress the *everyday* importance and the *local* dimension of the "problem" triggered by their social protests and practices of resistance. The "local" becomes important and relevant to political actors as a socially perceived "place", as "their place", and as being threatened. As social anthropologists working in the Mediterranean have shown, the significance of a specific village, town or region to the people who work and live there, is related to complex processes of identity formation and making the locality meaningful as their own "place" (see Kavanagh & Lauth Bacas 2011).

It seems that the observed Mediterranean protest movements managed to mobilize their participants; they were successful in linking the big issues of austerity and neoliberal politics to a notion of locality and to the everyday experiences, emotions and perceived needs of local actors. In all of these cases, protest is successful in the form of small local initiatives, which establish change through continuously challenging hegemonic practices. All of the protests are based on common acts of solidarity, locally-based strategies of cooperation and the establishment of (close) personal relationships.

Secondly, another common feature is the major role of face-to-face interaction and *mutual trust*. In all case studies, the interlocutors stressed the importance of close relationships and the relevance of trust within the group of actors. This observation that mutual trust is seen as a central concept for many actors engaged in the here discussed Mediterranean protest movements will be taken as a starting point for further arguing. The actors' viewpoint that mutual trust is an essential element and precondition for cooperation and practices of protest has to be understood in relation to the societal context their movement is situated in.

In the Mediterranean, the issue of personal trust is of special relevance; many Southern European societies have been described by ethnologists and social anthropologists as societies characterized by a "culture of public *distrust*" (Giordano 2007; Roth 2007). The ethnologist Klaus Roth (2007: 1) points to a basic dichotomy that runs deeply through these societies, namely the opposition between the public and the private spheres. Researchers familiar with the social worlds of actors in Southern Europe often agree with the statement that "the societies and their entire social life have a binary structure, consisting of two clearly separated spaces to which people attach very different values, the private space being viewed as familiar, friendly, and intimate, while the public space is perceived as unfriendly, dangerous or even hostile" (Roth 2007: 1). Therefore, acting in the public sphere (outside the private circle of family and close friends) is always related to a set of behaviours, attitudes and norms that teach actors to move carefully and with a generalized distrust in the Other in a potentially hostile surrounding.

To overcome this deep inner logic of a binary social order – said to be a relevant feature of most Mediterranean countries – and to enable actors to come together in "altruistic" protest activities and civic engagement in the public sphere, the rhetoric of mutual trust turns out to function as a relevant cultural code that is important for building political engagement beyond established party structures. In a more general sense, Giordano (2007) stresses this high relevance of personalized trust situated in an overall "culture of public distrust" as a very rational behaviour, given the historical experiences of actors in the Mediterranean with clientelism, nepotism, corrupt political elites, and "mafia-style" structures and practices. Personal trust in these specific socio-historical – Mediterranean – contexts can be understood not only as a useful cultural resource for building social networks of trustworthy persons beyond the private sphere. As Streinzer in his case study of the Volos-based TEM exchange networks shows, the rhetoric of trust (and of disappointed trust) can also be employed as a socially accepted code of control in relation to network members, who are accused of free-riding in the local exchange network (see Streinzer 2018 in this volume).

To sum up: Based on the concept of the Mediterranean as a patchwork of regions (and micro-regions) providing a basis for comparative reasoning and research, we argue that the esteem of trust and close relationships expressed by many movement members is related to the societal context they live in: that is the context of *generalized distrust* existing in transformation societies and Mediterranean societies towards politicians, institutions, and unknown groups, as explained by Roth (2007) and Giordano (2007). In societies of generalized distrust, people who are not part of already existing kin groups or close social networks are generally not trusted; in order to establish trust to such "strangers", social manoeuvres like face-to-face communication have to be employed. Therefore, an emic emphasis on trust and solidarity as normative code and behavioural expectation can be regarded as a relevant characteristic feature of protest movements within the Mediterranean.

Our suggested approach is supported by results from the research of other current movements within states surrounding the Mediterranean. For example, personal trust played a leading role as internal norm of the Italian feminist movement Se Non Ora Quando (When not now, when then?), founded in 2011, as shown in a study by Marion Näser-Lather (2015). The valuation of personal trust led to the feminist movement Se Non Ora Quando using restricted modes of digital communication on the local level such as closed Facebook groups only for trusted members who knew each other personally and in many cases were friends. However, on the national level, personal trust could not be established; instead, mistrust against leading activists who were at the same times influential members of political parties or trade unions dominated. General mistrust towards politicians – a characteristic of Italian political discourse – aggravated conflicts within the movement.

Other recent studies have pointed to similarities regarding communication practices. Daniel Trottier and Christian Fuchs argued in 2015 that in Southern European countries, stronger social networks exist and face-to-face interactions in these countries are very important. In addition, Dieter Haller has perceived similarities of the revolutionary movements of the Maghreb in 2011. He states that the collective engagement in spaces of social proximity where face-to-face interaction takes place plays a major role for those movements. Haller names the integration of sensual components and the construction of a "communitas" as necessary factors for success of these movements, meaning that bodily experience and social engagement come together. He comes to the conclusion that this is a Mediterranean characteristic, referring to the traditional importance of places in Mediterranean cities as space where conflicts are sorted out. It could, however, be argued that also within Occupy and other protest movements, which are not situated in the Mediterranean, physical co-presence plays a major role.

One might argue that characteristics such as the relevance of relationships and face-to-face interactions could be related to economic factors, for example the crisis and the scarcity of social services as well as the influence of organized crime. However, while this is undoubtedly true, those conditions are a characteristic of all the countries around the Mediterranean, and all these conditions lead to solidarity in little groups, which are of social and political importance for the involved actors in a larger sense.

These effects are reinforced, of course, by sociopolitical circumstances such as the crisis, but also – taking a long-term perspective – to developments taking place in the course of modernity. Nico Schrode links the growing importance of personal trust to the fact that societal trust in the system has collapsed in the context of reflexive modernization[6] because of the perceived fragility of social reality and of crises, of the lability of societal systems and the decreasing security (Schrode 2014).

In this respect, an anthropology of the Mediterranean, that is, the understanding of the Mediterranean as a relevant reference frame for comparison, could be useful for a better understanding of dimensions, structures and successful use of cultural resources and social capital of the actors engaged in the protest movements under study. To underline its non-essentialist meaning, we would rather speak of protest movements *in* the Mediterranean, stressing the contextualization that has to be taken into account in any anthropological analysis. On one hand, the movements and initiatives we refer to portray cases that are unique in their specific historical and socio-cultural context. On the other hand, they are situated in a wider framework, which is not only historically connected but also characterized by the present experiences of austerity and neoliberal politics that affect Mediterranean countries and its citizens in manifold ways.

In short, the contributions in this issue support the argument that resistance movements have to be understood in a context larger than anti-austerity movements; instead, these locally active resistance movements open up the space for creative actions and participation beyond the more classical core of opposing austerity and neoliberalism. The studies collected here show the emergence of a vivid plurality of resistance practices nevertheless characterized by some similarities: by their reliance on personal trust and their being rooted and being effective in local communities and locally-based practices. In evaluating their impact, we agree with Richard Sennett (2000: 203), who has pointed to the fact that change develops in small-scale, local practices, and not through mass uprisings. The movements and initiatives presented in this special issue accomplish this desire to actively contribute to social change through solidarity networks where mutual trust has been highlighted by the participants as the most prominent cultural resource of their resistance activities in reaction to the crisis situation they encounter.

Notes

1 The protest practices of the Spanish movement *15M*, also called the *Indignados*, and of the international movement *Occupy*, are characterized by not raising political claims in the parliamentarian arena, but by occupying public places for months, thus demonstrating alternative ways of living together and of basic democracy (see Corredera 2012; Hammond 2013).
2 For the distinction between macro-, meso- and microlevels of resistance, see Williams (2009).
3 A critical reflection and reevaluation of the concept of familism in relation to anthropological studies in Southern Italy is provided by Carlo Capello (2013).
4 Many different researchers have stressed the facilitation of protest through the use of digital media, e.g. Schönberger (2004), Benkler (2006), Shirky (2008), and Castells (2012).
5 The question whether activism only relying on online-practices can be successful in the sense of engendering change has been widely discussed (see, e.g., Ayers 2003; Hamm 2006; Morozov 2011).
6 The theory of reflexive modernization, established by Ulrich Beck and Anthony Giddens, thematizes the unintended effects of the global dominance of industrialized modernity, which question modernity itself, e.g. through the individualization of social inequality (see Beck 1986; Giddens 1997).

References

Abulafia, David 2005: Mediterraneans. In: William V. Harris (ed.), *Rethinking the Mediterranean*. Oxford & New York: Oxford University Press, pp. 64–93.

Arendt, Hannah 1968: *Über die Revolution*. Frankfurt am Main: Büchergilde Gutenberg.

Ayers, Michael D. 2003: Comparing Collective Identity in Online and Offline Feminist Activists. In: Martha Mc-Caughey & Michael D. Ayers (eds.), *Cyberactivism: Online Activism in Theory and Practice*. New York: Routledge, pp. 145–164.

Baskar, Bojan 2002: *Dvoumni Mediteran: Študije o regionalnem prekrivanju na vzhodnojadranskem območju* [Ambiguous Mediterranean: Studies of Regional Overlapping on the Eastern Adriatic Area]. Koper: Zgodovinsko društvo za južno Primorsko & Znanstveno-raziskovalno središče Republike Slovenije.

Baumgarten, Britta & Peter Ullrich 2012: *Discourse, Power and Governmentality: Social Movement Research with and beyond Foucault*. Berlin: Social Science Research Center Berlin (WZB).

Beck, Ulrich 1986: *Risikogesellschaft: Auf dem Weg in eine andere Moderne*. Frankfurt am Main: Suhrkamp.

Benkler, Yochai 2006: *The Wealth of Networks: How Social Production Transforms Markets and Freedom*. New Haven: Yale University Press.

Brumen, Borut 2000: *Sv. Peter in njegovi časi: Socialni spomini, časi in identitete v istrski vasi Sv. Peter* [St. Peter and its Times: Social Memories, Times and Identities in the Istrian Village St. Peter]. Ljubljana: Založba.

Butler, Judith 2011: Bodies in Alliance and the Politics of the Street, http://www.eipcp.net/transversal/1011/butler/en. Accessed July 9, 2017.

Capello, Carlo 2013: Southern Italy's Double Face: A Critical Reflection. *Journal of Mediterranean Studies* 22:2, 381–398.

Castells, Manuel 2012: *Networks of Outrage and Hope: Social Movements in the Internet Age*. Cambridge: Polity Press.

Corredera, Maria 2012: Die Indignados von 15-M. In: Jürgen Link & Rolf Parr (eds.), *Wieviel Kulturrevolution am Mittelmeer? Kulturrevolution* 61–62, 58–61.

Crouch, Colin 2008: *Postdemokratie*. Berlin: Suhrkamp.

Della Porta, Donatella 2015: *Social Movements in Times of Austerity*. Cambridge: Polity Press.

Dir, Yamina 2005: *Bilder des Mittelmeer-Raumes: Phasen und Themen der ethnologischen Forschung seit 1945*. Münster: LIT-Verlag.

Driessen, Henk 2001: People, Boundaries and the Anthropologist's Mediterranean. In: Ina-Maria Greverus, Regina Römhild & Gisela Welz (eds.), *The Mediterraneans: Reworking the Past, Shaping the Present, Considering the Future. Anthropological Journal on European Cultures* 10, 11–23.

Fernández-Savater, Amador 2012: "15. Mai": Eine Revolution aus Personen. In: Jürgen Link & Rolf Parr (eds.), *Wieviel Kulturrevolution am Mittelmeer? Kulturrevolution* 61–62, 62–63.

Foucault, Michel 2004: *Geschichte der Gouvernementalität: Die Geburt der Biopolitik*. Vorlesung am Collège de France 1978–1979. Vol. 2. Frankfurt am Main: Suhrkamp.

Giddens, Anthony 1997: *Die Konstitution der Gesellschaft: Grundzüge einer Theorie der Strukturierung*. Frankfurt am Main: Campus Verlag.

Giordano, Christian 1990: Is there a Mediterranean Anthropology? The Point of View of an Outsider. *Anthropological Journal on European Cultures* 1:1, 109–124.

Giordano, Christian 2007: Private Trust and Informal Networks: On the Organisational Culture in Societies of Public Distrust. A Glance at Southeast Europe. In: Klaus Roth (ed.), *Social Networks and Social Trust in Transformation Countries*. Münster: LIT, pp. 14–33.

Goddard, Victoria, Josep R. Llobera & Chris Shore (eds.) 1994: *The Anthropology of Europe: Identities and Boundaries in Conflict*. Oxford: Berg.

Graefe, Peter 2004: Personal Services in the Post-industrial Economy: Adding Nonprofits to the Welfare Mix. *Social, Policy and Administration* 38, 465–469.

Greverus, Ina-Maria & Gisela Welz 2001: Reworking the Past, Shaping the Present, Considering the Future: An Introduction to the Two Issues of The Mediterraneans. In: Ina-Maria Greverus, Regina Römhild & Gisela Welz (eds.), *The Mediterraneans: Reworking the Past, Shaping the Present, Considering the Future. Anthropological Journal on European Cultures* 10, 1–9.

Hall, Stuart & Tony Jefferson (eds.) 1976: *Resistance through Rituals*. London: Routledge.

Haller, Dieter 2011: Der Mittelmeerraum als Schauplatz von Empörungen, Revolten und Umbrüchen. Zentrum für Mittelmeerstudien. Working Paper No. 2, http://www.zms.ruhr-uni-bochum.de/mittelmeerstudien/mam/downloads/zms_-_wps_-_2.pdf. Accessed October 10, 2013.

Hamm, Marion 2006: Proteste im hybriden Kommunikationsraum: Zur Mediennutzung sozialer Bewegungen. *Forschungsjournal Neue Soziale Bewegungen* 19:2, 77–90.

Hammond, John L. 2013: The Significance of Space in Occupy Wall Street. *Interface: A Journal for and about Social Movements* 5:2, 499–524.

Hardt, Michael & Antonio Negri 2002: *Empire: Die neue Weltordnung*. Frankfurt am Main: Campus Verlag.

Herzfeld, Michael 1984: The Horns of the Mediterraneanist Dilemma. *American Ethnologist* 11, 439–454.

Hollander, Jocelyn A. & Rachel L. Einwohner 2004: Conceptualizing Resistance. *Sociological Forum* 19:4, 533–554.

Kavanagh, William & Jutta Lauth Bacas 2011: Issue Editors' Introduction: Special Issue "Unfolding Perspectives in Mediterranean Anthropology". *Journal of Mediterranean Studies* 20:1, v–xv.

Lauth Bacas, Jutta 2013: New Reflections on Anthropology

in the Mediterranean: Introduction to the Special Issue "Reflecting Anthropology in the Mediterranean". *Journal of Mediterranean Studies* 22:2, 215–228.

Lefebvre, Henri 1996: *Writings on Cities*. Cambridge, MA: Blackwell.

Llobera, Josep 1986: Fieldwork in Southwestern Europe: Anthropological Panacea or Epistemological Straitjacket. *Critique of Anthropology* 6, 25–33.

Marx, Gary T. 2009: A Tack in the Shoe and Taking off the Shoe: Neutralization and Counter-Neutralization Dynamics. *Surveillance and Society* 6:3, 295–306.

Morozov, Evgeny 2011: *The Net Delusion: The Dark Side of Internet Freedom*. Sebastopol, CA: Safari Books Online.

Näser-Lather, Marion 2015: Die reale Begegnung: Kommunikationsmodi und Infrastrukturnutzung in der Frauenbewegung Se Non Ora Quando. *Kommunikation@ Gesellschaft 16*, http://www.ssoar.info/ssoar/handle/document/45242. Accessed May 22, 2017.

Ortner, Sherry B. 1995: Resistance and the Problem of Ethnographic Refusal. *Comparative Studies in Society and History* 37:1, 173–193.

Peristiany, John George (ed.) 1963: *Contributions to Mediterranean Sociology: Mediterranean Rural Communities and Social Change*. Acts of the Mediterranean Sociological Conference, Athens, July 1963. Berlin: de Gruyter Mouton.

Pina-Cabral, J. de 1989: The Mediterranean as a Category of Regional Comparison: A Critical View. *Current Anthropology* 30:3, 399–406.

Rammstedt, Otthein 1978: *Soziale Bewegung*. Frankfurt am Main: Suhrkamp.

Roth, Klaus 2007: Trust, Networks, and Social Capital in the Transformation Countries: Ethnological Perspectives. In: Klaus Roth (ed.), *Social Networks and Social Trust in Transformation Countries*. Münster: LIT, pp. 1–13.

Sacchi, Paola & Pier Paolo Viazzo 2014: Family and Household. In: Peregrine Horden & Sharon Kinoshita (eds.), *A Companion to Mediterranean History*. Chichester, West Sussex: Wiley Blackwell, pp. 234–250.

Schönberger, Klaus 2005: Bericht des Ausschusses für Bildung, Forschung und Technikfolgenabschätzung (17. Ausschuss) gemäß § 56a der Geschäftsordnung. Technikfolgenabschätzung Internet und Demokratie – Abschlussbericht zum TA-Projekt Analyse netzbasierter Kommunikation unter kulturellen Aspekten. Deutscher Bundestag Drucksache 15/6015, http://dip21.bundestag.de/dip21/btd/15/060/1506015.pdf. Accessed April 15, 2018.

Schönberger, Klaus 2015: Digitale Kommunikation: Persistenz und Rekombination als Modus des soziokulturellen Wandels. Theoretische Begriffsarbeit in empirischer Absicht. *Zeitschrift für Volkskunde* 2, 201–213.

Schönberger, Klaus & Ove Sutter 2009: Zur Form des Protesthandelns sozialer Bewegungen. In: Klaus Schönberger & Ove Sutter (eds.), *Kommt herunter, reiht euch ein ... Eine kleine Geschichte der Protestformen sozialer Bewegungen*. Berlin: Assoziation A, pp. 7–29.

Schrode, Nico 2014: "Vertrauen" – Splitter einer umfassenden soziologischen Theorie. Soziologieblog 04/25/2011, http://soziologieblog.hypotheses.org/827. Accessed July 7, 2017.

Sciama, Lidia 2013: The Mediterranean: Topos or Mirage? *Journal of Mediterranean Studies* 22:2, 223–229.

Scott, James C. 1985: *Weapons of the Weak*. New Haven: Yale University Press.

Scott, James C. 1989: Everyday Forms of Resistance. *Copenhagen Papers* 4, 33–62.

Scott, James. C. 1990: *Domination and the Arts of Resistance: Hidden Transcripts*. New Haven: Yale University Press.

Sennett, Richard 2000: *Der flexible Mensch – Die Kultur des neuen Kapitalismus*. Translated from American English by Martin Richter. München: Goldmann.

Shirky, Clay 2008: *Here Comes Everybody: The Power of Organizing without Organizations*. London: Allen Lane.

de Souza e Silva, Adriana 2006: From Cyber to Hybrid: Mobile Technologies as Interfaces of Hybrid Spaces. *Space and Culture* 9:3, 261–278.

Stauth, Georg & Marcus Otto 2008: *Méditerranée: Skizzen zu Mittelmeer, Islam und Theorie der Moderne*. Berlin: Kulturverlag Kadmos.

Streeck, Wolfgang 2014: Taking Crisis Seriously: Capitalism in its Way Out. *Stato e mercato* 1000, 45–68.

Thiele, Alexandra 1992: Sozialer Protest: Die Hungerunruhen von 1847 als Beispiel eines kollektiven Protestverhaltens. *KulTour: Mitteilungsblatt des Volkskundlichen Seminars der Universität Bonn* 3:2, 5–15.

Trottier, Daniel & Christian Fuchs (eds.) 2015: *Social Media, Politics and the State: Protests, Revolutions, Riots, Crime and Policing in the Age of Facebook, Twitter and YouTube*. London: Routledge.

Ullrich, Peter & Reiner Keller 2014: Comparing Discourse between Cultures: A Discursive Approach to Movement Knowledge. In: Britta Baumgarten, Priska Daphi & Peter Ullrich (eds.), *Conceptualising Culture in Social Movement Research*. Houndsmills, Basingstoke: Palgrave Macmillan, pp. 113–139.

Vinthagen, Stellan & Anna Johansson 2013: "Everyday Resistance": Exploration of a Concept and its Theories. *Resistance Studies Magazine* 1, 1–46.

Wallerstein, Immanuel 2010: Social Crises. *New Left Review* 62, 133, https://it.clonline.org/cl 142.

Williams, J. Patrick 2009: The Multidimensionality of Resistance in Youth-Subcultural Studies. *The Resistance Studies Magazine* 1, 20–33.

Žižek, Slavoj 2012: *The Year of Dreaming Dangerously*. London & New York: Verso Books.

Jutta Lauth Bacas holds a doctorate in social anthropology from the University of Zurich with a special focus on migration studies. She has held teaching positions at universities in both Switzerland and Germany and also worked as a senior researcher at the Academy of Athens, Greece. Currently she is a research affiliate at the Mediterranean Institute of the University of Malta and conducts research on political culture and refugee reception in Greece.
(jutta.lauth.bacas@gmail.com)

Marion Näser-Lather, Ph.D. in European ethnology, has held postdoctoral positions at universities in Paderborn, Marburg and Innsbruck. Currently, she is a researcher at the Centre for Gender Studies and Future Feminist Research of the Philipps University Marburg. Among her research interests are protest research, gender studies, digitization, and critical military studies.
(naeserm@staff.uni-marburg.de)

MARSEILLE *VS* THE MEDITERRANEAN
Local Practices of Digital Resistance

Philip Cartelli, Wagner College, New York

This article discusses the creation of a participatory web documentary in Marseille in reaction to the spatial imposition and symbolic productions of two new cultural institutions in the city. Based on observations of the web documentary's producers and participants and an analysis of the final product, it argues that the former have produced a form of resistance in their empowerment of local individuals and perspectives. These perspectives operate in opposition to those of the new institutions that depict Marseille as a "Mediterranean" city while implicitly and explicitly excluding local particularities and practices, which have paradoxically contributed to the city's identity and international renown.[1]

Keywords: urban renewal, Mediterranean, web documentary, resistance, digital

In late fall of 2013, a group of individuals gathered in a small conference space adjacent to an art gallery in the Panier, a historic district in Marseille. Around the table sat members of a local video collective called Tabasco Video, representatives from the district town hall and the sub-regional "département" government, as well as public outreach representatives from two recently opened institutions: the Museum of European and Mediterranean Civilizations (MuCEM) and the Villa Méditerranée.[2]

The meeting's subject was a "web documentary" project conceived by Tabasco Video. Tabasco's members had already successfully solicited a first round of funding from local government bodies, but this event was intended to further solidify the support network needed to produce the proposed online series, entitled "Et le Panier dans tout ça?" (And what about the Panier?). As its members described it during this initial meeting, Tabasco Video's web documentary project would foreground the role of the eponymous neighborhood and its inhabitants in wider socio-economic changes taking place in Marseille through a series of three participatory workshops directed at distinct groups: students at a nearby secondary school, the Collège du Vieux-Port; members of a job training program for recent arrivals to France; and other Panier inhabitants of all ages who had already collaborated in previous Tabasco projects. In each of these workshops, participants were to be asked to formulate and document their own answers to the titular question regarding their position and that of their neighborhood amidst the panorama of wider change in Marseille.

Within these reflections the Panier was meant to assume a central role both as physical space and palimpsest of local concerns about identity and belonging in a transitional urban social sphere. Split into three sections corresponding to the workshops, the web documentary's format would include online videos, still images, and sound clips, all of which could be accessed by viewers. The viewers in turn would be free to advance, replay, or select a different path in their interactive online experience. Tabasco Video's members presented the project as an extension of their prior participatory video practice, an ongoing effort to empower residents to voice their opinions about urban processes and disseminate these opinions to local and non-Marseille audiences.[3] Gifreu (2011) defines the web documentary as "interactive applications, on- or offline, made with the intention of representing reality with its own mechanisms that we can call modes of browsing or interaction, relative to the level of participation allowed." Interactivity and participation are thus principle elements in this genre, which frequently permits its spectator to control the speed at which the work is experienced, or even to choose the direction of one or several possible narratives. In this way the project proposed by Tabasco Video was participatory regarding both its production and the medium to which it was destined: the former is the focus of this article.

The meeting itself was relatively low-key. As mentioned, Tabasco had already obtained a degree of funding from local authorities to begin the project and it had similarly drawn on pre-existing relationships with nearby schools and other social institutions. However, this was the first official meeting between members of Tabasco and the MuCEM and Villa Méditerranée, which is remarkable in itself since while they were mutually interested in working with one another, representatives of all three were aware of the forthcoming project's potential for institutional critique, one that would directly target the latter's contribution to the creation of a new physical plant in Marseille as well as changing notions of local identity.

"Digital Resistance"

In this article, I discuss Tabasco Video and its collaborators' engagement with a joint program of urban renewal and cultural development that has taken place in Marseille since 1995. With a focus on the first volume of the web documentary, I analyze

the conditions of its production and its final form. I argue that this process reveals a local practice of "digital resistance," which I define as the temporary creation of a counter-public, the perspectives and claims of which are transmitted in an accessible form whose primary limits are one's internet bandwidth. Tabasco Video's resistance model uses the means provided by the cultural institutions against themselves, in the process asserting local abilities and authority to define its own cultural prerogatives and to rightfully identify connections between economy, infrastructure, politics, and culture. In the body of this article, I situate this practice in its urban, cultural and regional contexts, all of which contribute to the project's specificity, before exploring Tabasco Video's background as an organization and the workshop in greater depth. Taken together, I contend that this example shows how a group of individuals who are not driven by strictly political goals are able to empower members of another social group to claim their right to the city through the medium of audiovisual culture.

My use of the notion of "digital resistance" builds on that of the Critical Art Ensemble collective's eponymous concept (2001), but also responds to subsequent developments in the field, reinvigorating this pre-existing concept by expanding upon its possible uses today. The Critical Art Ensemble's originary notion responds to the definition of "digital" as the potentially endless reproduction of content, while mine refers specifically to online media. While Critical Art Ensemble writers, artists and activists were concerned about the possible recuperation of their "tactical media" by capitalist structures, the majority of resistance movements today are linked to or dependent on such infrastructure through the use of social media. As I explore in the body of the article, however, the type of dissent in which Tabasco is engaged resonates with definitions of political resistance and claims-making through critique, particularly in its insistence on the rights of local citizens to question and challenge the representations and discourse of those in positions of authority. It also responds to recent conversations in between media and social movement studies. However, despite Downing's assertion that "social movements are variously defined, often hard to categorize, and – as a result of their 'unconstitutional' qualities – resistant to rigid theorizing" (2008: 43), I must underline the specificity of the Tabasco Video case, whose members would reject the terminology of a "movement" and who do not self-identify as activists. These members are employed individually by the collective for assignments which may include public or private commissions or those which they have developed on their own and sought out funding for, such as "Et le Panier dans tout ça?" Furthermore, while, in this article I am interested in the digital form of Tabasco Video's web documentary; I do not consider its reception to the same extent. The timeline of this research coincided primarily with the project's production phase; Tabasco members began post-production work on the web documentary after I had left Marseille and so the project's aftermath, including its impact, were not my central concern. Instead, I am interested in the element of Tabasco's process that engaged with what Milan calls "emancipatory communication practices," including "the power of participation, which refers to the *possibility* of making informed contributions to democratic decision-making and public life" (my emphasis, 2013: 2). Within this context, the unique contestatory element of Tabasco Video's project entails its collaboration and dependence on the financial support of the subjects of its critique.

A central element of Tabasco's digital resistance involves its questioning of the role of cultural institutions, where the latter can be seen as directly contributing to if not exacerbating local social and economic problems. Since their respective openings in mid-2013, the MuCEM and Villa Méditerranée's administrations had already considered the Panier as a central point of concern, directing outreach efforts to local residents. The meeting that I attended in late 2013 marked the beginning of their convergence around the "Et le Panier dans tout ça?" project, but it was only one element of a wider effort for which each institution had at least one dedicated employee and in the case of the MuCEM an entire department of public outreach. (The latter's responsibilities include the organization of group and school visits, as well as increasing access to members of social groups less likely to visit museums.) The proposed collaboration with Tabasco Video was thus precisely the type of mediated program that both institutions had already demonstrated interest in supporting.[4] However, the project that Tabasco Video produced was a de facto challenge to the very fabric of the MuCEM and Villa Méditerranée's existence, the notion that Marseillean and Mediterranean culture and society are one and the same.

As a contrast to a representation regime that positions Marseille and its inhabitants as a living diorama of Mediterranean identity, "Et le Panier dans tout ça?" went beyond mere questioning to challenge the root of these representations. It did so directly in its empowerment of minority and working-class perspectives on the changes being wrought in downtown Marseille of which the new cultural institutions are part. But it also did so in its refusal to accept the terms of a model of collaboration between powerful public culture institutions and smaller, locally-oriented associations. Even when they benefitted from material and in-kind support from institutional collaborators, Tabasco's workshop directors, editors and general team refused to shy away from asking uncomfortable questions or depicting the dichotomies between the discourse and practice or effects of cultural institutions. In this regard, they both allowed other voices to participate in the construction of counter-discourse and expressed their own sensitivity regarding the spatial reorganization of downtown Marseille.

The Neo-Mediterranean City

Marseille's twenty-six century-long history as a port city makes it a both real and symbolic center in Mediterranean commercial and cultural exchange, in turn binding its fortunes to the sea. In the years since the Algerian War of Independence and the economic downturn sparked by the oil crisis, in the 1960s and 1970s respectively, the city's prior significance as a key Mediterranean and French port diminished, while, conversely, its Mediterranean associations increased. These associations are characterized as an idealistic celebration of the city's "Mediterranean" history and its ethnically diverse residents, many of whom trace their backgrounds to former French colonies and protectorates in North Africa (principally Algeria and Tunisia). The recent uses of its Mediterranean identifications in turn have tended toward commercial purposes, entailing a rebranding of this former working-class city with a large unemployed underclass as both a cultural melting pot and a tourist destination with major potential for economic investment as Maisetti (2014) discusses. However, as De Moriamé (2012) notes, the colonial past frequently permeates so-called "Euromediterranean" relations, making local uses of Mediterranean terminology anything but anodyne.

While Marseille's historic role as a vital lynchpin between France and the Mediterranean had an initial commercial basis, a political dimension was also attributed to it in later years. The city's significance as a major colonial port established it as the site for exchange between France and its colonies or overseas territories and eventually as a point of contact for former colonial subjects and colonists (*pieds noirs*) after the mid-twentieth century independence of the former. It is in the post-independence period that both Marseille and the Provence-Alpes-Côte-d'Azur (PACA) region of which it forms a part began to develop more durable contact with entities in former colonies, which have laid the groundwork for current political cooperation, of which the Villa Méditerranée was conceived as one element (Carrière 2013). According to Visier (2005), Michel Vauzelle, the former president of PACA and the intellectual architect of the Villa Méditerranée, was convinced that a repositioning of European attention and investment toward the Mediterranean area would reap benefits for his constituents. In this regard, his thinking parallels that of the French officials behind the more high-profile Barcelona Process and ensuing Union for the Mediterranean. However, this type of internationalist approach has not always been universally popular in Marseille. Despite a bipartisan interest in developing such relationships in the past, today, notions of Mediterranean unity see politicians divided along party lines. One sign of this

is the vigorous partisan contestation of the socialist party member Vauzelle's Villa Méditerranée project. Since 2015, when Vauzelle was replaced at the PACA presidency by a member of the right-wing Les Republicans party the institution's future has been cast into doubt.

The colonial period was a particularly rich period for the inclusion of Marseille in French cultural imaginaries of the Mediterranean, whether concerning the Saint-Simonian utopian industrialists who used the city as a transit point and site for major infrastructure projects, or the artists and writers associated with the locally edited journal *Cahiers du Sud* (Temime 2002). The atrocities of the Algerian War of Independence and its aftermath dashed these dreams, but some were resurrected beginning in the 1980s by an unlikely union of figures from across the political spectrum, including the former mayor of Marseille, Gaston Defferre. Another one of these figures was Thierry Fabre, who had left the Institut du monde arabe in Paris in the early 1990s to set up an annual festival of Mediterranean culture and ideas in Marseille called Les Rencontres d'Averroës, named after the Andalusian philosopher. Several years later, Fabre was asked to participate in the organization of the new MuCEM project, within which he became one of its major intellectual backers, developing a project that would celebrate both the Mediterranean as a diverse yet complementary geographic area and Marseille's incontrovertible place in that space. While Fabre left his administrative post at the MuCEM a few years after its opening, the institution still bears his imprint in its orientation and idealism.

Since 1995, the primary framework for these interlinked efforts has been the aptly named Euroméditerranée urban renewal project, currently the largest of its kind under way in Europe. As Bullen describes it, Euroméditerranée "has the explicit ambition to influence the symbolic, material and spatial reorganization of Marseille" (2012: 168). Both the MuCEM and Villa Méditerranée fall within the perimeter and purview of Euroméditerranée and, while their aims are avowedly cultural (or in the case of the Villa Méditerranée combined with a complementary political focus), they both directly and indirectly contribute to the city's identity as a Mediterranean destination, whose novelty derives in part from the concurrent arrival of more commercial venues. My dissertation research in Marseille (Cartelli 2016), initially concerned with social politics of access and use to the Euroméditerranée zone, gradually adapted to the additional cultural and commercial context of this urban development project. This entailed an investigation of the creation, dissemination, and effects of the associated Mediterranean discourse at the level of those who generate it and among the city's inhabitants. During my research period, which came several years after the start of the global financial crisis, many of these inhabitants were still suffering from a downturn in employment and investment – not to mention their exclusion from earlier economic development – despite Euroméditerranée's intended counterweight to these effects. In addition to ethnographic fieldwork with the inhabitants and users of neighborhoods and public spaces, I pursued my research through interviews and interactions with political officials as well as institutional administrators and employees. I also regularly attended cultural programs and events at both institutions and visited their permanent and temporary exhibitions on my own and in guided tours. While I aimed to balance the perspectives of a variety of interlocutors, including those spatial users and those responsible for designing and administering redeveloped public spaces and their new institutions, this was not always so easy. Although I took care to consider the latter perspectives, the increased time that I spent with local residents and habitual users of the spaces in question meant that I tended to side with their perspectives, especially since my access concerned their daily existence and not solely their professional activities.

One of my primary observations in my larger research holds that the provenance and use of the Mediterranean concept in Marseille is largely confined to those who have tasked themselves with its dissemination. These include the new MuCEM and Villa Méditerranée's intellectual architects and administrators, who insist that their emphasis on Marseille's Mediterraneanism is a reflection of local perspectives and realities. By participating in the "Et le Panier dans tout ça?" project, they hope to create a more durable relationship between the institutions and their surrounding community, but they also hope that such a process will simultaneously prove their foundational assumptions regarding locals' identification as "Mediterraneans".

In one conversation, the director of the MuCEM's department of public outreach expounded on such an assumption, citing a 1999 study undertaken by the Mediterranean Laboratory of Sociology (LAMES) research center in nearby Aix-en-Provence. Led by sociologist Pierre Vergès, the study's research team attempted to ascertain the self-identifications of Marseillais (Vergès, Hajek & Jacquemoud 1999). In my interlocutor's summary of the project,

> When asked to specify their principal identity, they [Marseillais] respond 'Mediterranean' [instead of 'French' or 'European']… So at the MuCEM, we're in a mirror effect, because when they come here they discover a part of themselves…. [In this sense,] we're operating as the opposite of exoticism, we're in the 'near' instead [of the far]. This phenomenon of recognition really changes the [visitor's] experience… It permits a form of appropriation. (February 25, 2014)

This observation resonates with an idealized projection of the MuCEM's mission and its intended reception among a Marseillais public, but it fails to reflect frequent discrepancies between the Mediterranean label and local senses of belonging. It also neglects to consider the reality that, while the MuCEM's admission numbers during its first year wildly exceeded expectations, those of its visitors from Marseille, and more specifically from ethnically diverse and working-class neighborhoods such as the Panier consistently lag behind expectations.

As the subsequent discussion reveals, many locals do not conform to or agree with institutional visions. Marseille has a proud local identity, based on its port's past glories as a major shipping center and a fractious relationship with the rest of France (with a particular enmity reserved for Paris), frequently oriented around outsized support for the city's football team, Olympique de Marseille. As much as locals may relate themselves and their identities to the sea at their doorsteps or the influence of the wider geographic and cultural basin, they are cognizant of local particularities that preclude comparisons with Valencia, Istanbul, or Naples. In turn, the members of Tabasco Video, with their combined several decades of experience spent in the Panier, strongly believe that this small working-class neighborhood demonstrates its own unique traits, in part linked to its successive hosting of immigrants from Italy, Corsica, and Algeria, but also the Comoros Islands in the southern Pacific Ocean, which the label "Mediterranean" is far too reductive to accurately describe.

Tabasco Video's web documentary project constitutes one element of my research into the changing uses of public space in Marseille and the role of Mediterranean discourse within these processes. When approached by members of Tabasco Video, I was enthusiastic about the opportunity to share my ongoing research with local residents and involve them as independent agents and interlocutors. As a filmmaker myself, I was also occasionally able to assist members of the workshop with technical issues.[5] This experience ultimately provided an opportunity to observe an intermediary zone between local residents and cultural administrators, contributing to my eventual assertion that the Mediterranean depictions and discourse of Marseille's new cultural institutions operated at a significant remove from local inhabitants' perceptions of their city's cultural identity as well as their own priorities for the present and the future during a time of economic instability. At the same time, I observed that members of Tabasco Video responsible for the web documentary had developed similar conclusions.

Local and Regional Contexts

Contestations over the changing uses of urban space are not specific to Marseille or the Mediterranean. Indeed, Marseille's progressive "Mediterraneanization" is in many respects similar to the cases of other former industrial port towns elsewhere in the world.

The revitalization of the North American cities of Baltimore in the 1950s and 60s and Boston in the 1990s served as templates for the redevelopment of Western European urban waterfronts, such as the famous docks of Liverpool and London in England and Bilbao and Barcelona in Spain. Cultural-driven development models have shown a particular durability in a number of these cases. Liverpool, in particular, was European Capital of Culture in 2008, while Lille, another French city with a revitalized city center, owes much of its recent facelift to its 2004 tenure in the same program. In 2013, the year that also saw the openings of the MuCEM and the Villa Méditerranée, Marseille assumed the European Capital of Culture title along with its surrounding region of Provence.

The uneven development and gentrification that are part and parcel of urban renewal projects makes them frequent targets for critique on the part of those who perceive within them threats to sociocultural diversity as well as local lives and livelihoods (Smith 1996). In Marseille, the prevalence of such contestations is inconsistent when compared with the cases of other Mediterranean cities in recent years. One major example of urban contestation that stands out in the city's recent history is the activity of a local collective called Un Centre Ville Pour Tous (A Downtown for All). Founded in 2000, Un Centre Ville Pour Tous was initially comprised of concerned locals and those directly affected by mass evictions on the Rue de la République, a major thoroughfare bordering the Panier, which had been targeted for upmarket renovation by a conglomerate of private operators (Borja, Derain & Manry 2010). While the Rue de la République renovations ultimately took place (although the majority of its new apartments remain empty as of this writing), Un Centre Ville Pour Tous remains active, primarily as a source of information and support for residents of other neighborhoods and local housing advocates. More recently, a group of concerned residents organized protests to campaign against the town hall's efforts to "cleanse" the historically working-class weekly market in a different downtown neighborhood. In addition, local artists drove a number of contestations before, during and after Marseille's Capital of Culture period, frustrated by their exclusion from the yearlong programming. However, a general characteristic of all of these contestations is that, aside from a relatively small cohort of experts (lawyers, architects) and activists, those who participated in these movements did so because they were directly affected by the actions being contested.

In Marseille, while locals may share concerns about rising rents, municipal, regional and national political mismanagement, social segregation, and a perceived lack of attention paid to long-time residents, engagement with these issues tends to remain at the level of everyday discourse, aside from the examples of space-specific resistance mentioned previously. Such subtlety belies residents' awareness of what Rancière has called the "distribution of the sensible", defined as a "system of self-evident facts of sense perception that simultaneously discloses the existence of something in common and the delimitations that define the respective parts and positions within it" (2000: 12). With regard to the context of a changing public sphere (and accompanying spaces) in Marseille, such a system further determines "who can take part in the 'common' with regard to what one does, [and] to the time and the space within which one practices their activity" (ibid.: 13). In this conceptual framework, a critical consciousness is approved and engendered from a sensitive political awareness. Such is the case of Tabasco Video's web documentary, when it encourages local citizens to voice their own perspectives and challenge others' opinions regarding the transformation of a site that they have previously used as a common space and its reconversion for cultural purposes.

As I explore in the following two sections, the precise form of Tabasco Video's collaborations with area residents revolve around empowerment rather than education. By this, I mean that Tabasco Video's projects have not solely sought to teach their collaborators *how* to make their own videos, films, or web-based media; rather they have given them the necessary psychological and material tools to consider themselves as capable interlocutors whose opinions on a given subject are not only valid but also necessary. The workshop at the Collège du Vieux-Port provides a recent example of this evolving formula that is characterized by an investment in the perspectives and claims of city inhabitants, but that in this case places them side-by-side and head-to-head with those in positions of institutional and political power.

Documenting a Changing Urban Public Sphere

Like many local non-profit organizations in France, Tabasco Video is an "Association Loi de 1901", a legal status that allows it to receive government subsidies while paying salaries to its members, who are considered as contractual employees. Marseille has a relatively large number of associations and is as such reputed in France as a "ville associative", a status that is frequently identified as a sign of the city's vibrancy in spite of its widespread unemployment and poverty. Marseille's associations, of which Tabasco Video can be considered a representative example, tend to be concentrated in downtown areas that have seen the arrival of artists and other members of a "creative class" from elsewhere in France over the past two decades (Donzel 2014). Tabasco's members, in turn, are for the most part representative of this social class. They are also largely from outside of Marseille, although they were drawn to the city for a variety of reasons and its members are composed of French citizens and one Moroccan.

Tabasco Video's unique resistance practice in turn emerges from the group's goal to create and disseminate ideas through the medium of moving images and voices. Founded in 1999 by its current director, Benoît Ferrier, Tabasco Video initially existed to provide a legal and economic structure for its members' activities, namely the creation of documentary films. As Ferrier recalls, "Documentary film interested me… [and] I liked the idea of working with non-professionals to write and make unconventional films" (October 13, 2014). Unlike the larger part of their local working-class and minority collaborators, the majority of the members of Tabasco Video come from middle-class backgrounds, many of them from outside the city or its immediate region. Ferrier had arrived in Marseille in the 1990s and settled in the Panier, bordered on its southern side by the Vieux-Port, to the west by the city's foundering commercial port, to the east by the town hall and to the north by the third arrondissement. This placed the district directly between one of the poorest urban zones in Europe and the former Joliette dock areas, then in the process of being converted into a mixed-use office complex under Euroméditerranée's purview. As a primarily working-class neighborhood that had historically served as a point of arrival for generations of immigrants to Marseille, Ferrier found the Panier in the final years of the twentieth century to be a charged and contested urban environment, but also an attractive one in which to live, distinguished as it was by centuries of arriving and departing ethnic groups from around the Mediterranean basin.

Several years later, the Panier has already lived through its first stages of gentrification and growing attention as a tourist attraction. Its once cramped, dirty, and ominous alleyways and narrow streets have been largely cleaned of garbage and malingerers. Local bars have transformed into upscale restaurants, a motorized tourist train plies the cobblestoned alleys with international visitors on board snapping pictures of street scenes, and the popular annual Fête du Panier has had its funding removed by the regional government, in part due to complaints from newer residents that the event attracts undesirable elements who are noisy and leave trash behind. Most recently, with the opening of the MuCEM and the Villa Méditerranée, the Panier has seen its popularity with day-trippers grow, many combining a visit to the area's new institutions with a leisurely afternoon meal at one of the restaurants in the district's central Place de Lenche.

These recent factors have led to Tabasco Video's return to its original concern for the Panier as what Ferrier terms "a small village in the middle of a city." Ferrier explains the contemporary interest of "Et le Panier dans tout ça?" in the following terms: "[The Panier] is an attractive neighborhood, there's history there... And it's true that we've seen it change a lot in eight years. But Marseille has also been transformed" (October 13, 2014). Ferrier goes on to detail the ideological background to Tabasco's focus on local inhabitants and their perspectives:

> Their words should be taken into account. Theirs are perspectives that we don't hear and that are just as legitimate as others'. And that means that they deserve their place in society. I think that this is the political project ... in a sense it belongs to what we call participatory democracy. To help a local territory is to increase one's perspective on the world, which can help advance the debate. (Ibid.)

Tabasco's engagement in the Panier neighborhood began with Ferrier's work on a documentary film about a first wave of gentrification in the mid-1990s and expanded through further activities driven by collaborators, notably Tabasco's series of short documentaries hosted on their "Web TV". What began its life in 2004 on Tabasco Video's website as part of a project entitled "100 Paroles" (100 Words) eventually consisted of a compendium of all of Tabasco's short-form video projects on a freely accessible platform. These range from informational videos to impromptu cooking demonstrations to the type of critical perspectives on the changing neighborhood that would form the basis for "Et le Panier dans tout ça?" several years later.

The culmination of Tabasco's experiment with its "Web TV" was the mini-series "C'est Pas Joli Joli", a spoof of the popular French soap opera "Plus Belle la Vie", which, while based in Marseille, notoriously casts actors from elsewhere in France (remarkable by their accents) and is considered by locals to be a catalogue of Marseillean stereotypes. In Tabasco's series, scripted by members and local residents, inhabitants of the Panier play themselves, sometimes to a tee, through a sequence of vignettes that play off the soap opera's themes while relating them to local realities, including unemployment and gentrification.

The final episodes of "C'est Pas Joli Joli" were completed in 2013, leaving Tabasco Video in search of a new project. With several of its members having participated in a web documentary workshop earlier that year, this interactive form seemed to be a formally innovative way for the association to prolong their collaborations, while permitting them to remain within a similar critical framework. Another key impetus for the new project was implied in its title. While Tabasco Video's prior work tended to focus on the Panier as a singularly colorful neighborhood to the exclusion of the rest of the city, in "Et le Panier dans tout ça?" they consciously took a step back to consider the place of the neighborhood and its residents in the context of their wider urban context. In the first volume of the web documentary, which will be subsequently described in greater depth, the precise context was the neighboring J4 Esplanade, a former port quay recently transformed into a public space, and both the symbolic and physical center of wider changes afoot in Marseille.

The J4 was originally built in between 1949 and 1951 at the southern extremity of the Port of Marseille, but the era when it came into being was already one of transition. In the 1970s, much of Marseille's port infrastructure was shifted some fifty kilometers west of the city to the town of Fos-sur-Mer, where it remains to this day. The J4 subsequently became one of several embarkation points for ferries plying the Mediterranean Sea between Marseille and ports in Corsica as well as Tunisia and Algeria, which have continued to operate beyond the colonial period. During a time when Marseille enjoyed international notoriety as an overly porous city, a den of organized crime, and the "French Connection" in an international opiates trade, it was possible for locals to easily access the J4, along with the port's other principal quays, for licit or illicit purposes. Since it was no longer extensively used by shipping lines and its storage hangar had been demolished a few years earlier, it came as an inevitability when the J4 was decommissioned in the late 1990s, ceded by the Port to the City of Marseille under the authority of Euroméditerranée, which subsequently decided to participate in the space's redesign in tandem with the construction of the MuCEM and Villa Méditerranée.

Similarly, what ensued was not a clear-cut process of redevelopment, since the decommissioned J4 was an accessible space whose uses were yet to be deter-

mined. In this state, it quickly became home to an itinerant community composed of local residents and those from more distant neighborhoods. Many of the space's new users were remarkable for their illicit practices (smoking hashish, drinking alcohol, drug selling),[6] while others were simply attracted by the presence of an accessible swath of empty space along the sea in an overpopulated city center. During this period the J4 also attracted seasonal swimmers who dove into the sea from its pier, solitary city residents who came there to stroll or sit by themselves, and fishermen, groups of whom arrived before dawn while others preferred the period just after dusk.

Shortly thereafter the J4 was targeted by a landscaping project that sought to smooth some of its rougher edges, while keeping the space open and accessible. This provisional project saw the space attract even more visitors, including school students from the Panier, whose teachers brought them to use the J4 as a playground or football field, conveniently situated near to their cramped neighborhood streets. While the J4's initial redevelopment did not correspond with the imposition of new rules and regulations, this regime of open access changed when the space was gradually closed to the public beginning in late 2011. When it reopened in early 2013, its raked-gravel surface had been denuded of any structures, trees or protective spaces, aside from the edifices around which it was now to be oriented: the MuCEM, the Villa Méditerranée, and above-ground entrances to a five hundred-place underground parking garage.

While the presence of fishermen is generally tolerated on the redeveloped J4, theirs and other former practices such as swimming remain restricted and they report being hassled by security guards and police officers more than in the past. Among other things, an increased security apparatus has meant that those who used the J4 for illicit practices are not as welcome there. Many former users, from fishermen and swimmers to idle drinkers and hashish smokers, have confessed that the increased attention focused on their presence and activities has led them to stay away. Other members of the same categories of users continue to frequent the J4, although their presence is generally less remarkable among crowds of the site's new tourist users. In choosing the J4 as principal site for the first section of their web documentary, members of Tabasco Video were aware of its significance for Panier residents, but were simultaneously interested in refocusing local attention toward a contested site that has received less attention than other such spaces in downtown Marseille.

Producing Local Perspectives

The first volume of "Et le Panier dans tout ça?," entitled "The J4, the Panier, and Us," consisted of the results of workshops carried out with students in a single class at the Collège du Vieux-Port, located roughly between the Panier's central Place de Lenche and the J4 Esplanade. The workshops took place three times a week over twelve weeks from March through June 2014, excluding school holidays. In an explanatory note provided to school administrators and institutional collaborators (including those at the MuCEM and the Villa Méditerranée), Nicolas Dupont and Rémi Laurichesse, Tabasco's coordinators for the school project described it in the following terms:

> This part of the web documentary "Et le Panier dans tout ça?" will be presented in the form of successive video sequences through which the viewer will navigate to follow the students in their journey. We will ask them about their links to the J4 (public space and cultural places), and through the video medium, bring them to reflect on this environment in order to discover their neighborhood in other terms.

The primary method used in this process was video-recorded interviews, carried out by the middle-school students, in large part using questionnaires prepared by them along with Dupont and Laurichesse. The responses to these questionnaires, and the students' observations of parallel dynamics on the J4, provided an illuminating response to their initial perceptions regarding the J4's change for the worse. Students met a range of visitors, both inside and outside the MuCEM and the Villa Méditerranée.

Many of these people corresponded to pre-existent categories that they had expected to encounter: tourists with little interest in the J4's pre-transformation uses or embittered locals with nothing nice to say about the new buildings or renovated space. Others challenged preconceptions: for example, a woman living elsewhere in Marseille who regularly comes to the MuCEM to sit and relax in freely accessible areas on its roof terrace. Still others whom they encountered confirmed some of their own consistent challenges to the space's new rules for appropriate uses: a number of the boys in the class had frequented the J4 during warmer months to go swimming for years, and while they had altered their behavior slightly in the aftermath of the space's transformation, they did still continue to swim there whenever possible as they had in the past. Many of the interactions confirmed the students' particular perspective as members of working-class, ethnic minority communities struggling to make sense of their new social roles in a rapidly changing urban context.

In one of the sections of the first part of "Et le Panier dans tout ça?" two students restaged an encounter where one informs the other that he had been swimming near the MuCEM when he observed a number of police coming toward him. The student describes how he began to climb up the MuCEM's latticed concrete façade, but the policemen allegedly caught him, brought him to the MuCEM security director's office, from which he escaped and ran away, meeting back up with his friends at some distance from the J4. This certainly exaggerated story concluded with his interlocutor responding, "Hey, c'mon, let's just go back to the J4." The first student shrugs his shoulders, dismissing his own vow to stay away, and says: "OK, if you want." This exchange both reveals the students' ongoing engagement with the J4 and exposes their shared perspective that the MuCEM and Villa Méditerranée are primarily viewed as buildings (and either playthings or obstacles) rather than institutions. When they are considered as institutions, their cultural programming is considered secondarily (or not at all) to the increased security regime that accompany their presence on the J4.

While "Et le Panier dans tout ça?" did not appear

to alter students' practices on the J4, it provided a form for them to express their disagreement with the changes that had taken place there, contributing to the development of their critical and political perspectives. In some cases it became obvious to Dupont, Laurichesse, and myself, that students were voicing critiques that they had heard from their family members or older neighborhood residents, but in others (as in the questions of access regarding swimming off the J4) they had developed their own criticisms based on limits increasingly placed on their own experiences. However, during the making of the web documentary, the students were also confronted with social and professional categories they had not previously encountered – the tourists of whom they tended to speak with such disdain, but also professional representatives of the MuCEM and Villa Méditerranée, including architects and curators. While these interactions did not necessary alter their pre-existing perspectives, in some cases they provided students with an increased context for their criticisms as well as allowing them a forum to express these.

In one exchange with an architect affiliated with the Villa Méditerranée, a structure that has been widely denigrated by locals and outside observers for its odd shape, high cost, and minimal floor-space, one student explained that, to him, the building resembles a giant whistle. The architect initially laughed it off as a child's joke, but was eventually forced to acknowledge that many other locals have failed to grasp the Villa's subtle formal symbolism.

Through the use of footage such as this, the Tabasco Video team, in this case principally Dupont and Laurichesse, were able to use the form of a free and widely-accessible web documentary for which they had received support from local governance structures and the J4's institutions, to transmit a critique by a relatively precarious group of local residents that in many cases was directed toward those same institutions. In this way, Tabasco Video provided the form and means for a determined critique faithful to the perspectives of those who had made their opinions known. At the same time, however, Tabasco Video members made sure to link the questions of

urban spatial transformation to the culture concept, a connection that their collaborators may not have made on their own.

One item on the students' questionnaires wondered whether the changes on the J4 could be considered "cultural or touristic," a distinction that seemed relatively unclear to a number of the students as well as those whom they interrogated. Dupont and Laurichesse's editing made a point by resolving this sequence with the following transparent exchange:

Man: It's both.
Student: Why?
Man: Because culture attracts tourists.

Through the form of the questionnaires, "Et le Panier dans tout ça?" emphasizes the concerns of those posing the questions, by leading students to reflect upon their own attitudes as much as the responses provided to them, including their own occasional genuine confusion at the use of certain concepts or qualifiers. Among these was the meaning of the word "Mediterranean", which many students proved incapable of defining.

One sequence in the web documentary involved a number of students reflecting on a rhetorical question that had been posed to them by a fisher on the J4 in an earlier interview: "What's the point of talking about the 'Mediterranean' in Marseille?"

"We see it every day," the students claimed, alluding to the eponymous Sea. "Do we really need special museums for that?" In the subsequent video, student-interviewers stared off into space, bemused or confused, while their adult interlocutors no less awkwardly attempted to formulate answers equating a "mixing of culture", "port cities", and other standard yet stereotypical characterizations of Mediterranean identity. The last institutional representative to appear on screen in this sequence goes so far as to claim that "Marseille is the cradle of the Mediterranean," a hyperbolic statement at best. Tabasco Video linked these statements to students' own bemused attempts to reflect on the Mediterranean question, revealing that this terminology is to a large extent an external imposition and not a descriptor that they themselves readily use.

In the final sequence of their section of the web documentary, the students wonder about the repercussions of the J4's transformation on the neighborhood where the majority of them live. Back in the Panier, they meet a variety of interlocutors, some newcomers who claim that the neighborhood's superficial improvement has made them more comfortable there and helped attract tourist euros, while others complain about the unfortunate effects of an increasingly visible gentrification. But this reflection on their neighborhood assumes secondary status to the effects of changes on the J4, which in turn appear as an integral part of the Panier's common space. In this way, the first volume of "Et le Panier dans tout ça?" compares changes in access to the J4 to the effects of similar changes in spatial qualification and control in the Panier, but makes a particular point in linking these to the presence and effects of the MuCEM and Villa Méditerranée.

In an exchange following the completion of the first volume, Nicolas Dupont, one of the conveners of the Collège du Vieux-Port workshop, explained the relation of "Et le Panier dans tout ça?" to increasingly widespread Mediterranean discourse in Marseille:

> It's like that everywhere when they try to make a label or a brand… For everything that you make, there needs to be a precise entity, so that's what they're doing in Marseille with Euroméditerranée, making a label for what Marseille is today. But it's oversimplified and the approach of local participatory work is to be closer to the individual, particularities, and singularities. Of course it's different. (October 13, 2014)

With this statement, Dupont directly opposes what he terms the "label" or "brand" that is increasingly applied to Marseille, that of a "Mediterranean" city, with the more localized and less marketable realities closer to the "individual" level, which are less easy to generalize or simplify. This corresponds with Tabasco leader Ferrier's stated interest in "participatory democracy" and more specifically the opinions of a multitude of local residents, rather than the sound bite version of what he refers to with near-revulsion as the mainstream "media". However, if the Tabasco Video team may appear to be motivated by specific political convictions, they tend to deny that these are their own. Long-time member Élodie Sylvain explains,

> I don't let my own political perspectives in the project. What interests me when I interview a neighborhood resident is what he thinks. I can put my perspectives in, but that's just to start a debate. Regarding the changes in the neighborhood, I don't put my perspectives into the work that I do with residents. What interests me is what they have to say. (Ibid.)

Despite Sylvain's insistence on her objectivity, there clearly exists an imperative in considering the opinions of a certain population that in the context of their specific spatial contestations contributes toward the creation of a counter-discourse.

In a subsequent exchange, Ferrier and Dupont explain that they have no particular disagreement with the use of the Mediterranean label in general terms, but feel that Tabasco's project allows for the questioning of the effects of this type of terminology. Their project – both "Et le Panier dans tout ça?" and the works they have created over the years – have the benefit of emphasizing local specificities in the naming of identities and the corresponding granting of spatial access and authority in Marseille, as the following exchange reveals.

> Ferrier: Marseille is part of the Mediterranean's history. It belonged to this history… and it still does.
> Dupont: But you need to define what Mediterranean culture is.
> Ferrier: There's no single culture. There're *many* cultures.
> Dupont: Yeah, many cultures. And that makes sense to speak of Mediterranean cultures and to say that Marseille is a Mediterranean city. When

you hear that, you think of a mix of cultures. How does Marseille exist as a French city? It exists in a whole territory, of southern France, a Mediterranean territory. So obviously Marseille is going to be more Mediterranean than other cities... I think that it makes sense to give Marseille this specificity. But it's important not to fall into shortcuts. (Ibid.)

Here, Dupont demonstrates a tendency to resist the reduction of Marseille and Marseillais to a single identity, while accepting the utility of Mediterranean identity as a worthwhile descriptor for a diversity of cultures. This corresponds with the critique of the MuCEM and Villa Méditerranée that emerges in the web documentary. Through the inhabitants' opinions and in what Ferrier acknowledges are the political choices evident in Tabasco members' editing processes, a distinctly more critical and nuanced view of the localized use and effects of the Mediterranean label emerges, which Dupont's pronouncement serves to summarize.

Conclusion

In its use of the internet as an online platform for the dissemination of the final work, Tabasco Video takes advantage of a form that has been used to a large degree by social movements in recent years, including those originating in a number of Mediterranean countries during anti-austerity protests and the Arab Spring. The difference is that Tabasco's use of the form is primarily designed to provide wide access to the vision of Marseillean urban realities that emerged from the production of the web documentary. It is its dual desire to empower and depict – while avoiding an easy recourse to didactic or ideological discourse – that produces Tabasco Video's digital resistance model, which, in its wide online accessibility, provides a counterpoint and a counterdiscourse to Marseille's new cultural institutions' better-funded depictions of the Mediterranean as well as of the city.

The effects of this digital resistance remain unclear. A public presentation of the web documentary at the Villa Méditerranée in October 2015 was attended by the same institutional representatives from the initial meeting in 2013. Reportedly, all of their feedback was positive, which may initially be puzzling, although Nicolas Dupont has attempted to situate these reactions in the terms of the collaboration.

[In the web documentary,] both institutions are highlighted equally in terms of the link that they create with their surroundings, which lends them an image of proximity that they seek. I also think that the children's perspective allows them to say things that adults wouldn't be able to say. Their direct mode of address is funny and destabilizing at the same time (as in the interview with the Villa's architect). (September 7, 2016)

Dupont further wonders if the first section of the web documentary ultimately served to "introduce subjects with children... [before] investigat[ing] them with adults" in the subsequent sections. However, I argue that the first volume (to which I limited this article's discussion due to my comparative proximity to its process) represents something more singular than the other two: the innovation of "The J4, The Panier and Us" comes from its serious treatment of youthful points of view as worthwhile of engagement. In this regard, whatever the outcome of the project's effects, it has achieved its principal goal in providing a forum for the expression of local views. Furthermore, in empowering local youth more specifically it both asserts the value of their views and transmits a record of their engagement in a form that is widely and permanently accessible. Ultimately, the accessibility of this assertion of local values permits future uses of this and other projects by Tabasco Video and similar organizations elsewhere, including in applications that may extend beyond their initial digital context. In the meantime, the web documentary remains widely viewable in its online form to local residents as well as to others elsewhere who may be interested in pursuing similar projects, but also as evidence of their achievement in contradicting the dominant institutional perspective on local culture.

Notes

1 Thanks are due to members of Tabasco Video who generously allowed me to observe and participate in different stages of their web documentary project, which forms the basis for this article as well as a section of my dissertation: Mohamed Boubidar, Nicolas Dupont, Remi Laurichesse, Benoît Ferrier, Élodie Sylvain, Pauline Duclos, Gerard Brechler. I would also like to thank the guest editors of this issue and two anonymous reviewers, whose comments led me to clarify several important points in this article. Finally, I would like to thank Michel Peraldi for his support of my research in Marseille and Mariangela Ciccarello for the invigorating discussions and encouragement.

2 The latter, which at the time described itself as "a structure dedicated to cross-cultural dialogues," has since undergone a substantial reorganization in its mission and goals that has reoriented its focus away from cultural programming and toward cooperation between regional political entities and civil society representatives.

3 A sometimes incomplete English-language version of the first volume of "Et le Panier dans tout ça?" is accessible via the following link: http://www.lepanierdanstoutca.tabascovideo.com/volume1/.

4 The French notion of a "politique culturelle" (or national cultural politics) provides further background for this institutional support. As Brubaker writes, "French nationhood is constituted by political unity, [yet] it is centrally expressed in the striving for cultural unity" (1992: 1). One of the major characteristics of this French "aesthetic State" (Urfalino 2004) in the post-World War II period was its increasing encouragement of cultural democratization. Beyond the Ministry of Culture's gradual decentralization in the form of regional cultural centers, the long-term effects of this process include increased funding for local cultural organizations and support for their activities, even if the recent economic downturn has seen a reduction in these.

5 My own film about the changing uses of public waterfront space in Marseille, entitled "Promenade", had its world premiere at the FID-Marseille international film festival in July 2016.

6 While permitted in the majority of French municipalities, the public consumption of alcoholic beverages is currently illegal in Marseille. In practice, public drinking laws are unequally respected and enforced. The notion of "illicit" activities is meant to encompass those practices that would attract more attention from authorities if they took place in more central public spaces than the J4, in part due to the identity of their practitioners, physically identifiable by their North African descent.

References

Borja, Jean-Stephane, Martine Derain & Véronique Manry 2010: *Attention à la fermeture des portes! Citoyens et habitants au coeur des transformations urbaines: L'expérience de la rue de la République à Marseille.* Marseille: Éditions Commune.

Brubaker, Rogers 1992: *Citizenship and Nationhood in France and Germany.* Cambridge, MA: Harvard University Press.

Bullen, Claire 2012: Marseille, ville méditerranéenne? Enjeux de pouvoir dans la construction des identités urbaines. *Rives méditerranéennes* 42, 157–171.

Carrière, Daniel 2013: *À l'épreuve du doute, de la violence, et de la solidarité: Itinéraires méditerranéens entre la France et l'Algérie.* Paris: Le Publieur.

Cartelli, Philip 2016: *Becoming Euro-Mediterranean: Reframing Urban Space and Identity in Southern France.* Ph.D. Dissertation. Harvard University/Ecole des hautes études en sciences sociales.

Critical Art Ensemble 2001: *Digital Resistance: Explorations in Tactical Media.* New York: Autonomedia.

De Moriamé, Virginie 2012: La mémoire du passé colonial dans les relations euro-méditerranéennes: Une analyse du discours européen. In: Houma Ben Hamouda & Mathieu Bouchard (ed.), *La construction d'un espace euro-méditerranéen: Genèses, mythes, perspectives.* Brussels: Peter Lang, pp. 141–156.

Donzel, André 2014: *Le nouvel esprit de Marseille.* Paris: L'Harmattan.

Downing, John 2008: Social Movement Theories and Alternative Media: An Evaluation and Critique. *Communication, Culture & Critique* 1, 40–50.

Gifreu, Arnau 2011: The Interactive Multimedia Documentary as a Discourse on Interactive Non-fiction: For a Proposal of the Definition and Categorisation of the Emerging Genre. *Hiptertext* 9, https://www.upf.edu/hipertextnet/en/numero-9/interactive-multimedia.html. Accessed May 10, 2017.

Maisetti, Nicolas 2014: *Opération culturelle et pouvoirs urbains: Instrumentalisation économique de la culture et luttes autour de Marseille-Provence Capitale européenne de la culture 2013.* Paris: L'Harmattan.

Milan, Stefania 2013: *Social Movements and their Technologies: Wiring Social Change.* London: Palgrave Macmillan.

Rancière, Jacques 2000: *Le partage du sensible: Esthétique et politique.* Paris: La Fabrique.

Smith, Neil 1996: *The New Urban Frontier: Gentrification and the Revanchist City.* London: Routledge.

Temime, Émile 2002: *Un rêve méditerranéen: Des Saint-Simoniens aux intellectuels des années trente.* Arles: Actes Sud.

Urfalino, Philippe 2004: *L'invention de la politique culturelle.* Paris: Hachette.

Vergès, Pierre, Isabelle Hajek & Véronique Jacquemoud 1999: *Les marseillais parlent de leur ville: Étude de l'image de Marseille.* Aix-en-Provence: LAMES-MMSH.

Visier, Claire 2005: La "Méditerranée": D'une idéologie militante à une vulgate consensuelle. *Sciences de la société* 65, 145–163.

Philip Cartelli is Assistant Professor of Film at Wagner College, New York, where he also co-directs the Film and Media Studies program. His current interests center on the role of research in cinematic practice.
(pcartelli@gmail.com)

GREEN RESISTANCE OR REPRODUCTION OF NEOLIBERAL POLITICS?
Grassroots Collaborative Practices in Slovenia's "Green Capital" Ljubljana

Saša Poljak Istenič, Research Centre of the Slovenian Academy of Sciences and Arts

The article presents an ethnographic study of grassroots green resistance practices to neoliberalism and the visions of (a) more sustainable future(s) in the City of Ljubljana. It analyzes the acts and discourses of local alternative (anarchist) and mainstream ("creative") communities that oppose cultural and spatial policies at the municipal, national and EU levels. Their practices raise concerns about the instrumentalization of basic human activities and grassroots initiatives as well as NGOs' new responsibilities previously in domain of the state. Most of them get appropriated by the city in order to prove how it successfully abides by the neoliberal politics of the EU and therefore result in reproducing the system they oppose while communities are stripped of their power for effective resistance.

Keywords: creativity, resistance, neoliberalism, green politics, Slovenia

"Beet the system!" calls the banner of *Zadruga Urbana* (Cooperative Urbana), an association from Slovenia's capital Ljubljana formed by people dissatisfied with the current system of food production (thus the pun beet/beat). Their practices – which can be labeled "green resistance" that originated in the 1960s as a division of counter-culture movements – were triggered by the last austerity crisis, which highlighted social anomalies predominantly linked to neoliberalism and encompassing unsustainable attitudes (in environmental, economic, social and cultural sense; cf. Nurse 2006). In recent years, minor grassroots contestations, similar to the endeavors of Zadruga Urbana, increasingly supplement larger social movements in opposing neoliberal politics and austerity measures and offer solutions for problems previously addressed by welfare (but also cultural, spatial, environmental and some other) policies. They often address social values linked to left-wing (or socialist) political orientations and present the opposite pole of neoliberal characteristics, such as social equality, social justice, solidarity, reciprocity and collaboration/cooperation. This phenomenon is also distinctive for the Mediterranean, the region severely hit by the 2008 crisis. Although Slovenia is often referred to as "the land between" (Luthar 2008) due to its geostrategic position between the Adriatic, the Pannonian Plain, the Alps and the Dinaridic mountains, it is in certain contexts also classified as a Mediterranean country, as it has 43 km of coast-

Saša Poljak Istenič 2018: Green Resistance or Reproduction of Neoliberal Politics?
Grassroots Collaborative Practices in Slovenia's "Green Capital" Ljubljana.
Ethnologia Europaea 48:1, 34–49. © Museum Tusculanum Press.

line, 1.734 km^2 of terrain defined as Mediterranean (Kladnik 1997), and some Mediterranean characteristics – although "ambiguous" (Baskar 2002).

Most studies that focus on practices of solidarity, reciprocity and collaboration (which I understand as a more active involvement than cooperation; cf. English Language & Usage Stack Exchange 2011) deal with resistance to globalization or specifically address neoliberalism. However, as argued by David Featherstone, instead of treating neoliberalism as a "hegemonic" project that calls forth resistance with no tendency to disrupt its claims to hegemonic status, researchers should be attentive to the dynamic trajectories forged through grassroots resistances and be "sensitive to the very different ways differently placed struggles were conducted and articulated. [...] This allows a focus on the diverse terms, practices and spatialities through which neoliberalism has been brought into contestation" (Featherstone 2015: 15). My study wishes to follow this call, taking green initiatives as an example and pointing out that the majority of studied practices are not visible enough to be perceived as a protest and massive enough to represent a social movement. However, despite being mere grassroots social experiments, which stay marginal (or "alternative") per se, they indicate a wider tendency for a more just, equal, supportive, integrated, diverse and eco-conscious society, thus echoing a general ("mainstream") austerity trend to make life more sustainable (in all aspects of the term).

In recent years, Ljubljana has put great efforts into urban branding, striving for titles and awards with the aim to raise the city's profile and strengthen its position on the European and global cultural, tourist and (urban) political map. In June 2014, the city won the *European Green Capital 2016* award, which put the spotlight on diverse top-down as well as bottom-up green practices in Ljubljana with various agendas. The main goal of this article is to critically examine local green practices that implicitly or explicitly oppose recent austerity measures in the context of neoliberalism, which has dismantled the more socially oriented political and economic framework characteristic of former socialist countries. Resistance is thus understood here as a struggle of communities to overcome constraints, imposed upon them by current politics of cities, states and the European Union. I use the term to refer to actions that (attempt to) challenge neoliberal societal relations, processes or institutions. However, as pointed out by Akhil Gupta and James Ferguson (1997: 18), "[o]ne cannot decide whether something is or is not resistance in absolute terms; resistance can exist only in relation to a 'strategy of power,' and such strategies are shifting, mobile, and multiple." Turning the famous Foucault claim that power implies resistance into "where there is resistance, there is power" (Abu Lughod 1990: 42), special attention is given to the acts and discourses of communities that resist the "strategies of power" in the form of neoliberal green politics on different scales. In the context of Ljubljana, the article focuses on the following questions: What kind of communities develop from such collaborative practices? What change do they seek? How do they oppose the system and in what way do they reproduce it? By answering them, I will assess the resistance potential of "alternative" and "mainstream" green-oriented communities – where the adjectives indicate their culture as well as their social position – and the response of local authorities to their practices. In this way, the study aims to complement analyses of practices in the Mediterranean aimed at loosening austerity measures and protesting against the political handling of the crisis.

Resisting a Resistance: Theoretical Starting Point and Methodological Framework

Resistance as a concept attained "theoretical hegemony" by the end of the 1990s and has been strongly related to Foucauldian explorations of power in all manifestations (Brown 1996: 729). It evolved from an object of research in various academic disciplines even in the new millennium to a "division" of studies in its own right. The Resistance Studies Network (since 2006), the *Resistance Studies Magazine* (2008–2013) and the *Journal of Resistance Studies* (since 2015) represent forums dedicated to critically examining struggles against practices of domination, exploitation and oppression as well as freedoms that impose ethical constraints on individuals and communities (Resistance Studies Network – About 2016).

My research forms part of the postdoctoral project titled Surviving, Living, Thriving: Creativity as a Way of Life.[1] Not being primarily formulated as a study of resistance practices, the project was conceived as a protest (on the part of a researcher in humanities) against dominant international interdisciplinary analyses of creative cities, clusters, industries as well as the creative economy and the creative class perceived exclusively in neoliberal terms as a motor of economic development. These studies have as a rule placed creativity in relation to technology and innovation, thus reducing it to a mere product and disregarding the intangible, qualitative aspects of life in contemporary cities. In this light, my goal has been to explore creativity as an interactive social process, departing from the prevailing understanding of creativity either as the innovation or as the talent of the individual. My approach is inspired by anthropological accounts on creativity and following cultural initiatives that significantly contribute to the perceived "creativity" of the city but have not been recognized as creative (at least not in the sense of creative economy). In this way, I follow the call of Nick Wilson (2010) for a stronger social conceptualization of creativity, for creativity that is inherently inclusive and social in nature. When transgressing boundaries (of states and groups, industries, epistemologies etc.), individuals as well as communities reproduce or transform social values, resisting compliance with existing social anomalies and aiming to create a better (or different) world. I have focused on social creativity by examining livelihood strategies of various individuals and communities that resist neoliberal values and challenge prevalent notions that favor financial over human (social, cultural, symbolic) capital.

Given the progression of the economic crisis, I have paid attention to actions aimed at strengthening social actors' existential stability by increasing their social capital – which in concrete cases implied relying on social networks, being sensitive to cultural differences, and aiming for ecological sustainability. The buzzwords of my research therefore include

solidarity, justice, participation, ecology, and non-consumerism; however, resistance as a concept has not been at the center of my theoretical framework. On the other hand, various media and personal accounts have brought resistance to my attention, as social actors spoke of their motivations to oppose the neoliberal system, local authorities or prevalent ideologies. As a result, they have as a rule taken on alternative lifestyles because they did not want to submit to the hegemonic structures of the neoliberal world. This implies that the economic crisis has been indeed popularly understood as a crisis of values and explains why those who exercise alternative lifestyles pay so much attention to ethics.

My fieldwork of two and a half years in the Slovenian capital, which draws upon my fifteen years of living and researching in Ljubljana, was dedicated to mapping collective practices across the city, conducting participant observation of selected practices (where most of the informal conversations were taking place), and recording narrative interviews. I focused on a range of social actors – individuals that either were engaged in the city's social life, were affiliated in formal associations, joined informal initiatives, or worked in NGOs, social enterprises, other business entities, at the municipality or state ministries dealing with the cultural and creative sectors (47 altogether). Most of the practices I came across during my fieldwork have not been depicted as resistance. Some actors promote their practice as a cultural or social event, oscillating "on the verge between opposition and co-optation" (Leontidou 1990: 2). Others clearly express who or what they resist, but their acts stay out of the general public's limelight, covert or missed (cf. Hollander & Einwohner 2004: 544). Some acts stay unarticulated, inserted in the routine of everyday life (Scott 1985). The article is therefore based, firstly, on physical manifestations of "alternative" (or "resistance") green practices – in Foucault's words, "non-discursive domains" – and, secondly, on discourses, the "way of speaking" of their actors[2] (Foucault 1972).

To present the dynamic of resistance in Ljubljana, I structured the article into three ethnographic sections following an outline of the key counter-austerity grassroots narrative. The first focuses on marginal, "alternative" (i.e., anarchist) practices and discourses, which can be interpreted in the framework of the "right to the city" movement. The second presents "mainstream" (i.e., "creative") initiatives, which are more in line with general lifestyle and political tastes and often represent livelihood strategies of people working in the cultural and creative sector. In the third section, I contextualize both types of practices with branding strategies of the City of Ljubljana in order to assess their resistance potential. In conclusion, I summarize both modes of resistance, rethink the capacity of resistance practices to engender social change, and outline alternative future(s) they envision.

Solidarity: The Key Counter-austerity Grassroots Narrative

The recent economic crisis has stimulated the debates on responses *of* and *in* cities, the first of which focused on the macroeconomic aspects of urban austerity policies (e.g., Harvey 2012; Peck 2012) and neglected contestations from below. Grassroots resistance practices thus only recently came into attention of researchers. Among Mediterranean countries, Greece seems to be the most fruitful terrain for such studies (see, e.g., Arampatzi & Nicholls 2012; Rakopoulos 2013, 2014, 2015; Rüdig & Karyotis 2014; Arampatzi 2017), followed by Spain (Indignados movement), African shores and the Arab peninsula (the Arab Spring). Research in other Mediterranean countries (especially in Italy and Turkey) focused more on specific outbursts or on echoes of the massive movements mentioned above, including the Occupy movement. In Slovenia, resistance to austerity has not been a popular topic of research; if we disregard pure economic and political studies, it is mainly the domain of sociology (cf. Razsa & Kurnik 2012; Korošec 2014). In anthropology, Marta Gregorčič's work (2011) needs to be emphasized as it touches upon revolutionary anti-capitalist practices all over the world. Recent studies focused on Slovenia have been articulated mostly in terms of solidarity and reciprocity (cf. Simonič 2014; Vodopivec 2014).

Several Mediterranean researchers argue that the key counter-austerity grassroots narrative in Greece is indeed solidarity. Lila Leontidou (2015) draws attention to the ways "cosmopolitan solidarities" are forged through the use of information and communication technologies and how they can be implemented into neoliberal and mainstream conceptualizations of the city in order to reconnect to current "southern" (or Mediterranean) urban realities. Athina Arampatzi (2017) points out that solidarity-making "from below" empowers impoverished social groups to tackle their needs, while Theodoros Rakopoulos (2013) suggests that people's solidary activities actually comprise a wider political program that is more ambitious than simply attending to immediate hardships and that resembles the ideas of cooperativism and practical socialism.

In Slovenia, a former Yugoslav republic with its own, "soft" version of socialism and a relatively high economic and welfare standard, socialist ideas still permeate many practices that express disapproval with the current system burdened by austerity measures (mainly) in the welfare, health and cultural spheres. Such responses are often colored by nostalgia for times with no unemployment, affordable food and high social safety. However, nostalgia is not only a sentimental feeling but can be mobilized as "a resistance strategy of preserving one's personal history and group's identity … [and] an agent of liberation from oppression of contemporary hegemonic discourses and practices" (Velikonja 2009: 547). Most of the people who disagree with the current system allude to values linked to socialism and engage in critical creative activities that evoke "socialist" feelings of brotherhood, equality, social solidarity and stability as well as help reconstruct a utopian atmosphere of "good old times". People organize food-exchange outdoor events, which take the form of public socializing in front of the apartment buildings, an everyday event under socialism. They also set up cooperative urban gardening as an artistic research project that echoes post-war (but also older) agricultural practices. Others organize clean-up initiatives evoking the youth work brigades that built infrastructure all over socialist Yugoslavia. Although they actually conform to a neoliberal agenda – everybody should be creative and fulfill oneself in self-created "business" – they do express uneasiness or disagreement with austerity measures and compare the current situation with the times of higher welfare benefits as well as of stronger social (and personal) values. As I will show, anarchists[3] use a radical discourse (although some of their actions do not differ significantly from the "creative" projects), while "creatives" express resistance in an artistic way or with lifestyle choices.

"Alternative" Green Resistance Practices

In Ljubljana, and increasingly so all over Slovenia, resistance practices to neoliberalism – especially practices against modern consumerism and the commodification of everyday life – hinge on the collaboration of diverse inhabitants. These practices are as a rule officially (that is, in the mainstream discourses of public institutions and authorities) interpreted in a spatial way, as practices for the more efficient management of space. As such, they could have been classified as the "right to the city" movements. However, "[i]n many cases [the phrase] seems to mean just the right to a more 'human' life in the context of the capitalist city and on the basis of a ('reformed') representative 'democracy'" (Lopes de Souza 2010: 315). The same applies to Ljubljana's movements, which strive to "take back public spaces we forgot about." However, in contrast to similar movements in the Mediterranean and Latin America, most of them are not perceived or even recognized by the public as resistance, and they fail to gain sufficient power or human capital to enact the changes they are after. Materialized through initiatives engaging in community practices, co-working, community-led renovation, temporary use of space, urban gardening, local economies, housing communities and co-mobility, they merely represent social commentaries on urban spatial policy and are also interpreted as social experiments in the dominant discourse, as will be shown below.

The only exception among the "right to the city" movements, which is not incorporated into the mainstream discourse, is the anarchists' initiatives resisting municipal and global spatial policies outside the cultural/creative domain. Among them is *Zadruga Urbana* (Cooperative Urbana). While the organizational form of a cooperative can itself be seen as an element of socialist heritage[4] – although in this case the community is not registered as such but only tries to follow the principles of organization and functioning of cooperatives – its program also represents a vision to create a utopian society based on equality, social solidarity and shared economy (i.e., on socialist principles). The association perceives itself as an informal, autonomous "little urban-agricultural platform" that actively explores ways to operate non-hierarchically, inclusively and non-commercially. They mostly focus on the organization of activities linked to the sustainable production and consumption of food and include preparing public vegan dinners and crop barters as well as the transformation of abandoned urban places into collective gardens. They are usually most active at their headquarters in *Metelkova mesto* (Metelkova City), a part of Ljubljana that is the center of alternative culture, where they have also established a small collective garden because *"the place needed a sustainable moment."*

Collective action resulted in the establishment of another collective garden at an abandoned piece of land three kilometers from Metelkova mesto. The members of Zadruga decided to avoid applying for an official permit and paying rent. They have cultivated the land collectively and shared the crops spontaneously, and in these ways expressed resistance to the mainstream (Central European) gardening culture and especially to the city's policy on management of private gardens.[5] They also squatted on near-by premises to solve their housing problems. This created the basis for building a new community of approximately fifteen active gardeners in the center of the city, who experimented with autonomy to solve their needs, fulfill their aspirations, and develop their vision of society through self-organizing in a non-hierarchical way (Kilavo seme 2016). They have managed to gain sympathy from the local community; a farmer from the area even ploughed the occupied land on their request. The neighbors "on the one hand recognized [them] as people who will arrange disorderly surroundings; on the other hand, they knew that as long as the gardeners stay in the gardens, the concrete platforms for parking spaces will not be made and the buildings that would block their view will not arise" (Kilavo seme 2016). Their actions thus corresponded with the local vision of the place. However, when the land was about to become a construction site for a profitable real estate project, the gardeners failed to mobilize the broader community to raise their voices against the new construction plans in the neighborhood. The reason for this could be their specific narrative not resonating with the mainstream. Despite a professed openness to new members, the initiative is generally perceived as a subculture; the core community consists of young educated people with leftist political views. Furthermore, their public protest against demolishing the garden did not materialize on the site but took place mostly on social and alternative media. Whatever the outcome, the members publicly claimed they would not give up: "Maybe they will bulldoze our garden, but they will never be able to uproot our ideas and our activities. That is why we can confidently say that we will soon see each other in new gardens, and then we'll be better prepared" (Kilavo seme 2016).

In addition to the Zadruga, numerous individuals and communities disagree with the city's new vision of gardening on perfectly planned allotments; however, they complied with the legal forms of gardening in order to grow food near their homes instead of resorting to guerrilla tactics. In 2014, seven ways of such (i.e., non-guerrilla) gardening were identified in Ljubljana: gardening colonies, gardening as the continuation of tradition, legalized temporary use of land, gardening as area maintenance, gardening between houses and apartment buildings, gardening on a neighbor's property, and gardening in troughs (Simoneti & Fišer 2014). Although some of these forms were developed by creative initiatives with their own agenda, they have not grown into a wider social movement demanding greater authority and autonomy of the citizens to manage public spaces in accordance with their visions; instead, they (unwill-

ingly) serve the city's plans, as will be shown below.

Another prominent activity of Zadruga is organizing so-called alternative markets where participants exchange home-grown or processed food. It is an informal exchange market where most of the transactions are non-financial; however, money is allowed for purchasing those products in which producers invested their own resources (e.g., for packaging or processing). The participants include members and sympathizers of Zadruga who produce their own food or process crops into various products (juices, liquor, vinegar) as well as farmers who wish to sell their crops or products directly to consumers. The transactions mostly rely on trust; food is set up on the table, and participants are free to take whatever they want even if they did not bring anything to exchange as payment. These exchanges can happen without participants knowing who brought which food (if any), with the exception of the goods that have a fixed price; you can leave the money on the table. Despite allowing financial transactions, the gist of these markets is "*not the establishment of another consumerist chain, but to build social networks one can rely on*," as claimed by one of the participants. Their social capital is gained through community gardening, preparing public vegan dinners and participating in the food market. All these activities rely on solidarity with their participants and on reciprocity which can be delayed until one gets enough resources to exchange food or do something in return. Although Zadruga's members in this way try to ensure their basic existence, their actions also comprise a wider political program (cf. Rakopoulos 2013) that resists dominant social arrangements of food production and consumption and that embodies their vision of a direct economy.

This program is more consistently elaborated in the manifesto on the (de)institutionalization of gardening, which sums up the members' resistance to capitalism now developed into neoliberalism. They draw attention to the strategies of neoliberal policies to absorb alternative ideas into their own vision of the city and turn the fight against the destruction of environment into green capitalism. In this manner, protests against the global food industry have been

Ill. 1: Food to exchange at the alternative market of Zadruga Urbana. (Photo: Saša Poljak Istenič, March 17, 2016)

incorporated into eco, bio and fair-trade brands, and the fight for urban public spaces has been swallowed by policies to create designed gardens for rent and green jobs (Zadruga Urbana 2014). Such urban policies, especially characteristic for the "North" but also being imposed on the "South" despite different urban development trajectories (cf. Leontidou 2015), leave little space for spontaneous and informal social movements that would articulate their demands for social change as efficiently as they manage to do in the Mediterranean (cf. Arampatzi & Nicholls 2012; Pautz & Kominou 2013; Rakopoulos 2013, 2014, 2015; Cappucini 2015; Arampatzi 2017). The manifesto therefore in several ways reflects the critique of Mediterranean urban researchers, who draw attention to the fact that spontaneity and informality have been deeply embedded into the social fabric and are crucial for the urban development of the "southern" cities. However, they are now undermined through

the use of quasi-Orientalist discourses on the part of European Union power elites (cf. Leontidou 2014), who paint spontaneity and informality – at least in the case of gardening – as illegal, inappropriate, and non-exemplary (cf. City of Ljubljana quoted in Zadruga Urbana 2014).

"Creative" Grassroots Resistance

The European Union has opened up new perspectives for urban policies that demand citizen participation in initiatives for the improvement of urban issues (cf. Keresztély & Scott 2012). These initiatives are on the one hand in line with the neoliberal agenda of the city, the state and the European Union – and frequently supported with funds from these sources; on the other hand, they often publicly express dissatisfaction with current policies. The ones that are the most inclined to explore new possibilities of engagement in public spaces unite highly-skilled precarious workers who belong to the so-called creative class – especially because their activities, when proposed for funding, can be the means to ensure them an income. In the light of the current era of austerity, this often remains their only option to survive (in the market and existentially). However, in order to be eligible for funds, they have to comply with the rules of the system they work in: they need to register an entity with a formal legal status, invest time into bureaucratic work, provide enough human resources, and abide with other strict top-down rules. Is then any room left for critique of the system?

Although there are at least three areas in Ljubljana where gardening is a collaborative community practice, the most well-known is the garden named *Onkraj gradbišča* (Beyond the Construction Site), which materialized in the framework of one cultural festival in the summer of 2010. *Bunker,* a prominent NGO specialized in the performance and organization of cultural events, was in charge of the festival. At that time, it also participated in the Interreg

project Sostenuto that was revitalizing a prominent inner-city district. Project activities included a rearrangement of an abandoned construction site (from a chosen district) into a community urban garden for the purpose of the project and the festival. The Bunker association had enough influence to make a deal with the City of Ljubljana for the temporary use of the land and engaged a local creative initiative, the cultural and artistic association *Obrat*, which successfully converted their idea into reality. Due to the great interest of the neighbors, the site developed into a real community garden after the festival ended, again with the consent of the city.

The garden, although a site for community practice, has not been managed as spontaneously as Zadruga's garden, since the negotiations with the city to legally use the land require a registered organization to be involved. Obrat has taken care of such legal issues, but it transferred the management of the gardening activities to a self-organized coordination committee in 2015. As stated by one of the initiators,

Ill. 2: Spring work in the garden of Onkraj gradbišča. (Photo: Saša Poljak Istenič, March 12, 2016)

one person cannot be the leader forever, and the real challenge they have faced and now finally resolved is "*how you transfer this management to others. This is a process and it is hard [to transfer it], but this is sustainable. To make a project sustainable is that you ensure [there are] people who will continue this [activity].*" Despite the temporality of the garden, they too have plans for the future and intend to establish a new community garden when the construction works begin, as they believe they have managed to co-create a community capable of self-organizing and collaborating.

Approximately 100 persons care for 40 plots of land in the garden and participate in numerous public and community-based events that take place there or in other public spaces of the local community. The garden has become the site for establishing informal contacts and the solidary exchange of information, services and goods; however, since the gardeners have different social, ethnic and educational backgrounds, the garden operates as a space for sensibilization to differences as well as for practicing active co-design and sharing urban space. As such, it has been a popular location for various artistic and environmental projects, initiatives, events, for mass media coverage as well as for the local community. The garden community has also established various communication channels with the neighborhood and city authorities with a desire to gain public support, encourage people's participation and diversify socializing possibilities. Besides updating a fanzine, notice board and website, they also organize public events and workshops to revive local public life. It can be summarized that they, compared with the anarchistic initiatives that are more radical (guerrilla tactics, anti-dominance discourse, and subcultural characteristics), have gained stronger and more powerful public support.

As in the case of Zadruga, gardening in a creative framework occasionally serves as a political act against the management of public spaces or social insensibilities and inequalities. As explained by the creative initiative's spokesperson:

In a way we are enthusiasts, we are activists. We do not like how things in a society develop, we don't like how the place is treated and essentially we are insanely physical. I thought that I don't need another theoretical example of how good it would be if it was so and so, but that we need to make a practical case […] Let's look concretely at what that [garden] has brought about, what happened, did it really influence community cohesion, did it influence the safety of the neighborhood, are the people more connected. It did a little, but I don't know if it had a great impact.

By proving that an increasing number of people want to have a more active role in the co-creation of the city, the garden serves as a practical critique of the city's rigid, unifying policy of organizing and leasing small garden plots. It draws attention to the shortcomings of prevailing urban management of already scarce public spaces, which are also insufficiently supported by the proper mechanisms. By gaining local, academic and media support, the garden initiative pressures the city to ensure more places that are not earmarked for consumption and capital. However, as commented by the initiative's spokesperson:

The project did not bring about what we wished for. First, the city did not loosen the rules for the temporary use of places in such a way that people would have access to the land that is on hold. It is sick that we only have this project. I see this as bad, not as good. In fact, such projects should have developed all around Ljubljana.

The so-called *Mreža za prostor* (Network for Space), a network of various actors under the umbrella of the *Inštitut za politike prostora* (Institute for Spatial Policies),[6] now continue their efforts to loosen the rules for the temporary use of land; as a much stronger, bigger and influential initiative, they have hopes for gradual change.

The organized food and crops exchange outside the anarchists' initiatives have also gained much more support and many more followers than alternative markets organized by Zadruga Urbana and similar subcultural groups. The *Zelemenjava* (derived from "vegetable exchange") grew into mass public events of exchange not only of seeds, plants, crops, processed foods or food accessories, but also intangible things such as recipes and instructions. This initiative is now becoming a national socio-cultural movement as its events, which are organized locally by grassroots initiatives, are taking place in more than twenty towns around Slovenia. The only condition for participation is engaging in non-financial transactions based on the exchange of the material and the intangible according to personal preferences and negotiations. The organizational work is also voluntary; the founder and two colleagues do it as a hobby and seek places for events that are free of charge.

This initiative was not conceived with a resistance mindset but is continuously articulated as a critique of contemporary consumption. In the words of its spokesperson:

We are sick and tired that [consumption] is the only thing that exists. Every exit from the apartment is commercialized. Spending free time in public spaces cannot be unconnected with finances any more. [...] There are no pristine relations in a community any more, there is no habit of going to the neighbors for a coffee or playing in front of the apartment buildings, what we were used to do in our childhood and we now miss. And [Zelemenjava] is a parallel model; not that the people exit the classic economic model, but that they once a month build a parallel one.

This initiative – similar to the anarchist one – develops an organizational model of socializing and action that is not based on top-down principles but merely connects ideas and individuals to make transactions or events happen: "*You are not a participant in a passive sense, but everybody co-creates and co-organizes the event.*" Giving people equally important roles, the initiative tries to modify existing power relations and accord power to socially inferior or deprived individuals. This explains why these events are immensely popular among all social classes, from the unemployed to company executives, from cleaning ladies and migrants to intelligentsia with a Ph.D., as its founder explains:

But there they are totally equal because everybody has snails and are nervous because they eat their salads... You feel a sort of power in people with less income and education but who have twenty years of experience with gardening. Then somebody comes with clean fingernails and a super business card who tries it for the first time because it's a bit modern. Then a person can advise her/him and you see how proud she/he is.

Each gardener who participates in the events can also decide on the "exchange rate" – how much a vegetable or a product is worth and what he or she wishes in exchange; in this way, the events serve as a social corrective for poorer participants. They also empower people to actively participate in the food market and not submit to passive consumerism forced upon them by the neoliberal market economy, which is why such activities also gain the approval of the anarchist groups.

Such practices are often "swallowed up" by the city's spatial policies as role models of new governance of public places. Their initiators indeed seek the city's support so they may legally use public spaces. Yet they feel that there is a fine line between the city's support and its instrumentalization of "bottom-up" activities. For example, the city gives them the land for gardening without rent or allows the use of public premises for events without charge, but there is no steady financial support of activities. Even more, when there was the case of a procedural mistake in applying for the temporary use of the site, the city immediately issued an appeal for the removal of all activities from the garden without first contacting the organization in charge. This is why such initiatives are especially critical when the city usurps their activities to promote itself, as is the case of the *European Green Capital 2016* campaign.

Popular Resistance and the City Brands: Authority's Response to Offered Alternatives

In the last decade, the promotion of Ljubljana leans heavily on popular global brands such as "the city of culture", "the creative city" and, specifically, *European Green Capital 2016* and *UNESCO City of Literature*.[7] In 2016, Ljubljana focused on promoting the *European Green Capital Award*, which is a European Commission initiative aimed at recognizing and rewarding local efforts to improve the environment, the economy and the quality of urban life. Ljubljana's green policy is mostly concerned with maintaining green areas, eco-transportation, drinkable water and efficient waste management, but also includes the development of sustainable strategies to ensure the quality of life. For Ljubljana, the quality of life depends on factors such as safety and friendliness, recreational possibilities, preserved heritage, sustainable tourism and the development of brownfield areas into high-quality districts (cf. Poljak Istenič 2016).

Mobilizing grassroots creativity to fulfill the gaps created by austerity measures and promoting it to gain competitive advantage in the interurban rivalry is the newest neoliberal strategy of many cities struggling to position themselves on a global map of financial flows. Such strategies capitalize on the resourcefulness and ingenuity of citizens to adapt to the new reality of a crisis economy and refer to nostalgic feelings of community, authentic experience, and going "back to basics" (Forkert 2016: 11). Austerity has thus become the means to foster creativity while also encouraging or restoring relatively weak citizens' engagement. Such a handling of the economic crisis is increasingly criticized by anarchists, who claim that "[i]nstitutions themselves with the help of non-governmental organizations and non-critical individuals wrap most environmental issues in the shiny cellophane of popular culture" (Zadruga Urbana 2014). However, creatives and intellectuals are critical as well; as stated by an expert active in research and promotion of urban gardening:

The problem is that politics literally sits on such activities. This is a problem, the political usurpation of spheres, themes, styles, and then they praise themselves with these activities that become part of their PR. So you have people who actually fight a primal battle to carve a space for themselves and make something happen, and people who are paid by the system in order to demonstrate how good this system is and how it has listened to people.

When competing for the Green Capital title, the city invested significantly in green infrastructure. It built urban ecological zones and a regional waste management center, changed traffic regimes and refurbished the city accordingly, introduced electric vehicles and a bike-sharing system, and transformed brownfield areas into parks or allotment gardens. However, when promoting the award, the city issued a call for its inhabitants to "be active", appealing to them

not to ask yourself what the City of Ljubljana can do for green Ljubljana, ask yourself what you can do for it! The City of Ljubljana supports social initiatives, publishes their achievements and encourages activities on this website. Only when each inhabitant of our nice city lives green, sustainable and healthy, our mission will be fulfilled. This is a challenge that should be accepted by each of us. Inform us of your green achievements. (MOL 2014)

Although numerous creative initiatives submitted proposals to this call and had their events or projects featured on the city's websites, they are not keen on such appropriations and feel they are only used to promote the "festive atmosphere" we all are supposed to live in. "*This Green Capital is my pet hate, I am allergic to it anytime I hear something, the city calling us to tell them what we are doing,*" commented a spokesperson of one "creative" green initiative. "*They dedicated a pile of budget money to the Green Capital, but not to the program part. They sell it in a very cheap way but do not offer citizens many things.*"

However, in the absence of resources, people lack the autonomy – or power – to challenge this model of creativity so firmly incorporated into the cultural politics of austerity that increasingly revolve around social problems of exclusion, discrimination, passive citizenship, etc.[8] Submitting to official ideology is sometimes the only way to survive, as the cultural sector, at least in Slovenia, has suffered from the most severe budget cuts since the beginning of the economic crisis. This has affected the frequency of calls for cultural projects as well as the level of funding, which has put cultural producers into a seemingly "feudal relationship in which vassals – for three 'green working spaces' – promise rulers that they will organize the serfs and expand the control and the economy of the rulers with the help of those free human resources" (Zadruga Urbana 2014). So although creative initiatives embody critical social commentaries about current policies, they lack decisive oppositional or explicitly political aspects. Such "austerity creativity" therefore becomes prevalent in the absence of alternatives and large-scale social movements challenging austerity (Forkert 2016).

Studies on the global "North" show that current social movements are designed to encourage activation and self-responsibilization rather than actual political empowerment (Mayer 2013) and have lost the radical moment due to their appropriation by neoliberal urban policies (Forkert 2016). On the other hand, researchers of the Mediterranean point out that grassroots creativity as an alternative in the moment of crisis is "worth pursuing […] because of the opportunities offered for a way out of the crisis and into the development of a new and better society" (Leontidou 2015: 72). The *Creative City* debate has already turned toward grassroots initiatives with the adoption of the "creative underclass" in order to "'claw back' the meaning of creativity from the clutches of neoliberalism" and understands culture as a way of life embedded in the everyday rather than segregated into the fields of work or artistic practice (Morgan & Ren 2012: 128; cf. Morgan 2012; Gornostaeva & Campbell 2012). Grassroots creativity is also a fruitful basis to ground the *Smart City* concept into "southern" realities. As argued by Lila Leontidou (2015), its incorporation into the contemporary urban policies could be a prominent step toward development, smart growth, participatory democracy

and emancipatory politics. With one restraint: the initiatives should be properly supported instead of usurped by authorities in order to avoid more destructive resistance.

Conclusion

In Ljubljana, selected case studies of alternative food production and food markets show two modes of resistance to current urban politics, which can be – paralleled to a culture they represent, but also to a social position they hold – labeled "alternative" and "mainstream". The anarchist initiatives, belonging to the first, employ guerrilla tactics (occupying the land, squatting the buildings) to express their dissent with municipal and global policies. However, since they are perceived as a subculture and articulate their views (through alternative and social media) in a specific discourse, they fail to mobilize more supporters even in cases when they share the vision of a place with a local community or with citizens in general. They engage in gardening because they "believe that collective gardens raise people's awareness about producing their own food, consuming locally, being autonomous/productive, and enabling individuals without land of their own to produce food with sensitivity for their local natural environment" (Ljubljana [Slovenia]: What is Zadruga Urbana? 2016). Although highlighting the rights of people, this description in many ways echoes Slovenia's current agricultural and environmental policies (buying local products, preserving natural environment). Furthermore, the "headquarters" of the anarchists and other "non-mainstream" groups (homosexuals, "alternative" artists, activists, certain intellectuals) – Metelkova mesto – is promoted by the city as one of the main tourist attractions due to its "free creative spirit".

People seem more inclined to join the "creative" mode of resistance, as it offers desirable (and more mainstream) lifestyle opportunities. To financially provide for themselves, individuals working in the field of culture use various (although scarce) funding mechanisms to creatively/artistically explore alternative ways of acting (community-led activities) and managing public spaces (temporary use of land). Their activities often embed a social commentary of existing practices and urban politics. Although this is more or less a livelihood (or even survival) strategy, their resisting potential lies in their successful tactics to gain public attention and support. Despite being occasionally criticized that their inclusiveness is only a façade, citizens are motivated to engage and build a new community with aspirations to further co-create, collaborate and actively participate in public issues. The initiators at first act as the leaders of these communities, then usually strive to pass the managerial tasks on to community members in order to ensure the sustainability of these practices. However, because the initiatives belong to mainstream culture and more or less lack the autonomy and power (at least in the light of austerity measures) to more radically resist dominant urban policies, their actions become increasingly appropriated by efforts to prove how successfully the city abides by the neoliberal politics of the European Union: it ensures "green jobs", encourages "participatory practices", "includes vulnerable groups" and "revitalizes brownfields". Such "austerity creativity" (Forkert 2016) thus often reproduces the dominant system of neoliberal urban policies modeled upon the "North": in this concrete case, the initiatives have revitalized brownfields, managed public spaces, organized social life, ensured more decent living, and promoted Ljubljana's Green Capital image.

What is then the potential of grassroots creativity to engender social change? Mediterranean cities increasingly prove that fruitful alternatives leaning on solidarity, reciprocity and collaboration undermine the current austerity economy by creating alternative futures. The popularity of collaborative practices in Slovenia supports this claim as well; both modes of resistance – "anarchistic" and "creative" – in the green context build on socialist principles of social justice, equality, solidarity, and on characteristics linked to socialist times, such as collaboration/co-operation, mutual help, shared responsibility, common goods, personal contacts, face-to-face communication, and uncommercial socializing. Such values, expressed in their acts and discourses, paint a vision of more socially, culturally, economically and environmentally sustainable future(s). Furthermore, these practices challenge prevalent notions of "creative" and "smart" cities in a way that suits various cities in every part of the world and include much more diverse communities than is currently the case. This is especially important for Slovenia, which has underdeveloped mechanisms to support cultural producers. Considering that the collaborative practices described above did not transform into large-scale social movements, one could discuss whether they can be classified as resistance at all and what exactly their relevance is in the Mediterranean context. However, I believe that their resistance potential lies in their quest to find new forms of existential trust and security, which echoes the bottom-up contestations in the Mediterranean and beyond. They build communities that explore and embody positive social values jeopardized by neoliberal politics (including solidarity, reciprocity, collaboration/cooperation, equality, social justice and sustainability). Actors also consistently emphasize the increase of their social capital that they can count on in times of need and admit that alternative food markets represent a social corrective.

The positive alternative futures that the initiatives create to protest against the neoliberal system (such as self-management of public spaces, participatory decision-making, horizontal cooperation of various social actors, production of local food, and shared responsibilities) become incorporated into dominant urban policies to some degree – or, rather, get usurped by them – as the authorities offer no compensation (steady financial support, recognition of the initiatives) for the masterminds behind them, consequently stripping initiatives of their power for successful resistance. Current public administrations build on the transfer of services to civil society – as resistance practices prove that this is a fruitful alternative; however, this policy is especially problematic for Mediterranean and post-socialist countries with poorly developed non-governmental sectors. Authorities struggle to assess which public services could be transferred and to whom, yet they often refuse to admit that such services need to be systematically supported through infrastructure and financial funds if the functioning of the new system is to be ensured. The private-public partnership models have not been sufficiently utilized, which further affects the long-term stability of NGOs and vulnerability of services. The challenge that cities – especially in the EU-"South" – now have to face in order to build more large-scale alternative futures concerns establishing mechanisms to support the practices and organizations behind them that would successfully solve the anomalies of the current social and political order in a sustainable way. And last but not least, they have to find a way to convince the EU-"North" to recognize such grassroots practices as a legitimate and fruitful way out of the crisis.

Notes

1 The project *Preživeti, živeti, izživeti: Ustvarjalnost kot način življenja* (Z6-6841) was financially supported by the Slovenian Research Agency (2014–2016).

2 When I quote published texts of studied social actors, I only use quotation marks ("), but when I cite their words, recorded or written down during my interviews, I also use *italics*. I decided to keep anonymity of my collocutors due to their existential dependence on the authorities they criticize. I only disclose their function in the initiatives when judging that this will not compromise their character.

3 The word "anarchist" is an emic expression of the studied group. The members advocate ideology characteristic for anarchism and are also connected with A-Infoshop, self-declared social space for anarchistic movements.

4 Despite the fact that cooperatives date back to the middle of the nineteenth century, in Slovenian everyday discourse they are predominantly regarded as a socialist rural phenomenon, as the term and organizational principle were used by the Yugoslav communist party when introducing collective farming.

5 In 2007, the city began to remove illegal gardens on public land and put considerable effort into regulating urban gardening and arranging the allotments according to its vision of "orderly" landscape which includes defining "exemplary" gardens and gardening practices as well as "exemplary" urban gardeners (cf. MOL 2012; Pravilnik… 2016).

6 Institute for Spatial Policies is a non-governmental, consulting and research organization in the field of sustainable spatial and urban development.

7 The endeavors of the Mediterranean cities mostly revolve around culture. Several cities were successfully branded as the *UNESCO's Creative City* or have been proclaimed as the *European Capital of Culture*.

8 In urban policy, creativity is mostly understood in the framework of the creative industry, which in general encompasses economic activities focusing on the creation and use of knowledge and information; however, in Europe, creative industry most often equals cultural industry, i.e., culture or cultural production in its broadest sense. This conception disregards grassroots, more socially-oriented creativity, which is the main feature of "austerity creativity". However, since the state in crisis increasingly transfers its tasks and obligations to NGOs and volunteers without proper (or any) financial support, the development of the field is endangered either way.

References

Abu Lughod, Lila 1990: The Romance of Resistance: Tracing Transformations of Power through Bedouin Women. *American Ethnologist* 17:1, 41–55.

Arampatzi, Athina 2017: The Spatiality of Counter-austerity Politics in Athens, Greece: Emergent "Urban Solidarity Spaces". *Urban Studies* 54:9, 2155–2171.

Arampatzi, Athina, & Walter J. Nicholls 2012: The Urban Roots of Anti-neoliberal Social Movements: The Case of Athens, Greece. *Environment and Planning A* 44:11, 2591–2610.

Baskar, Bojan 2002: *Dvoumni Mediteran: Študije o regionalnem prekrivanju na vzhodnojadranskem območju* [Ambiguous Mediterranean: Studies of Regional Overlapping in the Eastern Adriatic Area]. Koper: Zgodovinsko društvo za južno Primorsko & Znanstveno-raziskovalno središče Republike Slovenije.

Brown, Michael F. 1996: Fórum: On Resisting Resistance. *American Anthropologist* 98:4, 729–735.

Cappucini, Monia 2015: Urban Space and Social Networks in Times of Crisis: A Local Perspective from the Exarchia Neighbourhood of Athens. *The Greek Review of Social Research (special issue)* 144:A, 129–134.

English Language & Usage Stack Exchange 2011: What's the Difference between "Collaborate" and "Cooperate"? http://english.stackexchange.com/questions/28752/whats-the-difference-between-collaborate-and-cooperate. Accessed January 14, 2016.

Featherstone, David 2015: Thinking the Crisis Politically: Lineages of Resistance to Neo-liberalism and the Politics of the Present Conjuncture. *Space and Polity* 19:1, 12–30.

Forkert, Kirsten 2016: Austere Creativity and Volunteer-run Public Services: The Case of Lewisham's Libraries. *New Formations* 87, 11–28.

Foucault, Michel 1972: *The Archeology of Knowledge*. London: Tavistock.

Gornostaeva, Galina, & Noel Campbell 2012: The Creative Underclass in the Production of Place: Example of Camden Town in London. *Journal of Urban Affairs* 34:2, 169–188.

Gregorčič, Marta 2011: *Potencia: Samoživost revolucionarnih bojev* [Potencia: Self-determination of Revolutionary Struggles]. Ljubljana: Založba /*cf.

Gupta, Akhil, & James Ferguson 1997: Culture, Power, Place: Ethnography at the End of an Era. In: Akhil Gupta & James Ferguson (eds.), *Culture, Power, Place: Explorations in Critical Anthropology.* Durham & London: Duke University press, pp. 1–32.

Harvey, David 2012: *Rebel Cities: From the Right to the City to the Urban Revolution.* London & New York: Verso Books.

Hollander, Jocelyn A. & Rachel L. Einwohner 2004: Conceptualizing Resistance. *Sociological Forum* 19:4, 533–554.

Keresztély, Krisztina & James W. Scott 2012: Urban Regeneration in the Post-socialist Context: Budapest and the Search for a Social Dimension. *European Planning Studies* 20:7, 1111–1134.

Kilavo seme 2016: Zgodba skupnostnega vrta [The Story of Collective Garden], http://radiostudent.si/dru%C5%BEba/kilavo-seme/zgodba-skupnostnega-vrta-na-ulici-velika-%C4%8Dolnarska-15. Accessed June 23, 2016.

Kladnik, Drago 1997: Slovenija: Narava. Naravnogeografska členitev [Slovenia: Nature. Physical Geographical Division]. In: *Enciklopedija Slovenije* [Encyclopaedia of Slovenia] 11. Ljubljana: Mladinska knjiga, pp. 306–307.

Korošec, Valerija 2014: Zgodba (predloga) o UTD v Sloveniji in njen kontekst [The Story (of the proposal) of the UBI in Slovenia and its Context]. *Ars & Humanitas* 8:1, 188–199.

Leontidou, Lila 1990: *The Mediterranean City in Transition: Social Change and Urban Development.* Cambridge: Cambridge University Press.

Leontidou, Lila 2014: The Crisis and its Discourses: Quasi-Orientalist Attacks on Mediterranean Urban Spontaneity, Informality and Joie de Vivre. *City* 18:4–5, 551–562.

Leontidou, Lila 2015: "Smart Cities" of the Debt Crisis: Grassroots Creativity in Mediterranean Europe. *The Greek Review of Social Research (special issue)* 144:A, 69–101.

Ljubljana (Slovenia): What is Zadruga Urbana? https://en.squat.net/2012/03/07/ljubljana-slovenia-what-is-zadruga-urbana/. Accessed February 22, 2016.

Lopes de Souza, Marcelo 2010: Which Right to Which City? In Defence of Political-strategic Clarity. *Interface* 2:1, 315–333.

Luthar, Oto (ed.) 2008: *The Land Between: A History of Slovenia.* Frankfurt am Main: Peter Lang.

Mayer, Margit 2013: First World Urban Activism: Beyond Austerity Urbanism and Creative City Politics. *City* 17:1, 5–19.

MOL 2012: Vrtičkarstvo v Ljubljani [Gardening in Ljubljana], http://www.ljubljana.si/si/mol/novice/77447/detail.html. Accessed February 21, 2016.

MOL 2014: Bodi aktiven [Be Active], http://www.ljubljana.si/si/zelena-prestolnica/bodi-aktiven/. Accessed June 7, 2016.

Morgan, George 2012: Urban Renewal and the Creative Underclass: Aboriginal Youth Subcultures in Sydney's Redfern-Waterloo. *Journal of Urban Affairs* 34:2, 207–222.

Morgan, George & Xuefei Ren 2012: The Creative Underclass: Culture, Subculture, and Urban Renewal. *Journal of Urban Affairs* 34:2, 127–130.

Nurse, Keith 2006: Culture as the Fourth Pillar of Sustainable Development. London: Commonwealth Secretariat, http://placemakers.wdfiles.com/local--files/theoretical-analysis-examined/Cultureas4thPillarSD.pdf. Accessed February 17, 2016.

Pautz, Hartwig & Margarita Kominou 2013: Reacting to "Austerity Politics": The Tactic of Collective Expropriation in Greece. *Social Movement Studies* 12:1, 103–110.

Peck, Jamie 2012: Austerity Urbanism: American Cities under Extreme Economy. *City* 16:6, 626–655.

Poljak Istenič, Saša 2016: Revival of Public Spaces through Cycling and Gardening: Ljubljana – European Green Capital 2016. *Etnološka tribina* 46:39, 157–175.

Pravilnik o urejanju in oddaji zemljišč Mestne občine Ljubljana za potrebe vrtičkarstva 2016 [Decree Governing and Leasing the Land of the City of Ljubljana for Gardening 2016]. *Uradni list RS* [Official Gazette RS] 19.

Rakopoulos, Theodoros 2013: Responding to the Crisis: Food Co-operatives and the Solidarity Economy in Greece. *Anthropology Southern Africa* 36:3–4, 102–107.

Rakopoulos, Theodoros 2014: The Crisis Seen from Below, Within, and Against: From Solidarity Economy to Food Distribution Cooperatives in Greece. *Dialectical Anthropology* 38:2, 189–207.

Rakopoulos, Theodoros 2015: Solidarity's Tensions: Informality, Sociality, and the Greek Crisis. *Social Analysis* 59:3, 85–104.

Razsa, Maple & Andrej Kurnik 2012: The Occupy Movement in Žižek's Hometown: Direct Democracy and a Politics of Becoming. *American Ethnologist* 39:2, 238–258.

Resistance Studies Network – About, http://resistancestudies.org/. Accessed June 2, 2016.

Rüdig, Wolfgang & Georgios Karyotis 2014: Who Protests in Greece? Mass Opposition to Austerity. *British Journal of Political Science* 44:3, 487–513.

Scott, James C. 1985: *Weapons of the Weak: Everyday Forms of Peasant Resistance.* New Haven: Yale University Press.

Simoneti, Maja & Darja Fišer 2014: Urbano vrtičkarstvo v Ljubljani [Urban Gardening in Ljubljana], http://prostorisodelovanja.si/urbano-vrtickarstvo-v-ljubljani/. Accessed February 26, 2016.

Simonič, Peter 2014: Solidarnost in vzajemnost v času recesije: Razumevanje starih in novih vrednosti in vrednot v poznem kapitalizmu [Solidarity and Reciprocity in Times of Recession: Understanding of New and Old Worths and Values in Late Capitalism]. *Ars & Humanitas* 8:1, 5–12.

Velikonja, Mitja 2009: Lost in Transition: Nostalgia for Socialism in Post-socialist Countries. *East European Politics & Societies* 23:4, 535–551.

Vodopivec, Nina 2014: Družbene solidarnosti v času socialističnih tovarn in individualizacije družbe [Social Solidarities in Times of Socialist Factories and Individualisation of Society]. *Ars & Humanitas* 8:1, 136–150.

Wilson, Nick 2010: Social Creativity: Re-qualifying the Creative Economy. *International Journal of Cultural Policy* 16:3, 367–381.

Zadruga Urbana 2014: (De)institucionalizacija vrtičkanja [(De)institutionalisation of Gardening], https://zadrugaurbana.wordpress.com/deinstitucionalizacija-vrtickanja/. Accessed February 22, 2016.

Saša Poljak Istenič, Ph.D. in ethnology, is a research fellow at the Institute of Slovenian Ethnology ZRC SAZU. Her research interests include creativity, sustainable development and heritage studies. She is the author of the book *Tradicija v sodobnosti* (Tradition in the Contemporary World [2013]). (sasa.poljak@zrc-sazu.si)

REINVENTING TRANSPARENCY
Governance, Trust and Passion in Activism for Food Sovereignty in Italy

Alexander Koensler, Queen's University Belfast

In an increasing number of realms in everyday life, informal personal relations of trust are being replaced by a constraining formalization of standardization and certification implemented in the name of transparency. Examining the repercussions of this process for small-scale farmers in Italy, this article offers an understanding of ordinary experiences with transparency and explores attempts to resist it. Based on ethnographic research with a neorural activist network that opposes official food-certifications, the article describes ambiguities in ingenious attempts to reinvent procedures to attest the quality and safety of "genuine" food products in more inclusive terms. Restoring the primacy of trust and solidarity, these cases illustrate how a different type of transparency can contribute to realizing a humanistic potential that is nevertheless not free of contradictions.

Keywords: transparency, food activism, Italy, certification, food sovereignty

Clandestine Red

Clandestine Red (*Rosso Clandestino*, in Italian) cannot be bought in a supermarket. Clandestine Red, a red wine of juicy and rustic taste, is distributed only by its producer in person; it can be found at informal markets, in squatted social centres and during alternative festivals. The producer of Clandestine Red – let's call him Ronnie[1] – sells his bottles while adding stories or jokes that conclude with a bright smile. Sometimes he also offers insights from his former life as a pub owner and traveller.

Clandestine Red, no surprise, is a relatively clandestine product. Ronnie never attempted to obtain any official certification, not even one that certifies basic hygienic standards such as HACCP.[2] Instead, Ronnie's bottles are certified as "genuine" by members of a local group that is associated with the Italian national network Genuino Clandestino (Genuinely Clandestine). Despite being a "clandestine" product, Clandestine Red is guaranteed by the movement to have been produced according to standards that are in many aspects higher than those for official organic or hygienic certifications, for instance in relation to ethical conditions and the use of artificial food additives. In addition, the product is guaranteed to have been produced without employing exploited seasonal workers on which mainstream agribusiness relies. The grapes were grown without any chemical treatment, not even those allowed by organic certifications. They were collected without using one of those machines that collect leaves and insects in addition to the grapes. Ronnie is well known within

Alexander Koensler 2018: Reinventing Transparency.
Governance, Trust and Passion in Activism for Food Sovereignty in Italy.
Ethnologia Europaea 48:1, 50–68. © Museum Tusculanum Press.

the Genuino Clandestino network, which was created in 2010 as an ironic anti-label. As an unprecedented success-story, the network spread throughout Italy in a few years and became one of the major contemporary Italian movements that oppose the neoliberalization of social relations. In an "era of transparency," in which trust seems possible, apparently, only through objective measurement and standardization, Clandestine Red offers a unique prism to understanding evolving modes of the governance of transparency and the possibilities for opposing and reinventing them.

This article[3] aims to examine the effects of transparency as a paradigm of governance in changing rural peripheries. How does the rise of regulations implemented in the name of transparency affect informal relations in the countryside? What are the prospects to counter the requirements of competition and standardization? In a broader sense, this theme addresses also more fundamental questions: How is it possible to recover humanistic relations based on trust and solidarity in a world of constraining formality and competition? Within their limits and constraints, can these activities become a counter-practice to standardization and competition? Beyond small-scale growers like Ronnie, these questions concern everyone who is caught in mechanisms of standardization and evaluation under the paradigms of neoliberal governance, including many public institutions such as hospitals and universities.

In order to discuss these questions, I will attempt to deconstruct the assumption that transparency necessarily conveys trust, as neoliberal ideology attempts to establish as common sense. Then, I will shift attention to activist practices of members of the neorural network Genuino Clandestino who appropriate the right to certify the quality and safety of food, reinventing the modes to certify in more democratic and inclusive ways. Following a visit for an alternative grassroots procedure to guarantee quality standards, I will explore "partial connections" (Strathern 1996) of social relations around forms of activism that start off at the visit and create new forms of experimental collaboration. I will show how these collaborations liberate a human-istic potential of trust that eludes many aspects of governmental transparency. Although not free of contradictions, these experiments undermine some implicit neoliberal ideological assumptions, such as that subjects obey standards only out of fear of punishment or act in order to maximize profit.

The idea to think about the relation between trust, transparency and solidarity derives from my ethnographic fieldwork with small-scale farmers conducted between 2014 and 2017 in central Italy, using long-term participant observation with a number of key informants, as well as participation in assemblies, events, and open-end interviews with key stakeholders. Since 2016, I am coordinating a major ethnographic project on activism for food sovereignty in Italy, the Peasant Activism Project[4], working with a postdoctoral assistant in visual anthropology. During our fieldwork, a hidden but vivid world of political activism in peripheral and isolated regions came to our attention. Some of these farmers and breeders had only a few animals, an olive yard or an orchard of a few hectares, others produced very little honey, jam or bread – often under conditions that seemed precarious, self-made and beautiful at the same time (see ill. 1).

Not all managed to make a living out of their passion, but almost everyone was deeply involved in political activism and engaged in heated debates about global agribusiness, neoliberalism and changing capitalism. Almost none of these small-scale farmers or food processors used bank loans, but relied on mutual aid, mostly within the network. A few had received small amounts of public funding from the European Union programmes for minor works, such as the restructuring of a stable for five cows, but these were exceptions.

During our shared working days in fields and stables and during assemblies or debates over coffee and cigarettes (smoking was quite common), my assistant usually attracted more attention than me. With his enormous camera, he became respected within a short time in his role as a "filmmaker". My own role as a participant observer remained more ambiguous. It seemed as if I was standing around uselessly, asking repetitive questions. Thus, people

Ill. 1: A makeshift small-scale goat farm in a forest area of central Italy. (Photo: Fabrizio Loce-Mandes, May 2017)

would frequently ask me to help out carrying wood, keeping control of wild goats or cleaning up vegetable gardens, not always with satisfying results. This experience gave me a particular insight into artisan production processes as opposed to standardized products, as we will see. Used to the fast-working path of journalism, many of our subjects frequently insisted on viewing our documentary and commenting on it. My own vague explanations of plans to write articles in unknown journals about governance and transparency was often met with silence or distraction. However, my own interest took shape in the course of our work, moving towards an attempt to understand the potential of humanist relations of trust and solidarity. These seem clearly to contrast with neoliberal paradigms based on the assumption that only competition, fear of control and cost-benefit calculations can be main drivers for human agency. In particular, within the growing anthropological literature on food activism, my aim is to develop further reflections on co-producing and affective

relations with local food products and to connect these themes more explicitly to issues of neoliberal governance and its inherent paradigm of transparency. At this point, some clarifications on the relation between transparency, trust and solidarity are needed.

Trust or Transparency?

"Trust relations provide the substance of everyday life," writes the philosopher Jay M. Bernstein (2011). Influenced by Annette Baier's seminal work, Bernstein defines trust as a "set of attitudes, presuppositions, and practices, which we typically fail to emphatically notice until they become absent" (2011: 395).[5] Over the past decade, anthropological literature began to pay attention to how trust and mistrust is embedded in everyday life. For example, this includes the interpretation of the rise of evidence-based policies as "audit cultures" and a crisis of trust (Strathern 2000a; Shore, Wright & Però 2011; Power 2007). However, the capacity to convey and destroy trust has been widely overlooked in analyses of the rise of the "society of transparency" with its demand for accountability and control, in particular in studies of rural change. Critical agrarian and food studies only marginally examine the impact on social relations of a pervasive market rationality and technocratic formality. In many ways, the undermining of trust also makes the experience of solidarity[6] more arduous – informal social relations that allow exchange of knowledge and goods as opposed to competition and individualism. Social theorist Jeffrey Alexander (2006: 13) describes the importance of the value of solidarity as "the feeling of being connected to others, of being part of something larger than ourselves, a whole that imposes obligations and allows us to share convictions, feelings, and cognitions, gives us a chance for meaningful participation, and respects our individual personalities even while giving us the feeling that we are all in the same boat." The challenges of accountability and regulations tend to undermine precisely this sense of solidarity based on trust relations. As we will see, the neorural solidarity in this study assumes forms that go far beyond the ambiguous function of welfare solidarity and creates parallel, alternative insurrectional spaces based on anti-capitalist narratives that create forms of "concrete utopias" (Cooper 2014) and contingent autonomous spaces that do not simply aim to oppose the state, but often act beyond existing categories of activism as conceptualized in post-anarchist thought (Newman 2015) and yet often unnamed figures of activism (Isin 2008 in a sense that go beyond the recent wave of activism in Mediterranean and North African countries (Žižek 2012).

The first time I noticed these profound implications was when helping to clean out a makeshift stable overlooking an uninhabited valley. Five cows were standing in the muddy dung in front of us, and we were sweating as we cleaned the cement floor. Taking a short break and checking a bunch of hay at the door, the middle-aged farmer, Claudio, explained that this was the first time that he had to buy hay. Claudio moved to the countryside from Rome in the 1980s with a first wave of neorural activists, and at that time he had access to pastures on a nearby hill belonging to his neighbour. "I used to bring him our fresh cow dung in a pick-up van." In exchange, he received access to these pastures as well as firewood and, once a year each autumn, a slaughtered pig. Since regional authorities implemented European regulations a few years ago, it became illegal to transport dung in pick-up vans. In the name of environmental protection, a "special waste" truck needs to be ordered from a subcontracted communal facility, and the dung needs to be recycled in another, distant, communal facility, all of which costs money. For a while, Claudio and his neighbour continued their practice and simply ignored the new regulations. But, after an informal visit by an official of the local hygienic authority (ASL),[7] his neighbour expressed anxieties about potential fees and further "trouble". Their collaboration and informal exchange ended; the informal solidarity between small-scale farmers had been undermined.

This short vignette exemplifies why Ronnie and his Clandestine Red is not the only small-scale farmer who feels "pushed into clandestinity", as someone said. Ronnie, Claudio and many others frequently narrate how they on a daily basis witness that regulations implemented in the name of transparency, food safety or environmental protection *de facto* erode informal relations and favour large industrial productions, thus fostering a continuing integration of farming into global agribusiness. Step by step, with every newly introduced standard or regulation, many people seem to experience the perils of undermined trust. Through a simple restriction on transporting dung to a neighbour, farmers are pushed into buying fertilizers, heating material and animal food, rather than exchanging these materials informally. Instead of visiting each other, they are pushed into visiting commercial venues in anonymous metal buildings on the outskirts of industrial zones that specialize in farming equipment. Here, transparency, as a governmental paradigm, remains inherently entrenched with the emergence of the "corporate food system" (McMichael 2009).[8] The emergence of transparency is one aspect of a broader dynamic that can be described as the "financialization" of more and more realms of life (Zerilli &

Heatherington 2016; Krippner 2005).[9] Unlike Claudio's informal exchange with his neighbour, trust is channelled through credit card or cash payment systems, ISO certified standards of products and professional marketing strategies.

During our ethnographic fieldwork, stories of how regulations had threatened and even ruined trust among neighbours were inexhaustible. For example, a goat-keeper with a stable a few kilometres outside a small village lamented the loss of times in which it was possible to bring a goat to a local festival for seventy euro without hiring a special animal transporter for an additional three hundred euro, thus pushing the organizers to buy frozen meat in a supermarket in the industrial zone instead. Another farmer described missing the times when it was possible to slaughter the pigs at home without paying for transportation and the services of a professional slaughterhouse, or when it was possible to make cheese in makeshift laboratories that did not comply with the complex food safety regulations such as HACCP. The common plot in all these stories focuses on the way in which informal relations of trust are rechannelled into formalized technocratic regulations. Community relations, neighbourhood friendships, and informal relations are threatened by a constantly growing regulatory regime based on governmental transparency instead of informal trust and solidarity. Claudio, like many others, is very aware of this process. He once described the financialization of agriculture as "perverse". I will call this type of transparency "governmental transparency".

Small-scale farmers and neorural activists are particularly vulnerable in the face of the impact of governmental transparency. Those who aim to create sustainable lifestyles and produce quality food often find themselves in difficulty with tightening regulations regarding food safety and the certification of standards that are considered by many as favouring large industrial productions. In contemporary advanced capitalism, transparency is emerging as a political paradigm and moral imperative from all angles. Transparency is defined as the physical property of allowing the transmission of light through a material, but this word is used metaphorically to imply visibility in relation to the conduct of individuals, groups or institutions. In common understanding, transparency aims to provide a basis for trust, but as we will see, governmental transparency in fact erodes and substitutes relations of trust in many realms of life. In the name of transparency and public safety, Claudio is asked not to personally bring his dung to his neighbour.

Transparency as a Governmental Paradigm

The value of transparency increasingly penetrates into more and more realms of everyday life, while at the same time transparency is not a common practice among the ruling classes. Introduced in the 1970s in high finance as a paradigm to promote the theoretical conditions required for a free market to be efficient (Epstein 2005), transparency has more recently become a requirement embraced in public administrations, service industries, family relations, friendships and love – all suddenly seem to need transparency in order to survive. In this way, transparency is becoming a moral imperative of how people and things should be governed, replacing previous forms of social relations, such as trust and solidarity. The paradigm of transparency has moved from financial services to the public domain with the neoliberal critique of social-democratic or socialist welfare practices (Shore, Wright & Però 2011; Strathern 2000a), while at the same time many decisions of the ruling classes are taken in the realm of opacity. According to the paradigm of transparency, basic trust in people's professionalism or ethical conduct leads to abuse and corruption. It is assumed that new mechanisms of control have to be implemented: We cannot trust those who receive welfare benefits; instead, we need surveillance practices to keep them in line. We cannot trust the post office employee on a permanent government contract, we need fixed-term postal employees who constantly fear for their working conditions and who compete with each other to provide good postal service. In other words, "trust" in people's ability is replaced by the creation of "quasi-market" conditions of competition based on the principle of transparency. This is the broader political importance of the idea underlying the reinvention of relations of trust in Genuino Clandestino, which is to rebuild a humanistic value system of trust instead of fear. In order to promote global agribusiness, the creation of "quasi-markets" requires, first, a standardization of objects and subjects, which are expressed as numbers, stars or points (as evident, for instance, in rankings), so that they can effectively compete.

"Transparency becomes a hell of sameness" writes Byung-Chul Han (2012) in his recent essay *The Society of Transparency*. Drawing largely on the thinking of Jean Baudrillard, Martin Heidegger and Walter Benjamin, Byung-Chul Han suggests that the increasing proliferation of practices associated with the concept of "transparency" is not casual but indicates a paradigm shift in contemporary governance – the illusion that democratic politics can be replaced by increases in technocratic measures of certification, standardization and evaluation based on the ideal of transparency. The implications of this illusion become evident in many everyday difficulties of small-scale farmers, like Claudio. Meeting the standards of transparency comes at a high social cost. In his thought-provoking essay, Han investigates the nexus of power and visibility.[10] For instance, in medieval Catholicism, particularly in certain forms of Madonna worship, religious cult statues were ascribed with value and power precisely because they remained invisible. Some statues were hidden during the year and brought out just once, for example, during a special performance. Other statues might remain hidden, access being given only to priests or special persons.

In contrast, for Han, power in the "society of transparency" is convened only through visibility. This observation leads Han to rethink the Panopticon, the most used metaphor for governance in the Foucauldian sense. This institutional building proposed by Jeremy Bentham (1791) in the late eighteenth century allowed all inmates to be constantly observed from a central watchpoint without the inmates being able to tell whether they were being watched. In short, the impression that "you can always be seen" makes the inmates act more responsibly, tending to incorporate social norms. As a metaphor for how power works in complex societies, Han contends that the Panopticon loses its centralistic perspective, becomes "a-prospective" with increasing transparency. For Han, the penetration of transparency as a governmental paradigm has severe consequences; he observes how the "society of transparency is a society of constant suspicion." "Where transparency exists, no trust can exist," he concludes (Han 2012: 80). Also other authors, such as Strathern (2000b), investigate the contradictory implications of the value of transparency. In other words, the critique of the value of transparency leaves no hope for a positive way out. However, this literature pays little attention to everyday practices that elude, subvert or reinvent the paradigm of transparency or to how people may circumvent or resist the paradigm of transparency.

Transparency in Changing Rural Peripheries

The rise of governmental transparency is only one aspect of a broader dynamic. Studies of agrarian change leave no doubt: irreversible shifts have occurred over the past four decades. The deregulation of financial markets, new technological opportunities and economic liberalization have profound impacts on social relations in rural areas. A growing body of critical agrarian studies has documented the pervasion of a professionalized, globalized and standardized agribusiness, now the dominant model for producing food in globally interconnected markets. Voices of authoritative figures in critical agrarian studies, such as Henry Bernstein (2010, 2016), Marc Edelman (2015), Philip McMichael (2012) and Jan D. van der Ploeg (2009), agree that these profound changes have affected how the role and the figure of the "farmer" itself is conceptualized. In *Globalization and Europe's Rural Regions*, McDonagh, Nienaber and Woods (2015) trace the challenges resulting from the restructuring of rural spaces throughout Europe. Especially in advanced industrialized societies, such as Europe, the current agribusiness model is considered largely dominant. In the words of Michael J. Watts (2008: 276), changes in the world economy have "irretrievably altered" traditional rural settings throughout Europe. In particular, as part of the broader process of finalization, the emergence of the contemporary global food economy relies on an increasing formalization of economic exchanges, leading to an "economization" of social relations in agribusiness in a way that reflects global corporate practices (Elder & Dauvergne 2015). This critique of financialization resonates with the debate in classical economic anthropology regarding the contested assumption of an increasing formalization and "contractualization" of social relations in the countryside, an area of studies inspired by Polanyi's (1957) classical work on the relation between rural transformations and economization. An often-overlooked aspect is that transparency, in this context, constitutes a prerequisite for the formalization of social relations. Transparency allows a veil of objectivity to be conferred on the value of objects, subjects and processes, thus creating comparable units based on standardized criteria that can be measured, evaluated, and put in competition with each other. In other words, the moral imperative of transparency is the last brick in the construction of global agribusiness based on competitive financial relations.

The overwhelming body of this literature pays little attention to those aspects that do not fit into the linear account of a rising industrialized agribusiness model. However, an increasing number of scholars have become interested in alternative or oppositional practices. A recent "peasant turn" (Bernstein 2016: 63) has emerged in the literature on agrarian change, focusing on a much-needed opposition to the industrial agribusiness model. Most notably, Van der Ploeg's (2009) concept of a "peasant mode of production" is influencing a line of analysis that investigates small-scale farming as a form of resistance against the pervasive imperial dimension of the global agribusiness system. According to Van der Ploeg, processes of "repeasantization" are complicating the process of agricultural industrialization. This scholar from Wageningen's renowned centre of critical agrarian studies distinguishes three ideal modes of production: peasant, entrepreneurial and industrial modes of production. "Repeasantization",

for Van der Ploeg, describes the process of transformation of non-peasants or former peasants into "autonomous", peasant-like forms of production that are articulated as struggles for autonomy and striving for self-subsistence. In addition, the peasant principle includes a different understanding of the interaction between humans and nature as well as cooperative concepts of work organization that allow peasants to overcome monetary and market constraints. However, many of these studies continue to be based unproblematically on the assumption of a relatively clear-cut opposition of "global agribusiness" and "peasants" and "traditional farming" (Edelman 1999; Kerkvliet 1993), which is often associated with activist discourses in food sovereignty movements (Morena 2014). However, the emphasis on "peasants" as an idealized and generic concept has come under scrutiny. Interestingly, Josh Brem-Wilson (2015) critically analyses the emergence and construction of "peasant discourses" as a homogenizing category.

Against the backdrop of this binary picture, a long-standing focus of social and cultural anthropology highlights marginal and often overlooked phenomena that are based around cultural aspects of food production and consumption.[11] In particular, this literature begins to examine the innovative potential of cultural productions that are positioned in a dialectic relation to those practices of mass production and consumption that are characterized by increasing integration into global economic circuits. These studies seem to provide a more nuanced account against that of the apparently linear and ineludible pervasiveness of global agribusiness. Food production has been recognized as a symbolically charged practice that creates and reproduces social categories, particularly in classical anthropological literature. Bernhard Tschofen (2002) explores the link between regional food production and issues of identity. Within his area, political food activism has received increasing attention as a particular instrument to negotiate power relations. The recent volume edited by Carol Counihan and Valeria Siniscalchi (2014) offers a broad overview of how activists, networks and ordinary people challenge agribusiness by negotiating and performing political relations through the prism of food. The work of Cristina Grasseni (2013) on solidarity-based purchasing groups in Italy has highlighted how these social groups help create new economic circuits that contribute to promoting sustainability on many different levels. Grasseni also discusses the ability of consumer groups to reinvent consumer–producer relations through the introduction of terms such as "co-production", which aims to change the consumerist imagination.

Importantly, *Ethnologia Europaea* has provided a forum for research highlighting the often-neglected practices of everyday forms of the contestation, subversion and re-creation of mainstream practices of food consumption and production. For instance, the special issue *Foodways Redux*, edited by Håkan Jönsson (2013), provides valuable insights into the ambiguous implications of the neoliberal politics regarding the branding of local or regional food. Sarah May (2013) discusses insightfully the politics of commercialization behind the regional branding of geographical indications. Fabio Mattioli (2013) offers unique insights into the political conundrum regarding different food labels in Italy, including the tensions between official organic labels, EU geographical indications and alternative "anti-labels". For Mattioli, the property labels of food should be understood as a form of meaning-making and as a site of conflict. In his discussion of the relation between food and the geopolitics of property labels, Mattioli thoughtfully uncovers the controversies and limits behind the politics of conferring geographical indications (GIs), the Presidia of Slow Food and its implicit class politics, and organic labels. Embedded in a rhetoric intended to provide "transparency", the proliferation of certifications, brands, logos and labels is ultimately connected to the "aggressive expansion of capitalist relations" (2013: 50).

The article of Pétursson (2013) published in the same issue discusses the ambiguities of "co-production", a term introduced by consumer-critical food movements to create more participatory and inclusive relations between food producers and consumers. In *Eduardo's Apples: The Co-Production of Personalized Food Relationships*, Pétursson clearly shows the limits and contradictions of attempts by commercial enterprises to create and maintain personal relationships between organic producers and consumers. In his case study, an online platform of a multinational organic food distributer attempts to create personal links between organic growers in the global South and wealthy consumers. Through the online platform, consumers can visualize a short self-presentation in video format by the growers of the products that they buy. Communication is mediated by a consumer relations team, and the grower remains strangely absent from discussions about sustainable apple packaging and nuances of apple taste. Pétursson's interesting case study shows the limits and contradictions of this attempt to create transparency using online tools and within commercial enterprises. For the author, storytelling remains a tool to create surplus value for the company's products rather than to enhance horizontal exchange. In summary, these studies do not explicitly address the ambiguous implications of transparency in food politics, but in many aspects these studies confirm the importance of transparency as a moral imperative and an ordinating principle, a tendency that penetrates more and more aspects of food politics, even in the realms of alternative food activism, local food networks and increased attention to ethical consumerism. However, the relation between transparency and trust is rarely addressed directly in this research, and more studies are needed to empirically understand the deeper political implications of the ways in which transparency penetrates how food systems are organized and practised in everyday experiences.

Genuino Clandestino: Beyond Governmental Transparency

In 2010, a group of small-scale farmers from Bologna were pushed out of an official organic farmers' market at the centre of Bologna. The farmers stated that they produced "organic" and "genuine" food and that everyone who wanted to come and see their facilities was welcome, yet they did not have the official certification. "Getting the certification" was too complicated and expensive, they stated, according to later accounts.[12] As small-scale farmers, they wished to focus on their main task, that is, to cultivate quality products and protect the environment, rather than keeping up with complex bureaucratic tasks. The farmers relocated to a nearby area.[13] Pirate-style flags and an ironic "anti-label", Genuino Clandestino, appeared on the alternative market to the official organic market. The group soon attracted the attention of other networks and local groups throughout Italy, many of whom had become critical and distant from the official practices required by organic certifications and the commercialization of local food, as evident in well-established networks, such as the Slow Food network or those who received specific labels as geographical indications (GIs). The anti-logo Genuino Clandestino group soon developed into a national campaign for the "free" processing of food, free of the restrictions imposed by regulations implemented in the name of transparency. Within a couple of years, the groups became a network with a national dimension and with local branches in almost every major region in Italy.

The rapid rise of the network of Genuino Clandestino poses interesting and unique challenges to the governance of transparency. Its innovative potential derives from its capacity to frame issues that are usually addressed in the realms of ethical consumerism as more straightforward problems of governance in wider, political terms. Put plainly, one of the underlying ideas of the network contests the idea that official standards of transparency and auditing are supportive and useful. The mobilizing drive of the "anti-label" Genuino Clandestino group is derived from its anarchic spirit and desire to appropriate the power to certify and label their products both as "genuine" and "clandestine". Within the network, the creation of alternative exchange circuits of food, including setting up local food-buying groups, often serve as a platform for the launch of broader political campaigns (for instance, against privatization, the redistribution of public land or neoliberal reforms). In many local groups of the network, independent, solidarity economic and alternative political circuits are set up to oppose the pressure of integrating the markets of small-scale farmers. For instance, in groups such as Terra Libera in Lazio (the region around Rome) and Campi Aperti in Bologna, these economic and political circuits are highly sophisticated networks of cooperatives and include the organization of alternative markets, the coordination of direct purchasing groups and a range of other forms of political activism. In both groups, these activities emerge from a decade-long activism on the margins of communist and anarchist ideologies. In more peripheral areas of Italy, groups exist more often as loosely tied associations between independent farmers with less frequent and less well-organized activities. Importantly, the movements and groups connected to Genuino Clandestino overwhelmingly revive anti-capitalist elements in their attempts to invent models and create spaces that are not subject to commodification and that are outside the realms of competition, market relations or commodification. Many groups have adopted creative names that allude to anti-market principles and ideas of sustainability, such as Terra Fouri Mercato (Land Beyond the Market), Spazio Fuori Mercato (Space Outside the Market), Utopie Sorridenti (Smiling Utopias), and Campo Libero (Free Fields). This anti-capitalist inspiration makes these circuits radically different from most other alternative forms of food activism.

The promotion of alternative certifications became a key feature of the network. In a first wave of experiments, most groups promoted so-called "self-certifications" of their products. Producers would exhibit written statements describing the way in which they produced their products, sometimes accompanied by photos or drawings. The concept of "self-certification" derives from rural experiences in Peru and Brazil with fair-trade associations and was designed to compensate for the lack of state authorities that could guarantee certification standards (Cabras 2013). In a second wave of experiments, many groups of Genuino Clandestino considered the need to develop more sophisticated alternative certification principles, with evolving definitions ranging from "participatory self-certifications" to "participatory guarantees". Terra Libera (Free Land) can be taken as an example of the shift from "self-certifications" to more participatory processes. The currently applied "participatory guarantee" is a collective process that involves fellow farmers, consumers (defined also by activists as "co-producers" in order to highlight their agency) and at least one food specialist of the products to be approved. After a visit by co-producers and activists, each participant drafts a short personal report to be published on the network's blog. Final approval is decided after a debate in the "general producer assembly". Having completed the procedure, new members have access to specific local markets that are organized by Terra Libera and can sell their products throughout consumer groups of the network. Terra Libera's certifications apply more stringent criteria related to ethical and quality standards than official organic certifications because they also pay attention to ethical labour relations and forbid any use of chemicals, even those that organic certifications allow. In the process, personalized forms of self-representations of the producers and his or her products are drafted, unlike the de-personalized mechanisms of official bodies.

"Where I Pass, wow, Everything Starts to Grow"

"Bring me one of Claudio's cheeses," Pedro reminded me a few days before the visit at Pedro's home for the "participatory guarantee". Originally from Spain, Pedro lives with Elena in one of the most isolated spots of central Italy. "I like to live where you can't find a highway close by," he once explained to me during a tiring drive through a seemingly endless number of small villages. Pedro's reminder to bring him cheese, is just a small indication of how "solidarity" relations can be re-established despite the perils of governmental transparency. But there is more. Pedro had prepared everything for a visit by Terra Libera activists to his home; he had cleaned up the garden of the old and isolated brick building, and lit a welcoming fire in front of the entrance. Usually distinguished by a long, uncultivated black beard and wild hair, for the occasion, he presented himself clean-shaven and with combed hair. The visit started with a presentation circle. First names

and the type of production undertaken ("Mike, beekeeper") was enough formality. Analogically, in the blog sphere of the network, contributions appear in the same format: as loosely connected interventions from single individuals known only by their first names – a practice of horizontal representation. Mike, the beekeeper, coordinated the event and briefly explained to newcomers the objectives of the visit: to meet farmers outside the markets and to establish new and personal relationships to collectively share the work.

Afterwards, we moved into Pedro's laboratory. In an abandoned stable with a wooden roof, we found a handcrafted distillery in bronze, a beautifully crafted artisan piece. In response to our signs of amazement, Pedro narrated his adventure in importing this utensil from Portugal. It was made by an old friend of him in such a way that it would fit perfectly into his small van. During the summer, Pedro frequently goes back to central Spanish highlands to collect herbs and distil them directly there, moving back and forth by ferry. He emphatically explained that he uses only a real wood fire to run the distillery. This makes the distillation a complex and work-intensive process. From these small indications, it became clear how Pedro embraces an almost poetic spirit in his work. He emphasized beauty and style over rationality and considerations of profit, and this dedication returns indirectly to him in positive terms. He seems to have a thoroughly romantic personality. On another occasion, I helped him carry a spacious, antique wooden suitcase to a market. The heavy suitcase contained just light bags of herbal teas. Despite the light content, the suitcase was so heavy that two people were needed to transport it. Such episodes showed that there is no evident emphasis on efficiency or market rationality in Pedro's work, as mainstream understanding would have it. Yet, everything flows in a way that is inspired by beauty, style, and love. This is one example of how the "solidarity economy" of the network goes beyond a rational cost–benefit calculation.

In Pedro's laboratory, a long series of huge glass bottles decorated the stone walls. Two "experts" or "co-producers" (two young women from a clandestine distillery in one of Rome's squatted spaces) began to ask detailed questions about Pedro's distillation techniques. With great openness, Pedro answered all queries; shortly, he started to speak emphatically about his work and his relationship with nature. "I am the contrary of Attila [the legendary leader of the Hunnic Kingdom who led devastating military incursions against the Roman Empire and is widely known through the computer game, *Total War: Attila*]," he stated. "Where I pass, wow, everything starts to grow." He moved on to explain his extraordinary care in the use of plants. In the meantime, we started to prepare an abundant lunch on a long buffet table outdoors. Many of the participants knew each other only from the markets. The lunch seemed to be an occasion for debating future ideas. Before officially ending the visit, the coordinator started a final round of discussion, asking whether anyone had observed something worth commenting on. At the margins, some participants began to propose informal exchanges. "Can I take this stick?" one participant asked Pedro, pointing to a piece of wood near the stable; "It seems to fit the carpentry work that I am doing right now."

The following week, Pedro's official admission into the Terra Libera network had been approved. Every participant during the visit had to draft a report that would be published after Pedro's successful admission. Over the past several years, virtually all small-scale producers who approached the network have been approved. Only in two cases did the assembly discuss the admissions in detail, expressing doubts. In one case, an asbestos stable roof had been discovered, and some argued that this was not consistent with the "genuine" standards. The farmer in question promised to remove the roof and was admitted after going through the process a second time. In another case, a national cooperative that employs disabled people in community-based agriculture projects applied to join the network. The project found considerable interest among Terra Libera activists, and the visit went well. However, during the assembly in Rome, some activists noted that a national government-subsidized NGO with strong relationships with the political elite was not compatible with the spirit of independent small-scale farming. Both cases demonstrate the process employed by the network and how enacting principles of grassroots democracy does not simply constitute another form of control but rather enables the forming of social relations of trust that otherwise would not have been created. At the same time, the process has become quite formal and resembles elements of state bureaucracy with reports that are collated and debated in a sophisticated two-stage process.

"Between Reality and Dreamy Imagination"

Compared to official certifications, what did the reports say about Pedro's work? Pedro received a long list of eloquent, encouraging words and compliments. Participants highlighted Pedro's passion and his respect for nature, as well as his exhaustive specialist knowledge. After an objective-sounding description of Pedro's professional abilities, Mike the beekeeper stated: "The hospitality of Pedro and Elena was exceptional, not to forget also our happy final social gathering at the thermal baths, at the margins of reality and dreamy imagination" (translation by the author). While I and my research assistant had to leave because of our two-hour drive home, a group of participants went to bathe at a nearby thermal bath. During that visit, the idea to revive a collective kitchen for a festival was discussed. In another statement, Ettore the vine grower expresses his appreciation of Pedro's work no less eloquently: "Sincere, pure and honest nature, an incredible dedication and passion for his work, that is fundamental and very present in Pedro and Elena's work. This visit could represent the essence of the 'participatory certification,' where transparency is the queen" (translation by the author).

Reading these words, I mused about the phrase: "Transparency is the Queen." What does this mean? In the midst of a pretty anarchist group, something of managerial jargon seems to have penetrated. Somehow, "Transparency is the Queen" sounds out of place here. Possibly, this expression may metaphorically stand for the ambiguous aspects of the "participatory guarantee". An element of an advanced neoliberalist consultancy philosophy seems to emerge behind the emphasis on naturality, direct relations of trust and the horizontal and the participatory nature of the process. This last point may lead to a reflection on the broader implications of this procedure. These episodes illustrate how some of the immediate effects reinforce the spirit of community and strengthen friendships. The visit created extraordinary enthusiasm and offered a forum for new possibilities of exchange. Probably more incisive are the motivational inspirations that offer the experience of participating in the process. Asked after a month about the reports that he had received after his visit, Pedro stated: "When I am sad, when I lose faith in my work; yeah, then what do I do? I take out the reports and read them. They give me strength; they make me cry." Similar experiences are also related by other members of the network. In open-end interviews, many members outline their particular deep emotional attachment to the network and its motivating power. For instance, Claudio similarly stated, "When I am feeling down, I read my reports and I cry out of happiness. They are so beautiful." Here lies one of the most interesting potentials of alternative certifications; they are able to create a dedication to work, a sense of belonging and a passion like no other official form of surveillance would be able to achieve.

On the other hand, the highly engaging "inner motivational" spirit of the "participatory guarantee" contains something almost suspect for scholars of neoliberal work ethics. This strong emotional attachment seems to realize a utopia of governmentality, realigning the individual spirit and mentality to a collective belonging, reflecting a post-Fordist shift in methods of social control and the production of motivation. Commercial actors, as well as many discourses on local or traditional products, emphasize the moral and relational attachment to products. Probably one distinction between neoliberal motivation techniques and the anarchistic network remains. In the words of one former movement leader, "They can copy our ideas and take over our slogans and knowledge about local products, personal relationships and co-production, but they cannot re-create our 'community', our collective way; they will

never be able to copy that sense of community and sharing."

A Delirium with Frictions

The visit at Pedro's house also had some more long-term, indirect consequences, one of which can only be called a proper delirium. The idea to set up a collective kitchen materialized on the occasion of Enofila, an effervescent festival by "independent" wine makers. With the kitchen project, the personal relations of trust developed at the visit for the certification at Pedro's laboratory created also more immediate forms of economic solidarity at the festival. However, this solidarity turned out to be more challenging and ambiguous than imagined, with a tension between informal trust and formal regulations, between a reproduction and rupture of neoliberal values of transparency. Until that point, members of Terra Libera had been selling their food at the festival individually. Compared to individual food stands, running a collective kitchen at a large festival requires a massive organizational effort and constitutes a qualitative step forward in terms of coordination. Collective kitchens have a long history at alternative festivals, demonstrations and other events around the world and are part of a globally interconnected movement comprising collective experiences in South America, Europe and North America (Bray 2013; Cabras 2013). However, it is unusual to find collective kitchens at alternative peasant or farmer markets, which are often based on individual or small-scale autonomous units.

Enofila has been a great success in recent years, attracting hundreds of alternative wine producers and thousands of visitors, but this year, according to rumours spread by the organizers, was going to become one of the biggest editions of the festival. And with these rumours the expectations of the kitchen members rose. To be able to display their products, wine makers had to be defined as "independent" and were preferably not part of the large commercial circuits of professional wine sellers.[14] Together with the wine sellers, concerts and food stands would complete the festival activities, attracting mostly a young crowd, in search of fun, amusement and low-priced wine. In recent years, Terra Libera has proposed documentary screenings, workshops and debate sessions related to issues of food sovereignty. In an informal meeting at a market, Claudio outlined why these activities should not be proposed anymore. "When we do something, a debate or a screening, I always see the same faces," he stated. "It's just us, the usual people who already know, who come to these kinds of events. The youngsters just flock in because they want to have fun and get drunk."

The festival takes place every year in one of Europe's largest occupied social spaces, an ancient Roman fortress in the eastern neighbourhoods of the Roman metropolis. The place in itself is a jewel of Roman military architecture. During the festival, its large open space surrounded by walls serves as a space for concerts and to relax. All kinds of sellers populate the area, such as small-scale artisans selling handcrafted jewellery, food or drink. The central open area is surrounded by long dark tunnels made of seemingly endless rows of small single cells, once the rooms for soldiers. Each cell hosts a different vine stand, offering free tastings. This is the main attraction of Enofila: visitors move from one cell to the next in small groups with glasses of wine in their hands, flirting, joking, and drinking.

Given this background, the project of the collective kitchen had to meet seemingly contradictory challenges. On the one hand, the kitchen should remain a political project based on personal and horizontal relations and, on the other, afford a reasonable opportunity to make money. These lines of friction came to characterize the organizational process, which was decided and debated collectively in assemblies of the kitchen working group. To create a collective and just system that would reflect individual needs and possibilities, the concept that finally received approval was highly complex. In previous assemblies, it was decided that small-scale farmers participating in the group would sell their products at subsidized prices to the group. Each member of the group who would contribute to the work of the kitchen would be remunerated according to the amount of time they put into the work. In a side discussion, in one of the assemblies, a motion

was approved that those who ate some of the food prepared during work would be charged for it. This motion was discussed particularly intensely since it entailed an implicit clash between different notions of solidarity. Does solidarity mean allowing free access to meals for those who work or does solidarity mean that everyone pays for what he actually consumes? Such questions reflect the broader political implications of collective organization and its contested ideological underpinning.

The collective kitchen was conveniently located at one of the main entrances of the squat. Along the tables of Terra Libera's stand, endless flocks of youths flowed into the dark tunnel entrances all evening long. While I was preparing bread with cheese, Pedro commented, "If I was not married, you know how many girls I would find here?" while two well-dressed ladies with opulent hairstyles and tight jeans were passing by. Most visitors are not visibly dressed "alternative", but people who are looking for cheap wine and fun; the festival assumes connotations of an almost mainstream enterprise. The group of the collective kitchen surrendered to the idea that Enofila was just a delirium, a collective ecstasy. At the same time, with such large, well-off crowds, it also represented a unique opportunity to make some money. This tension between the demands of solidarity and the values of the network and the attempt still to participate at the festival and earn some money became more and more salient. By evening, increasing numbers of visitors flocked into the festival stands. The members of the group became more and more excited. Vegetables, cheese and bread had to be carried from the store to the stand; the food had to be prepared and served (see ill. 2).

In the dark storehouse, it became difficult to find the products needed at the counter. Along other activists, I was searching in the dark for the needed products. At the beginning, there were no clear rules regarding who would do what; the lack of organization was obvious. The line of people ordering food became longer and longer, and things became more and more chaotic behind the desk. Under the pressure of mounting orders, the efficiency and coordination grew. At the same time, people of the group

Ill. 2: Food plates of "genuinely clandestine" products ready to be served at an alternative festival. (Photo: Alexander Koensler, July 2016)

frequently started to enjoy their work, and laugh. The ingredients that the kitchen offered were of exceptionally high quality. Some members of the kitchen group had prepared hand-made pasta, fresh cheese and bread for days. Someone also brought fresh meat, as if a wild pig had been slaughtered for the occasion, which created an outcry among the vegans and vegetarians. Finally, a subgroup of vegans created a separate cash desk, so that their income would not be "contaminated" by those who had been processing meat. Later in the evening, the group worked stunningly smoothly; there seemed to be a rhythm in the flow of movements. For most it had been great fun, the atmosphere was effervescent, full of jokes, laughing, and hugs. At a first glance, it seemed that this event was a successful step forward in the collective organization.

Definitely, participating in the kitchen project unleashed unique enthusiasm. More than the visit at Pedro's house, the attempt to create a "real solidarity economy", as one participant put it, the kitchen project appeared as an experimental practice that created strong emotions connected to a utopian imagination. However, in the following assemblies, members had to cope with some unexpected diffi-culties. For instance, the overall earnings were less than expected, probably because too many workers had to be paid. Additionally, many of the ingredients had not been processed, not because there was insufficient demand, but for simple organizational reasons, such as the fact that those in charge of carrying them to the sales area had not found them in the storage room. If a vegetable grower did not sell his vegetables simply because someone did not find his boxes in the storage room, how should he be compensated? These questions were debated openly in the assemblies. Although a way was found to redistribute the small amount of money such that everyone was satisfied, for many, the event turned out to be more of a voluntary service than a well-paid job. On this and many similar occasions, I observed how the spirit of solidarity and friendship had been able to soften or resolve frictions that might have threatened the collaboration in the group. As these ethnographic episodes have shown, this form of solidarity practices is an indirect result of the enthusiastic visit for the "participatory guarantee" at Pedro's laboratory. However, the tension between the attempt to earn some money and, at the same time, create a social and political adventure, was not completely resolved. The practical limits of the here-and-now of capitalist constraints, were challenged by the striving for enthusiastic solidarity and utopian aspirations in the way Monique Scheer (2017: 8–9) describes "emotional practices": Emotions are not always a conservative reflection of the existing world, but are relational practices in the Bourdieuan sense which can be a utopian performance. Understanding the experience of utopian solidarity within the limits of the crude reality of the festival sheds light on the role of such emotional practices for activists' reconstitution of the interconnections between enthusiasm, joy and solidarity (Zackariasson 2015) as a counter-concept to the cold rules of governmental transparency.

Conclusions: Liberating our Humanistic Potential

This article has followed the path from the dissolution of trust relations due to the pervasiveness of governmental transparency to the re-emergence of new, experimental attempts to establish trust and solidarity in neorural activism. The ethnographic episodes highlight the inventive potential of re-inventing the procedures of official certifications in more democratic, horizontal and inclusive terms. The event related to the alternative guarantee illustrated here, this has also led to the creation of other, more direct forms of collaboration and solidarity. Within the horizon of national networks for food sovereignty, the movement has created alternative modes to guarantee the quality and safety of local food products. This "participatory guarantee" is based on personal relationships, trust and passion – as opposed to the official principles of transparency that work on the basis of fear, surveillance and de-personalized relationships. Against the backdrop of a growing formalization and de-personalization, these selected episodes illustrate a form of vanguard resistance against the governance of transparency: the visit at Pedro's laboratory differs radically from the common practice of certification inspectors. A friendly, horizontal and benevolent atmosphere created new bonds of friendship and new ideas, strengthening the network. The final delirious visit

at the baths – unfortunately missed by the author – was a type of informal conclusion that is not easy to imagine in other certification contexts. Furthermore, the visit for the alternative certification at Pedro's laboratory led to the creation of a collective kitchen as a form of "solidarity economy". The work for the kitchen was possible only for a group based on trust relations, solidarity and cooperation. From my own participation, I experienced how the kitchen group at the festival is an extraordinary example of how trust relations can unleash enthusiasm with almost a utopian leap. These elements are rare, almost impossible to find in the pervasiveness of governmental forms of transparency. The often elegant and creative way in which various mounting difficulties were managed was surprising and indicates how the group was able to liberate a humanistic potential of agency unknown to neoliberal logics.

However, not everything worked out smoothly. An underlying tension between the attempt to "make some money" and the socio-political project with its layers of idealism could not be completely resolved. Similarly, the visit at Pedro's laboratory has subsequently been described in some reports using allusions to technocratic, neoliberal overtones ("Transparency is the queen"). In other words, the underlying truth that "transparency is needed", in one form or another, remains reproduced also in alternative counter-movements. In this way, transparency remains a key theme of contemporary governance, even if its principles are challenged by activism for alternative certifications like the one analysed here. In a broader sense, these experiences and practices touch important questions of evolving contemporary governance. It is a dynamic that has significance far beyond the agri-food sector; it concerns all aspects of contemporary governance. Alternative certifications do not simply constitute an alternative form of control, like self-control or the interiorized control described by the Panopticon. Alternative practices of certification, as the case above shows, can be embedded in a vibrant circuit of an alternative "grassroots" micro-economy that is able to liberate a humanistic potential based on trust and freedom, values neglected and repressed in neoliberal dynamics. Solidarity based on trust relations is presented by activists as a counter-concept to neoliberal principles, as a tool to counter the "loneness" of competitive agribusiness, as one informant put it. This solidarity is not just "another side" of an economic or ideological crisis (Rakopoulos 2016), nor does it fit neatly into a moral imperative of neoliberal individualism, as the interesting research of Muehlebach (2012) on welfare activism in northern Italy has convincingly argued. The forms of solidarity illustrated above go far beyond the rise of voluntarism after the withdrawal of the welfare state and are located in anti-capitalist and post-anarchist insurrectional autonomous, yet contingent spaces (Newman 2015) of "concrete utopias", yet they tend to reproduce some elements of hegemonic thought. The danger, here, is not to fill a vacuum of neoliberal desert, but to unintentionally reproduce an underlying, constructed "truth" that "transparency" is good.

Finally, let me stop here for a moment. Turning attention to a more fundamental insight, I have experienced through my own participation, to some extent, the importance of emotional practices that have some utopian elements in a society based on formalization and standardization. In opposition to the neat perfection of standardized products, it seems as if the roughness of artisan production allows and resonates complex emotional bounds. These experiences recall those "relations of resonance" that have been eloquently popularized by the sociologist Hartmut Rosa (2016) and describe an experience of fullness that people experience when listening to a beautiful song or are immersed in a prayer. Relations of resonance are based on respect and autonomy; they touch profound aspects of who we are (Walter Benjamin, in Rosa 2012: 318), a process that is undermined by the micro-political surveillance in the name of governmental transparency. In this article, the "resonance" is only one element that indicates the importance of fully recovering our human drive "to do something good" and not simply "better than others" (or more precisely, "to appear as better") as current hegemonic ideology would have it. In other words, with this article, I attempt to demonstrate

how yet "unnamed figures of activism" (Isin 2008) make their appearance beyond the pervasive governance of everyday life; their task is to affirm the content of life against the empty form.

Notes

1 Names of private persons, events, groups and minor localities are changed in order to respect the privacy of those involved, but names of some of the public figures, institutions or organizations remain unaltered.
2 Developed originally by US astronauts for their food supply, HACCP (Hazard Analysis and Critical Control Points) aims to offer a systematic preventive approach to the safety of food chains throughout all production stages. Since the 1990s, HACCP has been implemented in EU law and has become obligatory for all food processers, small and large. In short, the system aims to prevent hazards during all production stages rather than only at the finished product inspection. HACCP regulations became the centre of dispute in Italy following a critique of the Slow Food movement that HACCP regulations lead to a modern form of standardization that poses a threat to traditional small-scale and quality productions (Petrini 2012).
3 This article is based on a talk presented on July 29, 2016, at the SIEF summer school "Trusting Resistance: New Ethnographies of Social Movements and Alternative Economies," held July 24–30, 2016, at University of Tübingen. The summer school provided an extraordinary vivid forum to reflect on these issues and I thank the organizers and participants for their comments and feedback. I also thank Cristina Papa, Filippo Zerilli and Fabrizio Loce Mandes, the two anonymous reviewers and the two editors of *Ethnologia Europaea* for their feedback and comments on earlier drafts.
4 The Peasant Activism Project (www.peasantproject.org) is a major ethnographic research project that investigates innovative forms of neorural activism in Italy and is hosted by Queen's University Belfast. The project is financed by the Economic and Social Research Council, UK (grant number ES/M011291/1).
5 In a broader sense, trust is a cognitive attitude that anticipates that others will have and display goodwill towards me – or at least will not have or display ill will towards me. Annette Baier's definition places the issue of vulnerability in the forefront: "Trust (...) is accepted vulnerability to another's possible but not expected ill will (or lack of goodwill) toward one" (Baier 1995: 99). In the context of economic relations, the role of trust has been studied as a means of guaranteeing stability.
6 "Solidarity" remains a key concept in activist discourses. The term is notoriously hard to pin down and has often been used with different and often polyvalent

connotations. In a broad sense, in my fieldwork activists frequently emphasized that solidarity has to be understood as a social relation opposed to exploitation and competition, and thus as a clear counter-concept to contemporary neoliberalist ideology. Many neorural networks have established practices that help members to overcome financial limits or economic constraints without relying on bank loans. Importantly, a line of research has demonstrated the ambiguity of solidarity in neoliberal societies, where individual activism replaces welfare and state obligations (Muehlebach 2012), while others, like Rakopoulos (2016), have understood solidarity as a bridge concept to the "other side" of the crisis that allows to rethink the relation between democracy and economy or as a counter-practice in conflicts that can have unintended consequences (Koensler 2016).

7 Comparable to a national health service, ASL (Azienda Sanitaria Locale) is the Italian regional public administration body responsible for the provision of health-related services, including the running of hospitals and overseeing hygienic standards in the food business.

8 According to the critical agrarian scholar Philip McMichael, the term "corporate food system" describes the latest stage of the evolution of food systems, which began approximately in the 1980s with the rise of a global market of stateless money. The periodization and analysis of food regimes is widely debated in the *Journal of Peasant Studies*. For an overview, see also McMichael (2013) and Moore (2012).

9 Financialization describes the profound change that world economies have undergone for the past forty years, which is also characterized by the rise of globalization and neoliberalism. Some authors use the term to describe a mode of corporate governance focused on "shareholder value" as a guiding management principle and on processes of standardization that are used to evaluate company values (Krippner 2005). Russi (2013) analyses the financialization of the food industry as a process that is shaped by the growing power of multinational corporations that focus on economic profit rather than on concerns about sustainability, quality or safeguarding citizens.

10 Byung-Chul Han states that the "society of transparency" relies on the "value of exposition". In advanced capitalism, the Marxian concept of "value of use" is increasingly determined by its level of exposition rather than its actual "use". This is true, for instance, for companies whose shares are no longer related to the actual material value of their infrastructure but to their imagined global value (e.g. Youtube, Facebook).

11 Precursors of studies of food activism include analyses of how industrialization and globalization affect eating and culture (Counihan 1988). In studying reactions to industrialized food and its alienation, anthropologists have been at the forefront of those who investigate ethical consumerism. A growing body of research has analysed the role of ethical food activism, such as the Slow Food movement, in lifestyle changes (Wilk 2006), thus enriching a debate about important methodological issues regarding community and networks (Parkins & Craig 2006; Pink 2008; Allen 2006; Creed 2006; Martino, Giacchè & Rossetti 2016). This body of research has also begun to make a major contribution to considering relational political issues through food (Counihan & Siniscalchi 2014; Grasseni 2013; Papa 2004), in contrast to a more positivist strand that considers eating and culture as an issue in itself, as evident in *The Oxford Handbook of Food History* (Pilcher 2012) or the extensive writing on specific foods in circumscribed local contexts (Hirschfelder 2001; Wiegelmann 2006).

12 This anecdote was told by a founding member of the local network who later became member of Genuino Clandestino. Fieldwork diary notes of the author. Where not indicated otherwise, all further ethnographic descriptions are based on personal observations of the author, including event participation and informal conversations with activists.

13 According to another version of the founding story, the label Genuino Clandestino was invented by a group of small-scale farmers in Naples who criticized the institutionalization of organic agriculture.

14 According to my informants, this has been determined in assembly decisions of which they, however, have not taken part regularly themselves.

References

Alexander, Jeffrey 2006: *The Civil Sphere*. Oxford: Oxford University Press.

Allen, Patricia 2006: *Together at the Table: Sustainability and Sustenance in the American Agrifood System.* University Park: Pennsylvania State University Press.

Baier, Annette C. 1995: *Moral Prejudices: Essays on Ethics.* Cambridge, MA: Harvard University Press.

Bentham, Jeremy 1791: *Panopticon; Or, The Inspection-House: Containing the Idea of a New Principle of Construction Applicable to any Sort of Establishment, in which Persons of any Description are to be kept under Inspection: And In Particular To Penitentiary-Houses, Prisons, Houses Of Industry, Work-Houses, Poor Houses, Manufactories, Mad-Houses, Lazarettos, Hospitals, And Schools: With A Plan Of Management.* London: Payne.

Bernstein, Henry 2010: *Class Dynamics of Agrarian Change.* Black Point: Fernwood.

Bernstein, Henry 2016: Agrarian Political Economy and Modern World Capitalism: The Contributions of Food Regime Analysis. *The Journal of Peasant Studies* 43:3, 611–647.

Bernstein, Jay M. 2011: Trust: On the Real but Almost Always Unnoticed, Ever-changing Foundation of Ethical Life. *Metaphilosophy* 42:4, 395–416.

Bray, Michael 2013: *Translating Anarchy: The Anarchism of Occupy Wall Street*. New York: John Hunt Publishing.

Brem-Wilson, Josh 2015: Towards Food Sovereignty: Interrogating Peasant Voices in the United Nations Committee on World Food Security. *The Journal of Peasant Studies* 42:1, 73–95.

Cabras, Sergio 2013: *Terra e futuro: L'agricoltura contadina ci salverà*. Roma: Eurilink.

Cooper, Davina 2014: *Everyday Utopias: The Conceptual Life of Promising Spaces*. Durham: Duke University Press.

Counihan, Carole M. 1988: Female Identity, Food, and Power in Contemporary Florence. *Anthropological Quarterly* 61:2, 51–62.

Counihan, Carole & Valeria Siniscalchi 2014: *Food Activism: Agency, Democracy and Economy*. London: Bloomsbury.

Creed, Gerald W. (ed.) 2006: *The Seductions of Community: Emancipations, Oppressions, Quandaries*. Santa Fe, New Mexico & Oxford: School of American Research Press.

Edelman, Marc 1999: *Peasants against Globalisation: Rural Social Movements in Costa Rica*. Stanford: Stanford University Press.

Edelman, Marc 2015: Transitional Organizing in Agrarian Central America: Histories, Challenges, Prospects. *Journal of Agrarian Change* 8:2–3, 229–257.

Elder, Sara D. & Peter Dauvergne 2015: Farming for Walmart: The Politics of Corporate Control and Responsibility in the Global South. *The Journal of Peasant Studies* 42:5, 1029–1046.

Epstein, Gerald A. 2005: *Financialization and the World Economy*. Cheltenham: Edward Elgar.

Grasseni, Cristina 2013: *Beyond Alternative Food Networks: Italy's Solidarity Purchase Group*. London: Bloomsbury.

Han, Byung-Chul 2012: *Transparenzgesellschaft*. Berlin: Matthes & Seitz.

Hirschfelder, Gunther 2001: *Europäische Esskultur: Eine Geschichte der Ernährung von der Steinzeit bis heute*. Frankfurt: Campus.

Isin, Engin F. 2008: Theorizing Acts of Citizenship. In: Engin F. Isin & Greg M. Nielsen (eds.), *Acts of Citizenship*. London: Palgrave Macmillan, pp. 15–43.

Jönsson, Håkan (ed.) 2013: Foodways Redux: Case Studies on Contemporary Food Practices. *Ethnologia Europaea* 43:2.

Kerkvliet, Ben J. 1993: Claiming the Land: Take overs by Villagers in the Philippines with Comparisons to Indonesia, Peru, Portugal, and Russia. *Journal of Peasant Studies* 20:3, 459–493.

Koensler, Alexander 2016: Acts of Solidarity: Crossing and Reiterating Israeli–Palestinian Frontiers. *International Journal of Urban and Regional Research* 40:2, 340–356.

Krippner, Greta 2005: The Financialization of the American Economy. *Socio-Economic Review* 3, 173–208.

Martino, Gaetano, Giulia Giacchè & Enrica Rossetti 2016: Organizing the Co-Production of Health and Environmental Values in Food Production: The Constitutional Processes in the Relationships between Italian Solidarity Purchasing Groups and Farmers. *Sustainability* 8:4, 316–334.

Mattioli, Fabio 2013: The Property of Food. Geographical Indication, Slow Food, Genuino Clandestino and the Politics of Property. *Ethnologia Europaea* 43:2, 47–61.

May, Sarah 2013: Cheese, Commons and Commerce: On the Politics and Practices of Branding Regional Food. *Ethnologia Europaea* 43:2, 62–77.

McDonagh, John, Birte Nienaber & Michael Woods (eds.) 2015: *Globalization and Europe's Rural Regions*. Farnheim: Ashgate.

McMichael, Philip 2009: A Food Regime Genealogy. *The Journal of Peasant Studies* 36:1, 139–169.

McMichael, Philip 2012: Depeasantization. In: Guy Ritzer (ed.), *The Wiley-Blackwell Encyclopedia of Globalization*. London: John Wiley.

McMichael, Philip 2013: *Food Regimes and Agrarian Questions*. Halifax: Fernwood.

Moore, Jason W. 2012: Cheap Food & Bad Money: Food, Frontiers, and Financialization in the Rise and Demise of Neoliberalism. *Review* 33:2–3, 225–261.

Morena, Edouard 2014: Words Speak Louder than Actions: The "Peasant" Dimension of the Confédération Paysanne's Alternative to Industrial Farming. *The Journal of Peasant Studies* 42:1, 45–71.

Muehlebach, Andrea 2012: *The Moral Neoliberal: Welfare and Citizenship in Italy*. Chicago: University of Chicago Press.

Newman, Saul 2015: *Postanarchism*. London: Wiley & Blackwell.

Papa, Cristina 2004: What Does It Mean to Conserve Nature? In: Glauco Ortelli & Gherardo Sanga (eds.), *Nature Knowledge: Ethnoscience, Cognition, and Utility*. London: Berghahn, pp. 339–359.

Parkins, Wendy & Geoffrey Craig 2006: *Slow Living*. London: Berg.

Petrini, Carlo 2012: *Slow Food: Le ragioni del gusto*. Roma: Laterza.

Pétursson, Jón Þórn 2013: Eduardo's Apples: The Co-Production of Personalized Food Relationships. *Ethnologia Europaea* 43:3, 17–29.

Pilcher, Jean M. 2012: *The Oxford Handbook of Food History*. Oxford: Oxford University Press.

Pink, Sarah 2008: Re-thinking Contemporary Activism: From Community to Emplaced Activism. *Ethnos* 73:2, 163–188.

van der Ploeg, Jan D. 2009: *The New Peasantries: Struggles for Autonomy and Sustainability in an Era of Empire and Globalization*. London: Earthscan LLC.

Polanyi, Karl 1957: *The Great Transformation: The Political and Economic Origins of Our Time*. Boston: Beacon Press.

Power, Michael 2007: *Organized Uncertainty: Designing a World of Risk Management.* Oxford: Oxford University Press.

Rakopoulos, Theodoros 2016: Solidarity: The Egalitarian Tensions of a Bridge-concept. *Social Anthropology* 24:2, 142–151.

Rosa, Hartmut 2012: *Weltbeziehungen im Zeitalter der Beschleunigung: Umrisse einer neuen Gesellschaftskritik.* Frankfurt a.M.: Suhrkamp.

Rosa, Hartmut 2016: *Resonanz: Eine Soziologie der Weltbeziehung.* Berlin: Suhrkamp.

Russi, Lorenzo 2013: *Hungry Capital: The Financialization of Food.* London: Zero Books.

Scheer, Monique 2017: Die tätige Seite des Gefühls: Eine Erkundung der impliziten Emotionstheorie im Werk Bourdieus. In: Markus Rieder-Ladich & Christian Grabau (eds.), *Pierre Bourdieu: Pädagogische Lektüre.* Wiesbaden: Springer, pp. 155–167.

Shore, Chris, Susan Wright & Daniel Però 2011: *Policy Worlds: Anthropology and the Analysis of Contemporary Power.* London: Berghahn Books.

Strathern, Marylin 1996: Cutting the Network. *The Journal of the Royal Anthropological Institute* 2:3, 517–535.

Strathern, Marylin 2000a: *Audit Cultures: Anthropological Studies in Accountability, Ethics and the Academy.* London: Taylor & Francis.

Strathern, Marylin 2000b: The Tyranny of Transparency. *British Educational Research Journal* 26:3, 309–321.

Tschofen, Bernhard 2002: Celebrated Origins: Local Food and Global Knowledge. Comments on the Possibilities of Food Studies in the Age of the World-Wide Web. In: P. Lysaght, (ed.), *From Fasting to Feasting: Proceedings of the 13th Conference of the International Commission for Ethnological Food Research.* Ljubljana: SIEF, pp. 101–112.

Watts, Michael J. 2008: The Southern Question: Agrarian Questions of Labour and Capital. In: Haroon Akram-Lodhi & Cristóbal Kay (eds.), *Peasants and Globalization: Political Economy, Rural Transformations and the Agrarian Question.* London: Routledge, pp. 262–287.

Wiegelmann, Guenter 2006: *Alltags- und Festspeisen in Mitteleuropa.* Münster: Waxmann.

Wilk, Robert 2006: *Fast Food/Slow Food: The Cultural Economy of the Global Food System* (Society for Economic Anthropology Monograph Series 24). Lanham, MD: Altamira.

Zackariasson, Maria 2015: Loving and Forgiving? Emotions and Emotion Work in the Youth Organization Equmenia. *Ethnologia Europaea* 45:1, 42–57.

Zerilli, Filippo & Tracey Heatherington (eds.) 2016: Anthropologists in/of the Neoliberal Academy. *Anuac* 5:1, 41–91.

Žižek, Slavoj 2012: *The Year of Dreaming Dangerously.* London & New York: Verso.

Alexander Koensler is a research fellow at Queen's University Belfast. He has held postdoctoral and teaching positions at University of Perugia, University of Münster and Ben-Gurion University of the Negev. Trained as a socio-cultural anthropologist, his work aims to unearth the role of experimental political activism that, to a certain extent, innovates and transcends more institutionalised social movements. Currently he directs the ESRC-funded Peasant Activism Project (www.peasantproject.org).
(a.koensler@qub.ac.uk)

DOING ECONOMIC RELATIONS OTHERWISE
Everyday Politics of Solidarity in the TEM Currency Network in Volos, Greece

Andreas Streinzer, University of Vienna

Recent scholarship on Southern Europe focuses on economic crisis and contestations of hegemonic economic and political arrangements. Solidarity features prominently in these accounts as a notion of opposition to austerity and recession. This article uses solidarity as an entry point, and then shifts attention to the everyday politics of its enactment in the TEM complementary currency network. The article presents three sets of challenges faced by network members: moral discourses around debt, disregard of communal labour and hierarchies created through economic inequalities among network members. The discussion of these challenges places resistance and solidarity in larger discussions about capitalist economies and hegemonic thought and practice that go beyond the discussion of solidarity in Greece and Southern Europe.[1]

Keywords: solidarity, resistance, Greece, LETS, austerity

It is another market day, and we are sitting in one of the two buildings made available to the TEM currency network by a state organization. Giannis[2] turns his office chair towards me, away from the monitor that displays transactions in a banking online interface. He sighs and says: "We wanted a revolution and organized a central bank." His statement sinks in as we watch some network members go through a pile of second-hand clothes, arranging products for sale on their sales desks, cleaning them of the white flakes of paint that snow from the wall. (Fieldnotes, Volos, February 2014)

In this article, I examine the everyday politics of solidarity in a Local Exchange and Trading System (LETS),[3] a network for trading in a complementary currency. Network members organize the TEM (*Topiki Enallaktiki Monada* meaning Local Alternative Unit) as a form of resistance to eurozone capitalism and austerity policies. By invoking notions of solidarity (*allilengi*) as the guiding principle for their actions, my interlocutors attempt to create a new form of relational arrangement that would allow them to do economic relations otherwise than under the prevailing (euro) economy.

However, and as indicated by the opening quote, network members face serious challenges in enacting their differing ideas about what solidarity entails and how it should be practised. Focus on these challenges allows me to discuss the relation between dominant economic thought and alternative practice, which is especially significant when the conditions of provisioning are increasingly difficult everyday due to the fall of incomes in Greece. I argue that an essentialist view on solidarity and resistance, focusing solely on its bright sides, effects a narrow understanding of the everyday struggle of coping with deteriorating economic conditions.

In the article, I briefly introduce the euro crisis as economic and political context, and the TEM network as a strategy of resistance to the dominant (euro) economy. I then discuss resistance and solidarity in recent literature to argue for understanding these notions as both features of social relations and narratives that guide practices. This perspective allows me to present three major challenges that the network faces in attempting to do economic relations otherwise. These three – moral discourses around debt, disregard of communal labour and hierarchies created through economic inequalities among network members – are especially instructive for an analysis of hegemony, capitalism and an anthropology of living in austerity and recession beyond the Greek case. The ethnographic material I use in this article is from doctoral fieldwork undertaken in the Greek city of Volos between February 2014 and March 2016, where my fieldwork focused on urban household provisioning and economic strategies, among them the TEM network, to cope with recession and austerity.

Initially, some context should be provided regarding the recent developments that resulted in a downward spiral in household incomes in Volos and Greece at large. These political and economic developments are crucial as frames for understanding the TEM network and its economic and symbolic significance.

The Greek Crisis

From its beginnings as a political idea (Dodd 2005), the euro was designed to be an all-purpose money that served as a medium of exchange in global and domestic trade, a unit of account, a store of value and standard of payment (Holmes 2014: 593). The eurozone brought together countries that differed in their economic make-up (Dyson 2010: 598ff.), and one central aspect of the currency union was that the in-

terest rates on loans by which governments refinanced their debt to private and institutional lenders should converge. The strategy was to allow those countries that formerly had high interest rates to refinance with cheaper credit. Greece joined the eurozone in 2001 and for some years, it seemed as if this strategy was working out.[4] Yet, when the newly elected Greek government announced in 2009 that government debt was higher than previous governments had reported, international lenders reacted by increasing interest rates for the country's loans due to the growing risk that Greece would not avoid default.

European states stepped in to refinance lending banks, and the resulting admixture of private and state debt has been called the "eurocrisis" (Preunkert & Vobruba 2015: 219–220). However, another reason exists underlying the development of the crisis: the attribution of blame solely to debtor states, to the exclusion of creditors or other implicated parties (Lapavitsas 2012). In the case of Greece, the vicious cycle of debt refinancing was exacerbated due to the scale of debt (as of 2018 the loans offered by the European Union and the IMF to the Greek government exceed 323 billion euro), and by the attempts at economic restructuring through politics of austerity. Since 2009, the Greek state has reduced government expenses, and, since the signing of the first debt Memorandum with the so-called Troika – consisting of the European Commission, the International Monetary Fund and the European Central Bank – this has occurred on an unprecedented scale. Pushed by other European countries as well as the Troika, the Greek parliament has passed neoliberal reforms at a breath-taking pace. Such measures have included cutting state salaries, firing thousands of state employees, privatization of state assets, and extracting money from the social insurance system, among others. Many observers, including my interlocutors, initially welcomed reforms, as these had been promoted as necessary dissolutions of cartels, clientelist systems, and other economically undesirable entities. That was before an economic catastrophe unfolded that contracted the Greek GDP by 27.3% between 2008 and 2015 (ELSTAT 2016) and left many puzzled at the speed at which their jobs were rendered obsolete, their businesses failed, and their incomes dramatically decreased, to the point that most of my interlocutors in 2016 reported that their incomes had fallen over 40% from previous levels.

Greece slashed state spending on social programmes, including employment programmes, lowered wages and pensions, and reregulated social and economic policy. State spending was cut back mainly at what Bourdieu calls the "left hand of the state" (Bourdieu 1998: 1ff.), namely, social services, public health, and education. The effect was an increased burden on close social networks, and especially kin ties, to assume these former state functions (Hajek & Opratko 2013: 49f.). This is the structural context for the transformations currently affecting local economic structures in Volos, Greece, where my field site was located. Bereft of opportunities to raise their income, and sobered by the resource conflicts that developed in many close social networks, the members of the TEM complementary currency were mounting resistance to the consequences of recession and austerity, as well as attempting to support each other emotionally and economically.

The TEM Complementary Currency Network

In 2010, a group of people from different walks of life met at a demonstration against austerity measures planned by the Greek government in Volos. Some knew each other before but it was during their reflection on the protests that they came together as a group, united by their desire to "do something" to change their situation. Indignant about the harsh stance of the Troika and the Greek government, they concluded that the time had come to become active in organizing an economic mechanism that would grant them relative autonomy from the unfolding crisis. Ideally, it would allow them to establish economic relations between them that would bring about a more solidaristic way of doing economic relations. This was the birth of the Network for Exchange and Solidarity in Magnisia (*Diktio Antallagon kai Allilengis Magnisias*).

Meetings were held, and soon the group decided to begin a venture as a LETS (Local Exchange and Trading System), a mechanism by which they could create a new means of exchange to pay other members of their group for services and products. This means of exchange was named the TEM (Local Alternative Unit). A LETS is a trading network administered through online software. Each member is registered as a user with an account. Usually, as is the case of the TEM network, this account has a balance of zero when opened. Money is created by allowing these accounts credit up to a predefined limit. If two transactors agree on a service and its price, the service provider gets the amount in positive balance and the account commissioning the service is debited with the same amount, which may leave it with a negative balance. That means that the total sum of currency in the network is always zero, as accounts balance out (North 1999: 69). Whereas I have to leave aside discussions in the anthropology of money[5] here, these aspects of the TEM are key to the debates within the group of organizers about the TEM as money.

Besides the electronic infrastructure, the TEM network maintained two one-storey buildings where an open market was held twice weekly, a seminar room where lessons and workshops were given, and several living quarters for people who had been homeless.[6] Although the network was founded to administer the currency, many activities organized by network members became loosely associated with the TEM. Among these was the Solidarity Kitchen of Volos (*Kousina Allilengis Bolou*). Another activity organized by members of the TEM was a programme to support stray dogs, which were fed and given veterinary treatments by members.

Complementary currency networks are a recent phenomenon in Greece; most networks started in 2010, coinciding with the effects of austerity and recession. In her dissertation, Irene Sotiropoulou documented 33 groups (2012) and Thanou, Theodossiou and Kallivokas (2013) found 20 LETS and 11 time-banks. The TEM is the biggest of these networks. In early 2016, the TEM had 881 members, of which around 300 were active in trading. Around 50 members were regulars to the market, operating stalls there or coming to sell or buy food. The core group of people active in meetings, the running of the system and working groups were about 20 people. These were consistently aiming at including members in the decision processes of the network. The network aimed at being inclusive and democratic and most decisions were made through consensus. Yet, for running the technical infrastructure and public relations, one and at times two people were elected coordinators. Decisions were made mostly during meetings on Wednesdays, held when members sent requests for such meetings to the coordinators, or through a messaging board in the online infrastructure. Most of those were requested by members of the core group. Structural questions were discussed in general assemblies, which were held irregularly.

The membership base were people from lower classes or lower middle classes, around a third being self-employed, a third unemployed and a third public employees, students or retired (my observations match the work by Uesaka 2013: 23). Although there were some members in their twenties and thirties, the age of members tended to be forty and higher. In the core group, more women than men were active. Reasons and motivations for members were generally economic motives as well as social and political values and emotional support such as after a divorce or business default (for a more detailed discussion, see Flierman 2014: 23ff.).

The TEM founders also created a master account that would pay for communal work, for example work administrating the software, recording transactions, and maintaining the premises on which network members held their market twice weekly. While user accounts had a credit limit, the master account did not. Theoretically, unlimited amounts of money could have been created by this master account. To counter the possibility of inflating the value of the currency, the TEM was pegged 1:1 to the euro, and the organizing group kept an eye on how much the master account was in negative balance. Although discussions about using a form of paper money surfaced in summer 2015, the network's members decided not to pursue it, due to concerns about the cost of printing money, and the risk for fraud.

I joined the network in February 2014, which entailed filling in a form and paying a five-euro membership fee, whereupon I was permitted to post offers in the online directory of members where other members could see and request them. At that time, it was clear that the TEM membership was bound by more than merely economic relations, based upon their transactions. Social relations between a group of around 50 members, who were regulars at the market and meetings, had considerable non-commercial aspects as well. Often, members would give their services or products for free if someone could not afford their price, and would sometimes agree not to charge each other at all for services rendered among friends.

Fight the Power! But where is it?

The members of the TEM network framed their actions as resistance. When I joined the network four years after its foundation, their notion of resistance did not rest on a binary view of power or an "us versus them" attitude. Rather, resistance meant complex negotiation of the material and symbolic aspects of living in a capitalist economy in recession and with an austerity government. Whereas TEM members meant that their way of doing economic relations was in direct opposition to the prevailing capitalist economy, they were aware of the ambivalences of such a stance. As incomes fell and households needed to save themselves, TEM members struggled to provision themselves with necessary goods and services.

The TEM market mechanism thus was, in addition to being a community network and an attempt to enact solidarity, a way for members to substitute costs to better cope with the economic difficulties they faced. These difficulties were manifold, but the one that had direct consequences for the TEM was the lack of available income in euro. Household incomes had fallen drastically, leaving the larger part of my interlocutors with incomes reduced to less than 40% of their pre-recession income. Some lost all their income, while others struggled with a loss of customers, pressure at the workplace, or stagnation in sectors that employed day labourers. The dreams and aspirations of TEM members did not differ from those of other people in similar economic situations. Parents feared their children might not succeed in school, and thus suffer reduced economic prospects in general, and so some paid for private tutors. They used euro, TEM, and sometimes avoided payment, if they could recruit tutors to support them. They would go on time-consuming searches for second-hand clothing to project the impression they could afford new garments. Enterprises that advertised their products in TEM explained this decision as both a show of support and a relatively cheap way to advertise to customers who might pay in euro, if not during the recession, then perhaps afterwards. Given that access to basic necessities – housing, water, staple food, electricity, heating and transportation – was dependent on available money and liquidity, the fact that these households managed to cope can be considered a major achievement.

The TEM allows some to provide for themselves without spending euro, to an extent that gives them considerable autonomy from wage labour on the primary (euro) market. However, I met no-one who was altogether free from such labour. The households involved use the TEM as one strategy among others for making ends meet. As mentioned above, the retreat of the market and the state from offering or improving access to key goods and services has been answered by an increase in provisioning through kin and friendship ties. These involve a larger spectrum of practices that, in the case of the Volos households I worked with, included a reinforcement of gender roles, an increase in volunteerism, and a rise in the practice of women pooling resources to increase their purchasing power (Streinzer 2016), as well as structures such as the TEM. The situation comes close to what Manos Spyridakis describes in his discussion of labourers in declining industrial settings in Greece: the "culture of everyday resistance of the dominated through their conscious engagement in this asymmetrical power game and management of social reproduction" (Spyridakis 2012: 113). The TEM network attempts to resist hegemonic economic arrangements by organizing a membership-based trading network and creating economic relations that the members cannot realize in the mainstream economy. TEM members are well aware of their entanglement in the social, material and symbolic constraints of the broader society. The realization that localized resistance is intertwined in the politics of provisioning and thus in the mainstream economy, is clear in statements by group members such as Tonia, who says that:

> At first, we had [a] strong belief that we should do something to self-organize, to break with this corrupt politics that is all about bailing out banks and in which no-one takes care [of] one another. But then – we could not see this at this point – the crisis hit. And people lost their incomes, their way of life. And the network became something more serious – a mechanism to survive, basically. (Tonia, Volos, February 2015)

As the crisis deepened, the TEM's significance in members' everyday economic lives changed, and the TEM grew in importance to the social security of the households involved. That did not change the foundational character of the TEM as resistant practice, but it did influence the urgency of the network's economic functions. The increased provisioning stress on members had repercussions in debates about what means the network should use to achieve its double goal of relative autonomy from market provisioning and enacting economic relations with greater solidarity. Members of the network describe the way in which it differs from the dominant organization of means of exchange in ways that project the network's role on both large and small scales.

> Within the TEM, we have money, we exchange goods, we produce and receive in return. It looks like the larger economy. But what we have is the control over our money, we can issue some, we can decide about prices, we can invite others to join. The main difference is this – it is *our* money. And we are not capitalists, we support each other. (Giannis, Volos, March 2016)

Resistance and Solidarity in Recent Anthropological Scholarship

The concept of resistance in anthropology was developed to conceptualize mass movements and mobilizations (Ortner 1995: 174). James Scott then focused scholarly attention on everyday forms of rebellion and the hidden, often ambivalent nature of most resistance practices (Scott 1985, 1990). This ambivalence is worth taking serious as the inequalities underlying social hierarchies are maintained through a combination of coercion and consent (Jessop & Sum 2006: 368). By taking such a perspective, I develop Theodossopoulos' contention that "resistance may represent an astute critique of visible inequalities, but is not isolated from overarching hegemonic ideological influences that shape local interpretations of historical/economic causality" (Theodossopoulos 2014: 488). Resistance, therefore, is a messy process of opposing hegemonic normative frameworks and arrangements of power, which takes place between and within social groups with unequal power. This perspective is inspired by Poulantzas' understanding of political power (Poulantzas 2014: 147).

Sherry Ortner has remarked that there is more to resistance as a concept than the detection of opposition to domination. For Ortner, resistance is an ambiguous category, but one reasonably useful to "highlight the presence and play of power in most forms of relationship and activity" (Ortner 1995: 175). She writes that, ultimately, resistance offers a way to study politics and that these politics should be examined also with an analysis of the intragroup politics of the dominated: "Overall, the lack of an adequate sense of prior and on-going politics among subalterns must inevitably contribute to an inadequate analysis of resistance itself" (Ortner 1995: 179). I will develop this point and discuss the politics of resistance and its considerable tensions about how another, more solidaristic world ought to be built. The concept of "everyday politics" is useful to underscore these negotiations of interests, complicities, and contradictions, and to relate them to actually existing forms of attempting to do things otherwise: "The concept of everyday politics, as I define it, designates the practical encounter of common actors with existing cultural expectations and social power. It is, as it were, negotiation from below, not with only one's superiors but also with one's self or with significant others" (Kalb 1997: 22). Such conception of resistance – not as a straightforward property of a given practice or orientation but as the negotiation of power between and *within* groups – allows to investigate the complex play of power in the relational aspects of groups.

Recent anthropological scholarship, especially works on crisis in Southern Europe, has brought solidarity networks and volunteer organizations to the forefront of inquiry (Cabot 2016; Douzina-Bakalaki 2017; Muehlebach 2012; Narotzky 2012; Narotzky & Besnier 2014; Rakopoulos 2015). Rakopoulos defined the solidarity economy as one thriving on "conceptions of mutuality, reciprocal help, and self-organization – that is, on conceptions of struggle against austerity-driven policies and for alternative social spaces and structures to accommodate social justice" (Rakopoulos 2015: 88). Heath Cabot has conceptualized solidarity as the "contagious other" of austerity (Cabot 2016: 152). Yet Cabot finds among her volunteer interlocutors an unsettling feeling that, by taking over operations of the state, self-organized initiatives become part of a neoliberalization of society in which care is increasingly privatized. Such problematization of solidarity is crucial to understanding the challenges of contestation while being subject to a capitalist society in recession.

The TEM members use solidarity as a counter-narrative to exclusion, dispossession and austerity, and therefore as a narrative of resistance that they attribute to their practices. While they all strive towards solidarity as a focus of common struggle, they subscribe to different notions of what it entails and how to achieve it. The enactment of the already discursively differing narratives of solidarity into actual practice is fraught with contradictions and difficulties. In their attempt to do economic relations otherwise, they find themselves reproducing models of thought they had set themselves against. In exploring these ambiguities and contradictions, my research acknowledges the complexity of social relations and the normative power of hegemonic ideas and arrangements over the lives of my interlocutors. This perspective builds on the view of Papataxiarchis, who has argued that anthropologists should approach the topic of solidarity as an analytical tool to understand political movements (2016).

Yet I claim that we should aim to problematize how solidarity is actually done.

The argument of my article is that such an essentialized and purified account of solidarity initiatives leads us so far as to validate a generic version of social struggle. Such an account falls short of taking serious the complexities of coercion and consent that makes dominant models of thought and arrangements of social relations hegemonic. In such a perspective, Polanyi's point about the double movement that binds together the spread of free market capitalism and the reaction it creates – a push back or fight back from "society" (Polanyi 1944; for a longer discussion on Polanyi's work in economic anthropology today see Hann & Hart 2009) – can be used to describe phenomena such as the solidarity and volunteer networks in Greece. Yet, as Nancy Fraser points out, many scholarly accounts of such push-backs against market forces turn a blind eye to relations of domination within these attempts. She points to the residual "communitarianism" (Fraser 2014: 544) in such accounts, and calls on scholarship to find ways to address the frictions in emancipatory movements without shunning the complexities of such a venture. Such frictions occur in the ambivalences and contradictions of TEM members struggling with recession while attempting to act morally right. I argue for a critical engagement with the "modern revival of economic communitarianism" (Simonic 2014: 10), of which networks like the TEM are part, and a de-exoticization of romantic or idealistic notions of resistance as called for by Theodossopoulos (2014: 502).

Having clarified those intentions, I will now turn to the everyday politics of the TEM network. To do that, an analytical distinction between market forms is necessary, as proposed by Carrier who distinguishes "market" from "Market" (Carrier 1997: 14ff.). While the market is a form of exchange organization that has existed across societies and history (see also Polanyi, Arensberg & Pearson 1957), the Market is an abstraction (Carrier 1997: vii) that puts forth a world consisting solely of buyers and sellers, and contends that buyers always want to buy more cheaply, leading to competition among sellers. Car-

rier adds that Market is also "a claim and a belief that a certain sort of buying and selling benefits all those involved economically, politically, socially and even morally. And that that is the sort of buying and selling associated with the Free Market" (Carrier 1997: vii). While the TEM is a market mechanism that links buyers and sellers, members generally do not frame its operations in Market terms. Considerable interaction exists outside of buying and selling, and many services, such as childcare and skills training, and goods, such as meals, were given without resorting to the closed reciprocities of the transaction services the TEM mechanism offers.

Nonetheless, negotiations between members regarding the nature and purpose of the TEM, as well as what kinds of individuals should be admitted into it, often slipped into Market-oriented thinking. This happened most frequently during meetings where decisions about money creation, shortages of certain goods, or inequalities in access to the market were discussed. Such Market-oriented thinking arose as a rejoinder to abstract conceptions of the TEM and questions of what a market is and does. This is an important point, as the transformation of how people think about the economy and economic relations was often likened to conceptualizations of the Market as promulgated almost constantly through radio, television, and newspapers. Living in Greece at the time in question entailed being continually subjected to technocratic or monetaristic reasoning about eurozone negotiations, intricate details of the currency union, or the supposed legitimacy of spending cuts.

Creating a Secondary Market while Resisting the Primary One

I joined the TEM network in February 2014, at a time when debate was prevalent on the network over the prices of products being bought in euro and resold in TEM currency. Another controversy at the time concerned ways of expelling some of the network's members. Most network members with whom I interacted over two years repeatedly voiced concerns that "*kati den paei kala*" (something does not work well). Three clusters of topics were constant concerns for the network and its members, and were discussed at length in meetings, on market days, and in informal conversations. These three topics engage with crucial questions of the maintenance of the TEM network and exchange mechanism, and are subject to serious contestation and negotiation by network members. The first revolves around the creation of money through a certain kind of debt; the second around communal work needed to maintain the network; the third deals with consequences of the market mechanism and internal inequalities. In the next section I will show how these three topics each relate to my reading of resistance introduced above.

Debt, Credit and the Creation of Exchange Value

As mentioned above, organizing the currency required the establishment of membership, the setting up of the software, and other such constitutive measures, but to create units of the currency, there were further prerequisites: member accounts (or the master account) had either to be allowed to go into negative balance or given positive balance to start trading. Technically, having a credit limit of 20 TEM is the same as opening a new account with 20 TEM in positive balance, but the cultural meaning of being indebted was a heavily discussed issue amongst members.

The existence of the TEM currency is contingent upon agreement among the network's members that such currency exists, and secondarily upon its inscription in the online banking software. As with money in general (Gregory 1997: 254), the circumstances of the TEM currency's production are obscured by its appearing to be an object in its own right. Notions of private property enable people to think they can own a certain amount of abstracted value. This value can be either positive or negative, depending on the flow of value between the members' accounts. However, members interpreted the mechanism of creating money through negative balances as debt to the network or its members. This functional aspect of money creation was moralized by some TEM members in accordance with prevalent moralities regarding debt as "bad", compared to

credit as "good" (which matches most anthropological observations on the morality of debt, cf. Peebles 2010 and Gregory 2012).

Members' reasoning about what they construed as the network's early mistakes and the lessons that they drew therefrom are instructive. After having set up the software and they had begun to trade among themselves, the TEM founders decided to host a party to celebrate the introduction of TEM and attract potential members. Friends, family and local officials were invited, and media outlets were informed of the celebration. In order to kick-start circulation through potential new members, a credit limit of 300 TEM was set by founders, and during the celebrations, many signed up for the network. In hindsight, most members thought the credit limit of 300 TEM attracted members who were ultimately destructive to the network, also blaming the way the celebrations were announced in local media, as Giannis describes:

> We saw in the newspapers that if you register in this network [you] get 300 TEM for free. Not even a mention of a credit limit! [...] Now somebody comes to you with the mentality of: you are getting something for nothing. And that is not what you want, obviously. And they took the [300 TEM] credit, and took things from people, producers, people who had valuable stuff. And they went away and were never seen again. (Giannis, Nafplio, May 2015)

Two things are important in the above quotation: the understanding it represents of a credit limit and the notion that people took something from the network. It is well documented in scholarship about LETS that new members are met with the expectation that they should contribute to the LETS as a secondary market by offering goods or services (North 2007). As a trade mechanism, a LETS invites productive individuals who are actually trading. Yet in the TEM case, the credit limit was moralized as having taken away goods without giving back. A moral deficiency was attributed to these members because of their failure or unwillingness to offer products or services themselves. As a response, prior to my fieldwork, the credit limit was set at 20 TEM (where it stood in February 2014 and has since remained) but the narrative of the early free riders persisted. Interestingly, members did not connect this narrative of "credit flight" with the creation of money itself, though the practice of extending credit was integral to the creation of TEM currency. Rather, the narrative of cheap and easy credit attracting selfish people served as a strong normative line of argumentation categorizing those who carried a positive balance as givers and those with a negative balance as receivers – and thus debtors who had to pay back their debt (Peebles 2010: 226f.).

Maintaining the Network:
Communal Work, Anyone?

The maintenance of the software, handling of accounts, input of transaction data into the computer, maintenance of the premises and other such activities required work from network members. This work was paid for by the master account, at a fixed rate of 6 TEM per hour. This rate was agreed upon in long discussions in the early days of the network. Whenever I asked whether this rate would be raised or lowered, I was told that most members thought that it should remain fixed at the current rate. When I contrasted the 6 TEM per hour with the hourly wage paid for other kinds of work, which was sometimes as high as 20 TEM, the responses showed how communal work was framed in the network. The decision to pay members for communal work was meant to show appreciation for their work maintaining the network. As the TEM is a network operated for and by its members themselves, it engendered views about the merits of compensation that touched upon questions of how and why people work at all, and for whom. Dimitra, a TEM member, explained such views, criticizing volunteer organizations in the process:

Volunteers cannot maintain such a network as we are doing. At some point, they will get tired because it is a lot of work, and you also have to make sure how you will survive. So, people would have

to work [a job] in order to be able to work for the network for free. That is wrong. I think it is good that we pay people for these things. They can buy things [with that] money, and rightly so — they worked for it! (Dimitra, Volos, March 2015)

Besides this affirmative understanding of why the network pays members at all, I encountered a hard stance against raising the amount members were paid. The main argument for not paying more than 6 TEM for an hour was that communal work was supposed to be done because of an intrinsic wish to support the network, rather than as a source of profit. Members who performed a considerable amount of work sometimes refrained from claiming compensation for it, as they did not want their engagement to be seen as simply profiting from the network.

Tasks such as office work, typing in transactions, accounting and registering members were in high demand, and members competed to perform them. Less attractive tasks included conducting repairs on the buildings, gardening on the premises and the like. Some male members sought these manual tasks, particularly those with backgrounds as craftsmen or in construction. However, it was only on rare occasions that all necessary manual tasks were finished. At times, the search for members willing to perform these tasks was frustrating for the organising members.

Discussions about how to resolve this problem of finishing less-desirable tasks revealed the unequal power relations within the network, and the corresponding categorizations that led to some people being pushed into engaging in manual labour. Meetings usually included calls for communal tasks that needed to be performed, yet finding members to accomplish them was difficult and described as tiring by the organizers. Often, they then engaged in the tasks themselves. Frequently, the meetings also included discussions about how to counter this lack of engagement in communal work and attempts at sanctioning members were discussed. No agreement was reached on which kinds of pressure could be exerted on members to labour for the network, until the discussions settled on the decision that those granted housing by the network should work more. The argument was framed as a rightful extraction of labour in exchange for the temporary right to stay in the premises. It related to a general moralization of the situation. For example, one interlocutor, Stefania, said:

> I don't understand, why they don't do more. They can live here! They don't pay anything for rent or electricity, and so on. So why should they not do the garden[ing], or repair stuff in return? They should do something productively. Then they would be maybe in a better position than they are now. (Stefania, Volos, June 2015)

On another occasion, when one of the dwellers had been very active in clearing a plot in the garden and starting cultivation on it, this accomplishment was given a special mention in a discussion at one meeting:

> He should be a role model for the others. He took the shovel and just started. He is very active and industrious. The others are sitting around all day; they do not even bring out their garbage themselves. They should look up to him. (Leila, Volos, March 2016)

A boundary was drawn between "them" and "us", between the passive recipients of solidarity and the members granting it. The moralization of people's decisions on how to spend their time only became active arguments when there was a shortage of labour for communal works, and a group existed that could be pressured into doing more of the unpleasant work. The members that lived on the premises partly agreed with this framing of their situation, and to the view that they should reciprocate what was given to them. Yet, they were uneasy with the reading that they should engage in tasks that others had requested to be done but refused to do themselves.

Pooling as Result of the Market Mechanism

LETS are often praised for its potential to match local supply and demand. However, there is evidence that this aspect has been overestimated in the literature (Cooper 2013a: 32). Also in the TEM network, many members did not think their social or economic expectations were met. This point deserves closer attention, as a considerable number of the almost 900 TEM accounts did not actually engage in any trade in TEM during my fieldwork. In addition, a small number of members with a high frequency of trading held more money than the large remaining part of the membership base.[7] The available money in the system thus pooled into the accounts of a few members.

Although some were aware of this distribution of money circulating in 2015 and early 2016, a presentation by one of the founding members during the general assembly in March 2016 made this point explicit. He presented data from the backend of the software that showed the unequal distribution of money in accounts. In discussions that followed, the roughly 40 members present took three basic positions in response to the inequality. Some members who were less active in trading or rare visitors to the market found the data confirmed their suspicions that the TEM was a mechanism for an in-group of a few to profit from others' participation. Some of these had attempted to use the TEM to offer products or services, but received few purchases and eventually stopped engaging in the TEM. Others naturalized the inequalities. Mario, a market regular and one of the most active members said: "I told you that the TEM is like the economy everywhere – it's a natural fact. There will be some that have more and some that do not" (Mario, Volos, March 2016). Mario's opinion was widespread among the active members, in these discussions as well as in informal talk. He thought equality of outcomes was an aim the network should strive for but could not achieve. But there was another reading held by a minority of members. They regarded the inequality as a necessary motivation, as poorer members could see what could be achieved with harder work, observing members that were better off. If everyone had the same outcomes, they argued, that would result in decreased trading and less effort made to offer high-quality services.

Interestingly, those who did achieve higher incomes in TEM were able to do so because the specific type of services or goods they offered was in high demand. Their offers were ones that households wanted but could no longer afford in the primary (euro) market. In addition, these offers were relatively scarce, offered by only a few members at an attractive degree of quality. Furthermore, members who achieved higher incomes were very well connected to other members, had a high frequency of contact with others, and were thus known both in person and as providers to many other members. A useful illustration of this is provided by one of the most lucrative services offered on the network: private tutoring. The Greek educational system requires a great deal of work from pupils, most of whom receive private tutoring to cope with the high demands. Faced with uncertainty regarding what education or occupation would be a safe bet for lower-class families, such families invested considerably in higher education for their children. The market for private lessons to support pupils' performance in school is an outcome of an educational system that favours children whose parents can afford private lessons to achieve higher grades and test scores in the Panhellenic Exams, which determine whether students can enter the Greek university system and where and what they can study. Teachers who offered tutoring services through the TEM replaced labour in the primary (euro) market, and as demand was high, they could ask for wages of about three times as much TEM per hour as the network paid for communal labour. Other goods in high demand were high quality clothing (of which there was only a limited supply amongst the piles of less desirable second-hand clothing).

The patterns of goods and services in high demand reproduced the very mechanisms of scarcity that had initially driven people to find means of exchange outside the primary market. Within the TEM network, inequalities were reproduced: male manual labour was offered by many, as was female labour in such domestic services as cleaning or cooking. Neither was in high demand, as many households were self-provisioning this type of labour from household members who were already unpaid. Offers that did manage to attract higher

prices and remain in consistent demand were for things or services people could not easily acquire in the primary market[8] or replace by unpaid labour in the household.[9] However, some TEM members whose offers were not in high demand nonetheless managed to achieve high incomes. These members were consistently prominent and vocal during meetings, or had a high frequency of contact with other network members, such as through working in the kitchen during market days.

The mismatch of supply and demand was moralized in certain ways that put pressure on those who did not earn as much as the minority of accounts that held most of the money in circulation. Those who could not attract buyers were often referred to as not trying hard enough to find ways to render their offers interesting to others, and were sometimes said to lack a competitive and entrepreneurial attitude. This was seldom treated as an open topic for contestation or even discussion. Those, who could not attract demand for their services or products stayed in the network for other reasons, or they left. It was only in cases where a departed member had been offering interesting things for sale that disturbances and discussions arose about how to deal with membership loss.

Most of the members I talked to were aware of these tendencies, but most had naturalized these inequalities and, in general, the few who did not were also among those who had not done well in terms of TEM income. One interlocutor, Anna, said, "It will be always like that; some make all the money. We cannot change that. But we hope that they have a kind heart and buy our stuff anyway, even if they do not really need it" (Anna, Volos, July 2015). Anna gives an affirmative interpretation of her dependency on the goodwill of high-earners in the TEM network. As the most frequently interacting group of network users comprised only around 60 people, there might be good reason for Anna to resort to other forms of economic exchange for the betterment of her situation. Other members voiced expectations of trickle-down economics, among these a complementary currency consultant who came to meetings at least once a year to discuss strategies with TEM organizers. He proposed to put even more pressure on underachievers, as that would lead, he argued, to a kind of necessity-driven entrepreneurialism that would force them to produce more interesting offers.

Clearly, the framing of the challenges the network faced, and their potential solutions, sometimes fell back on models of economic thought that seem counter to the TEM network's rhetoric of solidarity and mutual self-help. However, in the everyday politics of the organization, these models were used to assign accountability, demand practical action from others, and avoid open conflicts.

Conclusion

I have presented the TEM as the organized economic practice of a group of people whose economic opportunities in the dominant market are slipping away. In conscious engagement with the constraints brought by the recession in terms of paying significant bills, maintaining dwellings, caring for one's children, and the like, network members chose to enact economic relations otherwise – in deliberate difference from the dominant market and yet in many ways modelled upon it – by creating their own money through a LETS scheme.

In the opening sections of this article, I have argued, with Theodossopoulos (2014), for a de-romanticization of resistance, and for directing attention not only to the relation between the dominant and resisting groups, but also to the internal workings of the resisting group in using Don Kalb's concept of everyday politics (Kalb 1997). I have shown that there are various layered ideas about the future, longings, fears and discourses that circulate among network members about the politics of the TEM. The everyday politics I set out to describe as part of the resistant practice of the TEM often revolved around differing interpretations of how this could be achieved, what steps needed to be taken, and what kinds of subjects would be most beneficial for achieving a goal that all network members agreed upon – more solidarity. Yet, instead of focusing on how network members worked together to counter dominant models of thought and economic practice, I focused on the challenges they faced in how to enact their visions of a counter-hegemonic project.

It is necessary to step beyond smooth presentations of how people connect their practices to ideas about a better future, more solidarity and mutuality. Living in a capitalist society entails more than the destructive forces that come with it. To understand and explicate the play of power through both coercion and consent, a thoroughly ethnographic take on alternative practice is needed. Therefore, in this article, I gave my attention to three challenges that the TEM network faces. These three point to major themes that caused fights, frustration and irritation among network members as their ideas of how these are connected to their visions of solidarity were severely different amongst members. The first challenge was the moralization of the way money was created in the network. Whenever a new account is opened for a new member, its balance starts with a balance of zero, yet the new member is allowed a certain credit. As several new members spent their credit limit without ever earning, some members denounced them as free riders who took without giving to the network. Here, a productionist bias and a moral devaluation of debtors was recreated that led to a categorization of members into lenders (who had positive balance on their accounts) and debtors who had to pay off their debt. The second challenge in the network circled around the difficulty of getting members to do the communal labour that was needed to maintain the network. Communal labour was paid for at a rate of 6 TEM per hour, which was about a third of for example an hour of tutoring lessons. The difficulties of finding people willing to do these unwanted jobs led to discussions about whether those granted living space at the premises of the network could be pushed into taking over the work in exchange for being granted housing. Here, a boundary was drawn between seemingly passive receivers of solidarity and those granting it. The third challenge was to account for the inequalities in earning. As some members offered goods and service that were in high demand, their accounts accumulated money. Failing to attract demand was moralized as a lack of competitive and entrepreneurial attitude. Inequalities between members were sometimes naturalized and even reinforced by community currency consultants who visited the TEM network to support building their market mechanism.

All three challenges are instructive in that they show the serious struggles of building a solidaristic economic network that provides a space for production and exchange meant to value the productive capacities and creativity of network members and the quest for more solidaristic economic relations based on mutuality. The puzzles posed by this question go well beyond a discussion of a LETS scheme in urban Greece. I argue that it is crucial to understand quests for alternative and ethical living under capitalism as sites of struggle in themselves, especially during times of austerity and recession. In alternative spaces such as the TEM network, the quest for living in relative autonomy of dominant forms of the economy is a complicated negotiation of material relations, ethical practice, and systems of thought. Taking such an approach supports the understanding of continuing hegemony of central tenets of capitalism such as its productionist bias, the naturalization of inequalities by referring to supply and demand, the moralization of debt, as well as inherent devaluation of communal labour.

The TEM is both a set of practices in a network of people trying to enact resistance, and a mechanism for furthering goals not restricted to the emancipatory and anti-capitalist logic of its representation in online texts, media reports, and the accounts of commentators. Indeed, in daily life with TEM network members, it soon became clear that the pragmatics of coping during a recession, when the aspirations and actual effects of economic growth were still present even as the means to attain them were not, are exactly that: pragmatic. But that does not mean that TEM members had given up or that their motivation to engage in the network was mere survival. The TEM was an opportunity to understand oneself as a productive person, of personal worth, offering something others wanted, and a chance to earn money. Those who did not earn much gave me this explanation for their continued participation: that it helped them feel less humiliated by their sudden rejection from the labour market.

Many reported that they received support from friends and family members when in need, but were frustrated by their inability to reciprocate, which carried them further into social humiliation. The calculative device of the TEM enabled them to replace their weakness in the primary market with something similar, but different. And this doing of economic relations otherwise created a space for imagining another future, for resisting and for mutual help. In the article, my aim was to observe these imaginaries of a better and more solidaristic future by focusing less on the promises of the future but the difficulties of the present.

Notes

1 This article is based on research carried out for a Ph.D., which was funded by a fellowship of the Austrian Academy of Sciences (DOCteam), as part of the project Practicing Values. Writing the article was made possible with funding from the Faculty of Social Sciences, University of Vienna.

I am grateful to Anna Wanka, Thomas Fillitz, James G. Carrier, Deniz Seebacher, the colloquium of the Department for Integration and Conflict at the Max Planck Institute for Social Anthropology, Brian Campbell, Tatjana Thelen, Evangelos Karagiannis, Peter North, Bob Jessop and two anonymous reviewers for comments on earlier versions.

2 All names of quoted interlocutors are pseudonyms.

3 LETS (Local Exchange and Trading Systems) are locally created trading networks that use money created and used by a group of members to calculate credit and debt among them. They are therefore special-purpose monies with a restricted membership tor those who accept them as payment. The operations of LETS are linked to the "claim that 'better' money can be created" (North 2007: xii), money that values cooperation instead of competition, contests artificial scarcity, and emphasizes local economies. Such networks have existed since the nineteenth century, but they have received the name "LETS" and undergone a contemporary revival due in part to the widespread availability of personal computers. Digital technology allowed for a wider reach and advertisement of members' offers and needs, which can now be posted on an online message board. In the scholarly literature of social anthropology, geography and sociology, LETS have been treated with an affirmative tendency, stressing their potential to bring about change (Maurer 2005; Hart & Ortiz 2014). Less research has focused on the downfalls and challenges that existing LETS networks actually face. Recently, more critical work has surfaced (e.g. Cooper 2013a; Evans 2009; North 2016). The more critical ap-

proach to LETS has not diminished its appeal as a new form of social cooperation, or as an alternative to the state and market creation of money (e.g., Federici 2012: 138; Hart 2005: 174; on the TEM, Holmes 2014: 598).

4 Yet, with lower interest rates, debt became cheaper and as a result, the Greek government debt increased significantly between 2001 and 2009.

5 A discussion might start from Hart and Sharp's book on money and power in the economic crisis (2015), Keith Hart's work on money as a memory bank, as well as his remarks on LETS and taxation (2000: 264ff.), to Bill Mauer's work on ethical finance and local currencies (2005), and Graeber's suggestion to reclassify currencies into e.g. social currencies (2012). In economic geography, much influential work comes from Peter North (e.g., 2016 on, inter alia, the TEM network), feminist scholarship (such as Seyfang 2001 on the articulation of female work as undervalued in capitalism and its valuation in community currencies), as well as economic sociology (Dodd 2005 on tendencies of homogenization of currency and diversification of money in the eurozone; Bandelj, Wherry & Zelizer 2017 on the relation of normative and cultural orders and money; Evans 2009 on the relation between values and currency).

6 The buildings that the TEM network has used since its inception were let by a government ministry through a local branch of an educational institution run by the state.

7 Each account had an upper limit of 1.200 TEM, which created a barrier to higher levels of inequality.

8 The example of tutoring or language courses points to significant characteristics of such services: they were rather expensive in the primary (euro) market, at least compared to the available incomes members had, but they were considered important for both children and adults. E.g., for the interlocutor Alexandra, taking English courses was a fun activity but also an investment, which could yield future employment opportunities.

9 The most prevalent of such services were cleaning, ironing, cooking and childcare.

References

Bandelj, Nina, Fredrick F. Wherry & Viviana A. Zelizer (eds.) 2017: *Money Talks: Explaining how Money really Works.* Princeton: Princeton University Press.

Bourdieu, Pierre 1998: *Acts of Resistance: Against the Tyranny of the Market.* New York: New Press.

Cabot, Heath 2016: "Contagious" Solidarity: Reconfiguring Care and Citizenship in Greece's Social Clinics. *Social Anthropology* 24:2, 152–166.

Carrier, James G. 1997: *Meanings of the Market: The Free Market in Western Culture.* Oxford & New York: Berg.

Cooper, Davina 2013a: Time against Time: Normative Temporalities and the Failure of Community Labour in Local Exchange Trading Schemes. *Time & Society* 22:1, 31–54.

Cooper, Davina 2013b: *Everyday Utopias: The Conceptual Life of Promising Spaces.* Durham: Duke University Press.

Dodd, Nigel 2005: Reinventing Monies in Europe. *Economy and Society* 34:4, 558–583.

Douzina-Bakalaki, Phaedra 2017: Volunteering Mothers: Engaging the Crisis at a Soup Kitchen in Northern Greece. *Anthropology Matters* 17:1, https://www.anthropologymatters.com/index.php/anth_matters/article/view/480/605.

Dyson, Kenneth 2010: Norman's Lament: The Greek and Euro Area Crisis in Historical Perspective. *New Political Economy* 15:4, 597–608.

ELSTAT 2016: Η Ελληνική Οικονομία. *The Greek Economy*, http://www.statistics.gr/documents/20181/1518565/greek_economy_19_08_2016.pdf/97c9116e-be71-4c2d-b00e-4a1392912a3b.

Evans, Michael S. 2009: Zelizer's Theory of Money and the Case of Local Currencies. *Environment and Planning* 41:5, 1026–1041.

Federici, Silvia 2012: *Revolution at Point Zero: Housework, Reproduction, and Feminist Struggle.* Oakland: PM Press.

Flierman, Kirsten 2014: *"A Journey to Ithaca": Motivations and Practices of Alternative Currency in the TEM Network in Volos, Greece.* Master Thesis, MSc Social and Cultural Anthropology University of Amsterdam.

Fraser, Nancy 2014: Can Society be Commodities all the Way Down? Post-Polanyian Reflections on Capitalist Crisis. *Economy and Society* 43:4, 541–558.

Graeber, David 2012: On Social Currencies and Human Economies: Some Notes on the Violence of Equivalence. *Social Anthropology* 20:4, 411–428.

Gregory, Chris A. 1997: *Savage Money: The Anthropology and Politics of Commodity Exchange.* Amsterdam: Harwood Academic.

Gregory, Chris A. 2012: On Money Debt and Morality: Some Reflections on the Contribution of Economic Anthropology. *Social Anthropology* 20:4, 380–396.

Hajek, Katharina & Benjamin Opratko 2013: Subjektivierung als Krisenbearbeitung: Feministische und neogramscianische Perspektiven auf die gegenwärtige europäische Krisenpolitik. *Feminina Politica* 22:1, 444–456.

Hann, Chris & Keith Hart 2009: *Market and Society: The Great Transformation Today.* Cambridge & New York: Cambridge University Press.

Hart, Keith 2000: *The Memory Bank: Money in an Unequal World.* London: Profile Books.

Hart, Keith 2005: Money: One Anthropologist's View. In: James G. Carrier (ed.), *A Handbook of Economic Anthropology.* Cheltenham: Edward Elgar, pp. 160–175.

Hart, Keith & Horazio Ortiz 2014: The Anthropology of Money and Finance: Between Ethnography and World History. *Annual Review of Anthropology* 43, 465–482.

Hart, Keith & John Sharp 2015: *People, Money, and Power in the Economic Crisis: Perspectives from the Global South.* New York & Oxford: Berghahn.

Holmes, Christopher 2014: "Whatever it takes": Polanyian Perspectives on the Eurozone Crisis and the Gold Standard. *Economy and Society* 43:4, 582–602.

Jessop, Bob & Ngai-Ling Sum 2006: *Beyond the Regulation Approach: Putting Capitalist Economies in Their Place.* Cheltenham, UK & Northampton, MA, USA: Edward Elgar.

Kalb, Don 1997: *Expanding Class: Power and Everyday Politics in Industrial Communities, the Netherlands, 1850–1950.* Durham: Duke University Press.

Lapavitsas, Costas 2012: *Crisis in the Eurozone.* London & New York: Verso.

Maurer, Bill 2005: *Mutual Life, Limited: Islamic Banking, Alternative Currencies, Lateral Reason.* Princeton: Princeton University Press.

Muehlebach, Andrea 2012: *The Moral Neoliberal: Welfare and Citizenship in Italy.* Chicago: University of Chicago Press.

Narotzky, Susana 2012: Europe in Crisis: Grassroots Economies and the Anthropological Turn. *Etnografica* 16:3, 627–638.

Narotzky, Susana & Niko Besnier 2014: Crisis Supplement Current Anthropology. *Current Anthropology* 55, Supplement 9.

North, Peter 1999: Explorations in Heterotopia: Local Exchange Trading Schemes (LETS) and the Micropolitics of Money and Livelihood. *Environment and Planning D: Society and Space* 17:1, 69–86.

North, Peter 2007: *Money and Liberation: The Micropolitics of Alternative Currency Movements.* Minneapolis & London: University of Minnesota Press.

North, Peter 2016: Money Reform and the Eurozone Crisis: Panacea, Utopia or Grassroots Alternative? *Cambridge Journal of Economics* 40:5, 1439–1453.

Ortner, Sherry 1995: Resistance and the Problem of Ethnographic Refusal. *Comparative Studies in Society and History* 37:1, 173–193.

Papataxiarchis, Evthymios 2016: Comment: Unwrapping Solidarity? Society Reborn in Austerity. *Social Anthropology* 24:2, 205–210.

Peebles, Gustav 2010: The Anthropology of Credit and Debt. *Annual Review of Anthropology* 39:1, 225–240.

Polanyi, Karl 1944: *The Great Transformation.* Boston: Beacon Press.

Polanyi, Karl, Conrad M. Arensberg & Harry W. Pearson 1957: *Trade and Market in the Early Empires.* Glencoe: The Free Press.

Poulantzas, Nicos 2014: *State, Power, Socialism.* London & New York: Verso.

Preunkert, Jenny & Georg Vobruba 2015: *Krise und Integration: Gesellschaftsbildung in der Eurokrise.* Wiesbaden: Springer VS.

Rakopoulos, Theodoros 2015: Solidarity's Tensions: Informality, Sociality, and the Greek Crisis. *Social Analysis* 59:3, 85–104.

Seyfang, Gill 2001: Money that Makes a Change: Community Currencies, North and South. *Gender & Development* 9:1, 60–69.

Scott, James C. 1985: *Weapons of the Weak: Everyday Forms of Peasant Resistance.* New Haven & London: Yale University Press.

Scott, James C. 1990: *Domination and the Arts of Resistance: Hidden Transcripts.* New Haven & London: Yale University Press.

Simonic, Peter 2014: Solidarity and Reciprocity in Times of Recession: Understanding the Old and New Values in Late Capitalism. *Ars & Humanitas: Revija Za Umetnost in Humanistiko / Journal of Arts and Humanities* VIII:1, 9–14.

Sotiropoulou, Irene 2012: *Exchange Networks and Parallel Currencies: Theoretical Approaches and the Case of Greece.* Ph.D. thesis, University of Crete.

Spyridakis, Manos 2012: Making Ends Meet in the Shipbuilding Industry of Piraeus: An Ethnography of Precarious Employment. *Social Cohesion and Development* 7:2, 105–117.

Streinzer, Andreas 2016: Stretching Money to Pay the Bills: Temporal Modalities and Relational Practices of "Getting by" in the Greek Economic Crisis. *The Cambridge Journal of Anthropology* 34:1, 45–57.

Thanou, Eleni, George Theodossiou & Dimitris Kallivokas 2013: *Local Exchange Trading Systems LETS as a Response to Economic Crisis: The Case of Greece.* Geneva: United Nations Non-Governmental Liaison Service.

Theodossopoulos, Dimitrios 2014: The Ambivalence of Anti-austerity Indignation in Greece: Resistance, Hegemony and Complicity. *History and Anthropology* 25:4, 488–506.

Uesaka, Asuka 2013: *The Quest for Social and Solidarity Economy in Greece: Case Study of the Exchange Network and Solidarity Magnesia.* Bachelor Thesis, University of Lund.

Andreas Streinzer is a Ph.D. candidate in social and cultural anthropology at the University of Vienna and DOCteam fellow of the Austrian Academy of Sciences. His research interests in economic relations have led him to pursue fieldwork in Volos, Greece, to investigate household provisioning under conditions of recession. Among his recent publications is Stretching Money to Pay the Bills: Temporal Modalities and Relational Practices of "Getting By" in the Greek Economic Crisis (*Cambridge Journal of Anthropology* 34:1, 2016). (andreas.streinzer@univie.ac.at)

FROM EXARCHIA TO SYNTAGMA SQUARE AND BACK
The City as a Hub for Strategies of Resistance against Austerity

Monia Cappuccini, University La Sapienza, Rome

This article will examine the relationships between urban space and social movements in times of economic crisis in Athens, Greece. I will focus my attention on the impact that the Syntagma square movement had on those grassroots mobilizations, which precipitated at a local level as soon as the occupation of the Parliament's square ended in summer 2011. Accordingly, the anti-authoritarian neighbourhood of Exarchia will provide the spatial setting for pointing out how, starting from "the origin of the conflict," which occurred in December 2008, *joie de vivre* (Leontidou 2014) is reflected in practices of resistance. I will briefly depict two empirical cases, the time-banking system and the Social Solidarity Network, in order to finally recount Athens as a relevant hub for incubating social movements.

Keywords: urban anthropology, ethnography, urban social movements, Greece, Exarchia

In 2008 the burst of the subprime mortgage bubble and the bankruptcy of the American holding Lehman Brothers dragged the entire planet in an endless spiral of political volatility and fiscal austerity. At the same time, however, a wave of transnational anti-capitalist protests spread spontaneously across the world's major cities, which appeared in various square movements: Tahrir in Egypt, the Occupy movement in the USA, the Indignados' *acampadas* in Spain, Syntagma Square in Greece, Taksim Square and Gezi Park in Turkey. Locally organized as protest camps, these movements firstly created the conditions for giving a new meaning to urban space. Secondly, identifying themselves as the 99% against the 1% of finance capital, they succeeded in giving a spatial form to an increasing scepticism as

to neoliberal globalization (Miller & Nicholls 2013). Thirdly, by gaining experience of and experimenting with direct democracy and innovative ways of communal life, they brought to light the issue of sovereignty within current financial austerity (Lopes de Sousa & Lipietz 2011; Martínez Roldán 2011; Kanna 2012; Occupy Wall Street 2012; Schrader & Wachsmuth 2012; Taddio 2012). As a whole, all these global insurgencies of the crisis have developed a bottom-up antagonism that has effectively formulated a contestation of the mechanism of "accumulation by dispossession" (Harvey 2012).

Far from representing an isolated case, Greece stands out as one of the most acute debt contexts seen internationally. Accordingly, the thousands of *aganaktismenoi* (*Indignados* in Greek) who in May

Monia Cappuccini 2018: From Exarchia to Syntagma Square and Back.
The City as a Hub for Strategies of Resistance against Austerity.
Ethnologia Europaea 48:1, 84–98. © Museum Tusculanum Press.

2011 gathered in Syntagma Square in Athens can be understood as an extreme response to the attempts being made by international financial institutions to restructure their lives. In this article, I will examine the impact that this urban macro-scale protest had on those grassroots mobilizations that precipitated at a local level as soon as the occupation of the Greek Parliament's square ended some months after its very beginning. The spatial setting is provided by the district of Exarchia, which since its origins in the late nineteenth century has stood out as a historical space for radical politics in Athens, and still continues to act as one of the city's most vibrant areas. In December 2008 its antagonistic character once again came into the global spotlight with the revolts sparked off by the murder of the young man Alexandros Grigoropoulos.

In this article I will point out how, starting from that "origin of the conflict", the *joie de vivre* (Leontidou 2014) expressed by Greek *aganaktismenoi* fundamentally provided a source of inspiration and training for the local realm of political activism. The arguments discussed draw on almost two years of ethnographic investigation in the neighbourhood; accordingly I will shortly depict two different initiatives that emerged from my empirical fieldwork, the time-banking system and the Social Solidarity Network. Based on first-hand interviews with the social actors involved, both of these "urban solidarity spaces" (Arampatzi 2017) are amply instructive as to how their local practices are connected within a broader scenario of urban struggles, thus contributing to configuring the city as a hub for strategies of resistance against austerity politics.

Europe, the Shock Must Go On: The Age of Austerity and Resistance in Greece

After the initial burst of the Spanish speculative housing bubble, the moment that truly brought Southern Europe to the centre of the world's financial map arrived in October 2009, when Greek government made a shocking announcement: the country's real budget deficit was four times higher than the EU's specified limit, while its national debt was calculated at nearly twice the reference rate

(over 112% of GDP). From that moment on "the prospect of a Southern sovereign debt default had entered the agenda [so much as that] in April 2010, Greece became the first eurozone member to have its sovereign credit rating downgraded to junk status, effectively pricing it out of the markets" (Bosco & Verney 2012: 134).

The rest is no more and no less than a chronicle of our times. Well before the third tranche of assistance was agreed upon during the summer of 2015, on February 12, 2012, the Greek government ratified the second Memorandum of Understanding, thus securing an International Monetary Fund/ European Union/European Central Bank (IMF/ EU/ECB) bailout amounting to 130bn euro, largely aimed at supporting debt restructuring negotiations with Greece's private sector creditors and re-capitalizing domestic banks. In much the same way as the former 110bn euro agreement, signed in May 2010, this second package of financial support was provided on the condition that a new round of austerity and privatization measures be pursued. Although Greece's poverty rate was already the worst in the eurozone prior to 2009, the implementation of austerity measures aggravated the recession in the country, dramatically leading to side effects consisting in a sudden increase of social inequality and spatial injustice. Under the rescue programme, the unemployment rate skyrocketed from 7.3% in 2008 to 27.9% in 2013 (UN Human Rights Council 2013: 12–13), even more people were pushed into poverty, with an approximate 11% of the population living under extremely difficult conditions (ibid.: 20), while the statistics concerning suicides showed a 37% rise (from 677 in 2009 to 927 in 2011), largely ascribable to the financial and social strain imposed on individuals by the economic crisis (ibid.: 18).

At the same time, however, Greek society developed mass mobilizations throughout the period of the European sovereign debt crisis. The urban space of Athens, above all, played a strategic role in this long-lasting round of anti-neoliberal struggles. Simply to provide a few numbers, from May 8, 2010, until the end of March 2014, out of a total 20,210 demonstrations that came to pass in Greece, 6,266 took place in the region of Attica, most of which in the centre of Athens. These figures could be translated into 5,100 protests per year, or approximately 14 marches and/or rallies on a daily basis, including Sundays (Stangos 2014). Moreover, no historical account of the four-year Memoranda period can avoid considering the escalation of self-organized urban assemblies and networks that spread throughout Athens's many neighbourhoods, especially during the post-Syntagma period. As is well illustrated by two different maps drawn up by Omikron Project (2012), by 2014 grassroots practices in Greece had covered a large number of different topics, with involvement encompassing solidarity initiatives responding to social needs (food, health, education), experimentation of alternative economies (exchange systems and cooperatives), local participatory processes (neighbourhood assemblies and democracy projects) and political creativity (artistic and cultural environments, social media activism). Overall, "the age of resistance" (Douzinas 2013: 8) has been characterized by centralized mass mobilizations that stood alongside more dispersed and interconnected forms of small-scale opposition. On the whole, they have no doubt succeeded in spatializing the anti-austerity discourse within and throughout the city of Athens.

Investigating the Times of Crisis in Athens: An Empirical Approach

In the lapse of time from November 2012 to early 2015, the neighbourhood of Exarchia provided the spatial setting for my Ph.D. research in engineering-based architecture and urban planning; according to my socio-anthropological background, essentially I developed an ethnography of the grassroots mobilizations that emerged in the area as a response to the economic crisis. Even though this central neighbourhood in Athens is amply recognized as a hub for anarchist and anti-authoritarian activism, its distinctiveness has attracted a variety of passing comments that, however, generally pay more attention to the phenomenology of its alternative lifestyle. On the contrary, I strived to experience Exarchia's social

and political everyday life, thus offering a detailed examination of its conflictual nature.

A well-pondered theoretical framework, together with adequate ethnographic research tools, contributed to achieving this latter aim. Investigating "ordinary" living in such a peculiar territoriality called for the analytical discernments focused on urban grassroots and social movements provided by the social sciences. The insights offered in particular by scholars such as David Graeber and Manuel Castells helped develop the empirical research according to a perspective as critical as possible. Actually stepping into and gazing at the neighbourhood, understood as an "area of cultural improvisation" (Graeber 2007: 19), proved to be a well-oriented take on fieldwork. Firstly, using this key concept favoured interaction with those social figures whose interplay reinvents tactics and strategies of opposition, aimed at consolidating and reinforcing reciprocal communitarian bonds. Secondly, and as a consequence, it allowed the qualitative observation to go within those "trenches of resistance and survival" where social actors build and strengthen their sense of belonging, thus revealing the production of Exarchia's "resistance identity" (Castells 2010). Lastly, and even more importantly for this contribution, the social usage of the neighbourhood has also been related to the "age of resistance" in Athens, in order to emphasize the relations between forms of protest that precipitated on a local level, and the narratives and desires of transformation scattered over the cityscape as a response to the neoliberal restructuring of social and urban life. This spatial transfer was made possible by giving a more extensive sense to Henri Lefebvre's original concept of "the right to the city" (1968), that is, by conceiving the city as a means through which specific political goals can be pursued, rather than an end unto itself. Hence, referring to the "right *through* the city" (Arampatzi & Nicholls 2012), the case of Exarchia was used as a strategically key space, or as a main actor, aimed at recounting Athens as a relevant hub for incubating social movements during the IMF/EU/ECB era.

Spatially speaking, my fieldwork primarily unfolded along a small pedestrian street found quite close to Exarchia Square, Tsamadou Street, where various social centres and political activities are located. One of these is the Steki Metanaston, literally the "migrants' house", which provides support for refugees and irregular migrants. During two consecutive sessions, I attended courses in modern Greek for migrants at Piso Thrania, the teachers' collective that participates in the Steki; the latter gradually became the operational base for my fieldwork in Exarchia. Basically, I unfolded my research according to a sort of road trip through the neighbourhood; in particular, I went into the details of each social space that are found along Tsamadou Street, describing their usages and initiatives while interacting with their protagonists. Among them are the Residents' Initiative and the Social Solidarity Network, whose political activism takes place in (or is tied to) the occupied building located at number 15, right next door to the Steki. With the aim of recounting the environment of sociability and reciprocity that permeates Tsamadou Street, at least 40 semi-structured interviews were carried out with the social actors concentrated along there, in addition to other relevant persons (e.g., writers, researchers, anarchists), who had gained affinity with the area of Exarchia. Most of them also shared their experiences of urban anti-austerity mobilizations in Athens, for example Syntagma movement and "the day of Marfin Bank", providing evidence as to these events.

On a more general level, my empirical investigation was inspired by "the method of crack (as) the method of crisis [in order] to understand the wall not from its solidity [...] but from the perspective of its crisis, its contradictions, its weaknesses" (Holloway 2010: 9). Paradoxically, the "crisis" reflexively shaped my ethnography via different meanings and perspectives: as a topic, a method and a concrete interaction with Exarchia. With the aim of gaining a close and intimate acquaintance with the neighbourhood, the ethnographic technique of participant observation furthermore turned into a participatory research-action in Piso Thrania. Indeed, this experience marked my entire approach to the fieldwork: essentially, since the difficulty of the language called for a demanding and perhaps even daring ef-

fort, Piso Thrania eventually became a remarkable, pivotal point through which my moments of powerlessness and discouragement gave way to a more constructive attitude (Cappuccini 2017).

A Neighbourhood for a Clash of Urban Identities

Set in the heart of the Greek capital, Exarchia covers a triangular-shaped area corresponding to only 0.21% of the entire metropolitan surface. As regards to its social composition, it is not known as a place for the elderly: almost half of the inhabitants (45.3%) are between 15 and 44 years of age, and the largest group is between 25 and 34 (19.4%). In terms of occupational status, even three years after the outbreak of the economic crisis in Greece, 43.1% of the district's residents had proved able to hold down a job: at least a good third of them are professionals (35%), followed by technicians and assistants (9.6%), office clerks (7.8%) and managers (4%). On the whole it is a predominantly low- and middle-class district that, by way of its proximity with the Polytechnic and a few Faculties of the University of Athens, also comes across as an enclave for students (Panorama Statistics 2012).

Having substantially maintained its high urban land value, Exarchia has been less struck by the processes of urban depopulation and depreciation of property that have generally afflicted Athens' city centre. Actually, one should not forget that the neighbourhood is also widely recognized as an entertainment hotspot mainly intended for young people and alternative city-users. Although its fashionable atmosphere would seem to make it well-suited for attempts at social eradication, however, the complete transformation of Exarchia into a bohemian quarter, lively but harmless, does not yet seem to have fully succeeded.

On the contrary, if "the city air makes us free," in Exarchia one breathes a tradition of libertarianism. Its political identity can actually be depicted as a mixture of different experiences, at least as many as there are groups who all conceive of it as a true *steki*, the Greek term commonly used to indicate a familiar place in which one socializes. The life of the neighbourhood largely revolves around its main

Ill. 1: Memorial for Alexis in the corner of Tzavela and Mesologgiou, Exarchia. (Photo: Monia Cappuccini, 2014)

piazza, Exarchia Square, found in the centre of the district; passing through one can find anarchist and autonomous collectives, activists of the extra-parliamentary left, tribes of various underground cultures, socially marginalized people, migrants, young rebels and mavericks. At the same time, a swarm of social activities and urban practices give the entire area strong political connotations, with Exarchia's clear ACAB (acronym for All Cops Are Bastards) matrix largely contributing to portraying the place as an anti-authoritarian enclave.

Given the high concentration of all these different features, it would be difficult to single out, in other European capitals, a neighbourhood found in such a central urban position whose political identity is still equally entrenched. Similarly, Exarchia can hardly be tied down to a single representation, except perhaps the one unanimously provided by public opinion and the mainstream media, which has historically depicted the district as a place of widespread lawlessness and rebellion. More recently,

a comparative content analysis conducted by Vradis (2012) clearly indicates how the media coverage of issues involving Exarchia is still extremely at the service of its perception and stigmatization as a sort of "enemy within".[1]

With a quick glance at the country's modern history, the neighbourhood played a prominent role both during the student opposition against the Junta dictatorship, which culminated in the 17 November 1973 popular uprising in the nearby Polytechnic, and during the riots that beginning on December 6, 2008, spread throughout Athens and all over Greece, sparked off by the murder of Alexandros Grigoropoulos, a fifteen-year-old high-school student from an upper-class family, killed by the police in Exarchia.

The Days of Alexis, an Origin of Conflict

This fateful date was a Saturday night like any other, with the usual lively assortment of people hanging out in taverns, bars and cafés, or along the neighbourhood's many pedestrian streets. Alexandros Grigoropoulos was with his friends at the corner between Mesologgiou and Tzavela streets, when two policemen approached them during a patrol in the area. Following a minor verbal argument, while the officers were leaving the spot, however, for no specific reason one of them turned around, drew out his gun, aimed at the youths and shot Alexis dead. Without even having the time to think, Exarchia had already exploded. All of Athens and other major Greek cities were soon involved in violent clashes when the news of the murder quickly spread out from the neighbourhood (Vradis & Dalakoglou 2011).

During those days of revolt, for the first time in Greece's contemporary history the key actors were young high-school students, unmistakeably associated with Alexis. Migrants, especially from the second generation, similarly flanked their peers on the barricades. An unprecedented combination of "unusual suspects" irrupted onto the scene of the protest, thus concretely marking December 2008 as a generational transition. Dubbed by the media as "generation 700" (meaning "euro per month", as an average wage) and commonly referred to as *koukoulofori* (hoodies) or even with the epithet of *bachali* (an expression that roughly corresponds to 'hooligan', 'troublemaker'), they represented those whose expectations for a better future had been disappointed ahead of time, betrayed by an economic perspective of growth and wealth never delivered (ibid. 2011).

Largely dominated by anti-police and anti-capitalist sentiments, the days of Alexis went on for three consecutive weeks, with a sharp peak during the first. Occupations of public buildings and universities, demonstrations and open assemblies on a large scale stood alongside one another, in a climate characterized by "an acceptance and tolerance of violence even by those who did not engage in it" (Mentinis 2010: 199). The daily newspaper *Kathimerini* labelled those days of unrest as "the worst rioting that Greece has seen since the restoration of democracy in 1974" (2008), and in a similar vein the international media broadcast images of the fierce violence that broke out in the streets in country's major cities.

Due to its immediate and deep impact on society, a large number of researchers have described December 2008 as a breakdown rather than proposing a simplistic interpretation of the phenomenology of the riots. Overall they have stressed that, although the explosion of a priorly peaceful Greece was mostly age-related, it was not in the least restricted to the actions of *koukoulofori* teenagers. That eruption, in fact, brought together "sections of the working class that expressed their dissatisfaction with the culture of consumerism, individualism and indebtedness," continuing to maintain not simply that "'we don't like you', but also that 'we don't like what we have become'" (Mentinis 2010: 200). Essentially, those events arose as a generalized challenge of the structural basis of neoliberal society *tout court* and later developed into "a new common collective identity" (Psimitis 2011: 130). Not by chance, December 2008 influenced the urban anti-austerity movements to come in their "exercise of free expression in open spaces at the level of everyday life" (Petropoulou 2010: 221). Therefore, from that moment on, "the city was not simply the setting of collective actions and initiatives but became, more and more, a potential collective claim" (Stavrides 2010: 133). Intermingled with each other, ultimately the "origin of the conflict" signalled "the beginning of massive movements and protests against accumulation by dispossession as the debt crisis was deepening" (Leontidou 2012: 303).

From Exarchia to Syntagma Square and Back

In the wake of the appeal launched by the citizen grassroots organization Direct Democracy Now! on social networks, on May 25, 2011, hundreds of Athenians found themselves in the Parliament's central square and began to create a permanent occupation. Over a period of three months, thousands of demonstrators passed through Syntagma Square, including both young adults who were novices to street protests and fifty-year-olds who returned to this kind of experience after a long period of disenchantment. Surely, no one would ever have imagined such a huge level of collective involvement, nor that new methods of self-organization would have been peacefully invented. As has been established by various scholars (e.g., Leontidou 2012; Stavrides 2011; Douzinas 2013; Massarelli 2013; Mavrommatis 2015), the Syntagma occupation stood out for its spontaneity and introduced an absolute novelty within the realm of social opposition against austerity in Greece. Rooted in cosmopolitan networks as well as in the previous uprisings witnessed after December 2008, in particular, Leontidou developed the concept of *piazza* "in order to denote [Syntagma] as an openness and a nodal centre of material and virtual communication, rather than an enclosed square and its defined landscape" (2012: 302).

From a spatial point of view, occupied Syntagma Square was divided into two areas, upper and lower, each of which with its own distinct atmosphere. In the first, located just under the stretch of Vasilissis Amalias Avenue that runs in front of the Parliament, the "apolitical" *Indignados* had come together, animated by feelings of rage and exasperation against the establishment, expressed with slogans such as "Thieves, thieves", accompanied by the *mountza*, a traditional offensive gesture consisting in extending one's hand with the palm open. Moreover, part of them waved Greek flags and sung the national anthem, in a sort of rediscovered patriotic pride that partly signalled the presence of right-wing forces, not including however the extremist party of Golden Dawn. Much larger than the first, the pedestrian area of Syntagma Square was dominated instead by an openly left-wing approach to politics and brought together people with different backgrounds and belongings, who experimented with no-stop assemblies, participatory ways of living, daily workshops, open debates, information stands and spaces for discussions on issues ranging from debt to forms of direct democracy.

Evacuated and reoccupied on a number of occasions, Syntagma Square was definitively dismantled in early August. Above all on June 29, while the Parliament was voting on the second Memorandum, the demonstrators were subjected to a brutal violence unleashed by the police. Thereafter, anti-austerity movements survived on a local level in more fragmented and decentralized forms. Their spontaneity reemerged in Syntagma one year later, to honour Dimitris Christoulas – a retired Greek pharmacist who, due to severe difficulties in paying for his medications, shot himself in Syntagma Square in April 2012 (Kitsantonis 2012) – and yet received the very same repressive treatment. A further and more vigorous episode appeared in June 2013 when the Greek government targeted the public state-owned radio and television company, ERT, labelling it "a haven of waste" (*The Guardian* 2013) and announcing its immediate closure by an overnight legislative decree.[2] As a response, journalists, technicians, employees and protesters got together and took over the network's offices, thus continuing to go on air on a volunteer basis via a cooperative online TV station. Throughout five months, ERT's courtyard was packed with an atmosphere of vibrant cultural resistance that actively reproduced the same *joie de vivre* (Leontidou 2014) expressed and experienced by the *aganaktismenoi* in the Syntagma occupation. However, during the following November, riot police stormed the occupied building, forcing the demonstrators to leave.

On a general view, in contrast with a scenario of social control, Greek urban movements have given origin to an opposite portrait of vitality and desire in the context of the debt crisis. In fact, if on the one hand austerity activated a rhetoric of security aimed at disciplining the citizens' discontent, on the contrary spontaneity, participation and self-organization were stimulated as singular features of political resistance and social solidarity. The case of Exarchia is illuminating as to this movement, as if the "origin of the conflict" in December 2008 had scattered enough seeds of rebellion to support a longstanding collective action. From that uprising on, social struggles in Athens actually continued without pause at least until the second Memorandum agreement in February 2012, both on a micro- and a macro-scale. Urban anti-austerity mobilizations and local grassroots organizations both influenced and were influenced by this spatial inter-changeability, thereby strengthening their own affinities, alliances and networks. The Syntagma Square movement in 2011 above all encouraged this relation of reciprocity, mostly nurtured by an interaction with the city intended as a means through which different political goals could be pursued.

It is in fact noteworthy that the Greek piazza movement marked, after December 2008, another crucial step for urban protest in Athens. In particular, Douzinas has summarized the main differences as follow: "December was characterized by time, Syntagma by place, December by transience, Syntagma by permanence, December by (limited) violence, Syntagma by a repudiation of violence, December by mobility, Syntagma by a static presence" (2013: 150). However, examining more deeply their common traits, the final result is more a product rather than the sum of a series of distinctive features. Fundamentally, both of these insurgencies were made possible by the gradual emergence of "new subjectivities committed to resistance, justice and equality"; in getting rid of the dominant trian-

gle of "desire-consumption-frustration" (Douzinas 2013: 143), they were able to emancipate themselves and break away from the body of social passivity. This new-found political awareness was rooted in, and bonded through, "collective experiences" which took place and were radically shared within public urban spaces, conceived and lived "as a potentially liberating environment" (Stravrides in Brekke et al. 2014: 209). Furthermore, with regard to another series of events, not insignificantly this last self-empowerment process came after "the day of Marfin Bank", which regrettably spread a wide sense of collective guilt in the movement.[3] This paralysis of massive common actions finally came to an end as soon as the Greek citizens gathered in front of the Parliament. Just as in December 2008, all at once, thousands of "unusual suspects" started once again to get out of their homes and take back the square.

Ill. 2: Graffiti in Exarchia. (Photo: Monia Cappuccini, 2014)

Time-banking, New Ideas in Motion

As soon as the Syntagma occupation ended in August 2011, a time-banking system was "exported" in Exarchia by the Residents' Initiative (Epitropì Protovoulias Katikon Exarchion). The latter is a local assembly formed in 2007 to counter the telephone company Vodafone's attempts to install antennas in the neighbourhood. Their activities, as well as those promoted by the Social Solidarity Network, take place at the building located in 15 Tsamadou Street,[4] that is a beautiful late-nineteenth century neoclassical villa with a single floor, occupied in November 2009 thanks to an initiative of the Steki Metanaston, located just next door. While formally belonging to the Dromokaitio (a hospital for people with psychological disorders), before becoming a social centre, 15 Tsamadou Street had been rented to a private businessman, who turned it into a bar. When this commercial activity ceased in 2005, the building remained abandoned for four years, soon becoming a refuge for the area's drug addicts. The occupation came at the end of a series of fruitless negotiations between the Steki Metanaston, the Network for Social and Political Rights (Dyktio) and the ownership to put the space at the service of the public interest once again. New attempts were made after November 2009, with no less than three meetings dedicated to defining a reasonable rent for the building, taking into consideration the six thousand euro already spent in renovations and in creating a soup kitchen for irregular migrants. Unwilling to seek reconciliation, the Dromokaitio was quick to reply and three activists closely involved in the occupation later faced charges of appropriation of public property.

The Residents' Initiative is a sizeable group, whose base of roughly twenty stable members operates within a collective that counts up to fifty members. It does not have a well-defined political label, and is open to any and all identities: it includes people who have been involved in the movements for many years, and those who have their first experiences of this kind in the neighbourhood. Like Olga, who has been a member in the assembly since not long after December 2008. Now forty-one years old, born and raised in Crete, she moved to Athens at nineteen with the dream of living in Exarchia, which she has done since 1999. She tells me:

> I liked it there because everyone knows everyone else. There are other areas of Athens where you can also breathe the atmosphere of living in a small community, but they are home to the middle-class. Not that I am saying that Exarchia is a working-class neighbourhood, but here you can meet interesting people and even the families are more emancipated compared to the average in Greece.

When I ask her about the Residents' Initiative's relations with the neighbourhood, she answers:

> the assembly is very much respected, we don't use the hard-core political language that you hear in other local organizations. Another one of our strong points is that we succeed in talking with everyone here in Exarchia. We don't always collaborate, but we remain on good terms.

Since 2007 the local assembly has maintained a stable form. It was however soon faced with the need to confront one of the most critical periods, if not to say the worst, for Exarchia. Before they even had the time to celebrate their victory over the installation of the telephone antennas, two unexpected events occurred that accelerated the course of history: the homicide of Alexandros Grigoropoulos in December 2008, and the economic crisis that appeared soon thereafter. Olga explains to me that, not by chance, one of their first interventions took place in the area around Mesologgiou Street, exactly where Alexis was killed. Since 2008, adolescents from all over Athens had been gathering there, but at a certain point the atmosphere became so tense, that even just walking through could be dangerous. She points out:

> It was now somewhere to be avoided, so we held two assemblies and a few happenings there to get the residents involved, because we didn't want to come across like vigilantes or some kind of Zorro.

There was a more relaxed feeling, with lots of people in the street. Soon after, we started a campaign against petty crime in the square and called an open assembly in a theatre in Exarchia, precisely because we didn't like being labelled politically and give everyone the chance to speak up. The neighbourhood's other political groups also took part, and a few shopkeepers lent us some tables, acting on their own initiative. For a few months we set up a stand in the square and continually read announcements over the megaphone. In the meanwhile, we coordinated our efforts with the other stekia and once a month each of us was asked to organize activities. For our part, the Residents' Initiative set up a playground for children and a basketball hoop. For six or seven months it worked, the square changed its character and it was such a success that it was even reported in the media.

This all took place between 2010 and 2011 but then, as a consequence of the economic crisis, the number of homeless people and drug addicts sky-rocketed, and in 2014 the situation was even worse than before. She continues:

These days we still keep on proposing activities, but then reality strikes and our agenda priorities change. Lately, for example, we've been working on an initiative to keep the neighbourhood clean, but then two weeks ago someone was killed by a gunshot in Exarchia and we gave up on it. You can't do a campaign against littering when people are getting shot here! Not to mention the presence of the police!

However, an impartial view of the situation would likely be less catastrophic than one might imagine, at least for those who, like the members of the Residents' Initiative, have chosen to live in Exarchia to roll up their sleeves and to leave no room for feelings of powerlessness or resignation. One of the challenges they have overcome, for example, is the creation of a time-banking system. A few examples of this kind of free exchange based on hours "deposited" or "withdrawn" might include helping someone clean their garden and receiving language lessons for one's children in return, or getting some work done on the house in exchange for cooking or looking after someone's dog. A network of mutual support, in these times of economic hardship, has become a precious resource that operates as a complementary trading system. According to the Residents' Initiative blog (2008), until December 2013 in Exarchia 159 people took part, with 115 offers and a total of 183 hours exchanged with an invaluable gain in terms of interpersonal bonds created in the neighbourhood. Olga clarifies that:

the time-bank is based on the quality of personal relations. We've really accomplished something in convincing one and all to trust one another. I had met at least ten people that I could leave my house keys with.

In Exarchia roughly fifty activists are now involved in operating the time-bank, which has recently expanded to include the soup kitchen of the Autonomous Steki.[5] An offer of two free meals for each hour of time went very well. As Olga said:

new people, including sixty-year-olds, came inside the Autonomous for the first time, changing their minds about it as soon as they discovered that it's not a place where people go to make Molotov cocktails.

The idea of an alternative micro-economic environment grew out of a single seed: Syntagma Square. In no time at all, the concept of time-banking spread throughout the city of Athens and even contaminated areas and communities that had previously been immune to social experimentation, such as for example the rich neighbourhood of Kifissia. Olga explains that:

there are at least thirty-two initiatives similar to ours, plus about a hundred more that work on the same criteria of solidarity.

Then she comments by way of conclusion:

> Syntagma was a very important moment. A huge amount of people participated that had never been out in the streets before. There was a change in mentality, in the sense that many began to understand that the time to think only about buying goods and spending money was over. In the current scenario of the crisis, the time-bank might seem like a drop in the ocean, a grain of sand in the desert, but it really does mean that it's possible to imagine another way of living. We ourselves don't believe that we can change the world, but things like this give us optimism and hope.

A Network for Social Solidarity

The Social Solidarity Network takes action against houses either having their electricity cut off or being forfeited to banks, both of which are possible consequences for not paying the *charatsi*. The latter is a property tax introduced in 2011 by the government as a "special" austerity measure; until 2014 it was charged directly on electricity bills, and later calculated as part of annual individual tax return statements. Due to situations of insolvency of this new fiscal charge, it has been estimated that at least thirty thousand homes had their electricity cut off each month (Elafros 2013), and the activists in Exarchia were looking for a way to stop this. Among them are Stratoula and Babis, who are members of the Social Solidarity Network. Stratoula is forty-two years old, has been living in Exarchia since 1988, she speaks fluent Italian and is a film director. Babis is a few years younger, has been living in Exarchia for a while and is a sociologist, even though when asked about his work situation he simply says that "this is not the best of times for research here in Greece." They are the ones who told me how the Social Solidarity Network works and how the idea was born. Babis introduces:

> it is a local assembly created in September 2011, after the Syntagma movement, in the wake of which many other similar experiments were created all over Greece. In the beginning we focused our activities on the electricity cuts in the area around Exarchia, but now we're trying to widen our agenda and our range of action. We get together once a week at 15 Tsamadou Street. Our assembly is free, officially speaking there are no political parties and whoever participates does so under their own name. At our strongest, there were 30 or 40 of us, now there are a few less. We keep in contact by way of a mailing list with about 120 members.

Stratoula continues explaining that they started up just after the *charatsi* was introduced, as their first reaction aimed at "defending ourselves, to unite and protect one another against this attack." The Social Solidarity Network began to get organized in a very simple way: a cell phone was assigned to one member, and every time the DEI (Δημόσια Επιχείρηση Ηλεκτρισμού, Public Electricity Company) sends someone out this activist texts everyone on the list, after which whoever is available goes to the location. Usually all they do is set up a picket line to stop the authorities from cutting off the electricity. Until now it has worked fairly well and they have never had to resort to violent resistance. Stratoula goes deeper into their motivations, saying that:

> When the government announced the charatsi, they promised that it would be charged only for one year. But we all know this isn't true, and we're trying to tell people: "Don't believe these lies, this tax will be around forever and if you start paying it they'll keep applying it!" In the beginning they didn't believe us, but then they became aware of what was happening. Some people have been living without electricity for a year,[6] even if they only owe the DEI 250 euro. When we don't succeed in preventing cuts, we try to find a way to hook it back up for those who are determined to do so. It's not legal, but it's ethically correct, it's our duty! These are families with small children, how can we ignore them? We've even had support from the DEI workers' union, in extreme cases they have helped us because they themselves realize how absurd all of this is. If we all stopped paying any kind of tax or anything outstanding that goes to the banks for a

month or two, maybe the government would start to understand that what they are doing is completely insane.

This last statement leads us to a long digression on the anti-austerity movements, their phases and recent evolution, caught between waves of innovation and retreat. One of the first thought goes naturally to the "origin of the conflict". As Babis points out:

it was an amazing insurrection that strengthened political mentality in Exarchia. December 2008 was not an answer, but a question: what could we do against this system that after having ruined our dreams and destroyed our future, now kills our people? A kind of response was the Syntagma movement. Even our assembly came out from the necessity to reflect upon the political situation all over again.

Then, we briefly skim the sequence of the following events, passing through the Greece's mass demonstrations, its endless general strikes, its heavy social conflict and the violent riots that even held the Parliament under siege. Since all of this has had little or no effect, how is it possible, I asked, to invert this tendency using local practices of civil and fiscal disobedience? I don't even have time to finish formulating my question as to future developments when Babis lashes back:

Future? What do you mean, future? At the moment we can't see one. The movement is at point zero, and in terms of our own economic or employment stability we can't predict anything. All I can see is a multitude of troubled people who still try to react, and continue to fail. The future might be even worse than the present, but the real problem is that we have nothing at all to look forward to, and many feel frustrated. There has been a rise in mental illnesses, widespread depression, and suicide and the use of drugs have also increased. This is the true impact that the crisis has had!

Stratoula adds, raising the tone of the discussion:

We went out on the streets every day, facing the tear gas, clashing with the police… and nothing has changed. I don't know what's going to happen in the next five years, but for me every day is a struggle. Personally, I try not to give in to fear, because that is exactly what they want to instil in us. It's disgusting to think about how they've succeeded in creating this widespread feeling of guilt, convincing people that they've received too much and now it's time to pay. I'm shocked! This world is not for everyone. Many here are so frightened that they have shut themselves off. Everyone tries to protect their own families and there's a huge amount of despair, especially among people who are around fifty and have lost their jobs. It's hard to fight back when you live under such psychological pressure, lots of people think that it's impossible to change anything.

Babis concludes:

Everyone seems to be confused, they would like to respond but don't know how. After Syntagma, we were defeated. Even though it seemed much too pacifistic or nationalistic, Exarchia sustained the aganaktismenoi movement,[7] but we realized that we had lost our first battle and now we're looking for more creative ways to promote new ideas. Of course, after Syntagma many solidarity networks were built, and initiatives that promote bottom-up social economy, but sometimes their range of action is so limited that it's hard to see how much of an influence they have. It's a continuous battle between two feelings, between hope and desperation.

Conclusions

This article has discussed the impact that the Syntagma Square movement had on those grassroots mobilizations that precipitated at a local level as soon as the occupation of the Parliament's central square ended in August 2011. In particular, it has stressed how, starting from the "origin of the conflict" in December 2008, the *joie de vivre* (Leontidou 2014) expressed by the Greek *aganaktismenoi* fundamentally provided a source of inspiration in locally spatializing the anti-austerity discourse within and throughout the city of Athens. The empirical cases reported, such as the time-banking system and the Social Solidarity Network, both of them based in the Exarchia district, gave evidence to this relation of affinity and reciprocity.

Even though an unequivocal relation between the days of Alexis and the anti-austerity mobilizations in the IMF/EU/ECB era is still hard to discern, these two events created such wide fractures that their common aspects cannot be considered merely coincidental. Retrospectively, underneath the spectacle of the riots, "the origin of the conflict" seems to have signalled a growing awareness of the turbulent future that the Greek country was forced to face immediately afterwards. Overall, it has been embodied by and in Exarchia to be extended to the entire city of Athens as soon as the economic crisis was officially declared in 2009.

As a consequence of this latter spatial opening, the Syntagma movement definitely helped broaden and bring forth "the right *through* the city" (Arampatzi & Nicholls 2012) as an urban strategy aimed at claiming the city rather than conceiving of struggle as an end unto itself, thus configuring Athens as a relevant hub for incubating social movements during the IMF/EU/ECB era.

If, as Leontidou has argued, spontaneity in urban movements has come closer to Gramsci's definition but with new methods, including digital ones (Leontidou 2012), the Syntagma Square occupation well embodied this "revitalization", that represented an unexpected novelty for the realm of Greek political conflict as well. Thereafter, on the account of the vibrant atmosphere that mixed indignation with creativity, particularly in the ERT occupations, *joie de vivre* appeared as a distinctive cultural feature in the renewal of the anti-austerity experience, acting furthermore as a counter-discursive response to the "Quasi-orientalist offensive" (Leontidou 2014) launched by austerity politics towards Greece as a corrupt Southern Europe country. Finally, the first-hand interviews with Exarchia's activists proved how *joie de vivre* stands both as a trait of creativeness and as the expression of urban and social move-ments, as well as an anti-hegemonic statement of dignity, pride and self-respect, therefore representing a counter-discourse of living in crisis-stricken Southern Europe.

Notes

1 Referring to a total of 108 articles selected in three nationally circulating Greek newspapers – specifically, *Eleftherotypia* (Freedom of the Press), *To Vima* (The Tribune) and *Ta Nea* (The News), having respectively a moderate left, moderate right and centrist political inclination – and published over two distinct time-spans of five years each (1981–1985 and 2001–2005), Vradis has detected to what extent the neighbourhood has been negatively targeted by keywords such as "violence, crime, chaos, anarchy, hoodie-wearers, drug-dealing/drug-dealers" (2012: 90).

2 A total of 2,780 people were put out of work. The Greek government established the New Hellenic Radio, Internet and Television (NERIT) as the ERT's heir, which operated until June 2015, when the new Prime Minister, Alexis Tsipras, finally restored ERT as a national public broadcaster.

3 On May 5, 2010, only a few days after the approval of the first bailout program, thousands of people poured into the streets of Athens for the largest protest in the country's history since the end of the dictatorship. In a social climate already put to the test by popular discontent, the situation worsened along Stadiou Avenue, a central business street between Omonia and Syntagma, in front of a branch of the Marfin Bank, which had remained open on the day of the strike. As the march passed by the building, the windows of the main entrance were shattered, drenched with petrol and then targeted by Molotov cocktails thrown by a group of protesters. A fire broke out, leading to a significant death toll: three employees, including a pregnant woman, died of asphyxiation, trapped inside the bank while attempting to rescue themselves by reaching the roof. The widespread feeling of rage turned into shock and, if on the one hand a considerable number of demonstrators retreated from the streets, the rest of the protest rapidly evolved into a series of fierce clashes in the centre of Athens (Kolb 2011). As the result of a trial, in July 2013, the administrator of the Marfin Bank, the branch's manager and vice-manager, and the head of security, were sentenced to twenty-two years of prison for manslaughter. The reasons involved negligence and failure to comply with safety standards (*Kathimerini* 2013).

4 As of 2015, the Residents' Initiative left 15 Tsamadou Street. Owing to internal divergences, the group split into two distinct collectives.

5   Located in the upper side of the neighbourhood, since 2001 this social space has been run by a communist collective, whose political background is rooted in the tradition of autonomous Marxism and, more specifically, in the Italian *operaismo* (workerism). Recently it took the name of Perasma, 'Passage', following changes in the group's internal organisation.

6   As highlighted by Lekakis and Kousis, these emergency situations have worsened due to the increase in the price of heating fuel as a state revenue-raising measure demanded by the second Memorandum package. This led "to a massive substitution of central heating oil with wood, other fuel and, by some, even dangerous but available materials including, for example, old furniture and plastics. The result has been a new smog over Greek cities on all cold nights, containing particulate matter (PM2.5), sulphur dioxide, carbon monoxide and other harmful pollutants, at least five times higher than acceptable levels (National Observatory of Athens 2013), with considerable health and climate effects" (2013: 315).

7   In more than one informal discussion with other residents and activists, I was told that, the quarter's anarchists above all had snubbed Syntagma Square, because they felt it was naïve or not sufficiently radical and therefore politically irrelevant.

References

Arampatzi, Athina 2017: The Spatiality of Counter-Austerity Politics in Athens, Greece: Emergent "Urban Solidarity Spaces". *Urban Studies* 54:9, 2155–2171.

Arampatzi, Athina & Walter J. Nicholls 2012: The Urban Roots of Anti-Neoliberal Social Movements: The Case of Athens, Greece. *Enviroment and Planning A* 44:11, 2591–2610.

Bosco, Anna & Susannah Verney 2012: Electoral Epidemic: The Political Cost of Economic Crisis in Southern Europe 2010–11. *South European Society and Politics* 17:2, 129–154.

Brekke, Klara Jaya, Dimitris Dalakoglou, Christos Filippidis & Antonis Vradis (eds.) 2014: *Crisis-Scapes: Athens and Beyond*. Athens: Synthesi.

Cappuccini, Monia 2017: *Austerity and Democracy in Athens, Crisis and Community in Exarchia*. Cham: Palgrave Macmillam.

Castells, Manuel 2010: *The Power of Identities*. London: Blackwell.

Douzinas, Costas 2013: *Philosophy and Resistance in the Crisis: Greece and the Future of Europe*. Cambridge: Polity Press.

Elafros, Yiannis 2013: Some 30,000 Households a Month Have Power Supply Cut. *Kathimerini*, http://www.ekathimerini.com/150138/article/ekathimerini/business/some-30000-households-a-month-have-power-supply-cut. Last access May 31, 2017.

Graeber, David 2007: *There Never Was a West: Or, Democracy Emerges from the Space in Between*. Oakland, CA: AK Press.

The Guardian 2013: Greece Shuts Down State Broadcaster in Search for New Savings [online]. Available at: https://www.theguardian.com/world/2013/jun/11/state-broadcaster-ert-shut-down-greece. Last access May 31, 2017.

Harvey, David 2012: *Rebel Cities: From the Right to the City to the Urban Revolution*. New York: Verso.

Holloway, John 2010: *Crack Capitalism*. London: Pluto Press.

Kanna, Ahmad 2012: Urban Praxis and the Arab Spring. *City* 16:3, 360–368.

Kathimerini 2008: Police Killing of Youth Sparks Explosive Riots [online]. Available at: http://www.ekathimerini.com/60987/article/ekathimerini/news/police-killing-of-youth-sparks-explosive-riots. Last access May 31, 2017.

Kathimerini 2013: Three Bank Executives Convicted of Manslaughter for Fatal 2010 Marfin Fire [online]. Available at: http://www.ekathimerini.com/152363/article/ekathimerini/news/three-bank-executives-convicted-of-manslaughter-for-fatal-2010-marfin-fire. Last access May 31, 2017.

Kitsantonis, Niki 2012: Pensioner's Suicide Continues to Shake Greece. *New York Times* [online]. Available at: http://www.nytimes.com/2012/04/06/world/europe/pensioners-suicide-continues-to-shake-greece.html. Last access May 31, 2017.

Kolb, Bob 2011: *Fuoco Greco: La rivolta di Atene del 5 maggio 2010*. Lecce: Bepress Edizioni.

Lefebvre, Henri 1968: *Le Droit à la Ville*. Paris: Éditions Anthropos.

Lekakis, Joseph & Maria Kousis 2013: Economic Crisis, Troika and the Environment in Greece. *South European Society and Politics* 18:3, 305–333.

Leontidou, Lila 2012: Athens in the Mediterranean "Movement of the Piazzas": Spontaneity in Material and Virtual Spaces. *City* 16:3, 259–312.

Leontidou, Lila 2014: The Crisis and Its Discourses: Quasi-Orientalist Attacks on Mediterranean Urban Spontaneity, Informality and Joie de Vivre. *City* 18:4–5, 551–562.

Lopez de Sousa, Marcelo & Barbara Lipietz 2011: The "Arab Spring" and the City. *City* 15:6, 618–624.

Martínez Roldán, Sergio 2011: Movimiento 15M: Construcción del espacio urbano a través de la acción de Multitudes Inteligentes. *URBS* 1:1, 60–81.

Massarelli, Fulvio 2013: *La forza di piazza Syntagma: Voci di insurrezione da Atene*. Milan: Agenzia X.

Mavrommatis, George 2015: Hannah Arendt in the Streets of Athens. *Urban Studies* 63:3, 432–449.

Mentinis, Mihalis 2010: Remember, Remember the 6th of December... A Rebellion or the Constituting Moment of a Radical Morphoma? *International Journal of Urban and Regional Research* 34:1, 197–202.

Miller, Byron & Walter Nicholls 2013: Social Movements in Urban Society: The City as a Space of Politicization. *Urban Geography* 34:4, 452–473.

Occupy Wall Street 2012: *Occupy Manifesto: Dal popolo e per il popolo.* Trieste: Asterios.

Omikron Project 2012: *Omikron Project's Official Website* [online]. Available at http://omikronproject.gr. Last access May 31, 2017.

Panorama Statistics 2012: *Greek Census Data* [online]. Available at: https://panorama.statistics.gr/en/. Last access May 31, 2017.

Petropoulou, Chryssanthi 2010: From the December Youth Uprising to the Rebirth of Urban Social Movements: A Space-Time Approach. *International Journal of Urban and Regional Research* 34:1, 217–224.

Psimitis, Michalis 2011: Collective Identities versus Social Exclusion: The December 2008 Youth Movement. *The Greek Review of Social Research* 136:C, 111–133.

Residents' Initiative 2008: *Residents' Initiative's Official Blog* [online]. Available at: http://exarchia.pblogs.gr. Last access May 31, 2017.

Schrader, Stuart & David Wachsmuth 2012: Reflections on Occupy Wall Street, the State and Space. *City* 16:1–2, 243–248.

Social Solidarity Network 2011: *Social Solidarity Network's Official Blog* [online]. Available at: http://dikaex.blogspot. it. Last access May 31, 2017.

Stangos, Angelos 2014: The Cost of the Protests. *Kathimerini* [online]. Available at: http://www.ekathimerini. com/159821/article/ekathimerini/comment/the-cost-of-protests. Last access May 31, 2017.

Stavrides, Stavros 2010: *Towards the City of Thresholds.* Trento: professionaldreamers. Available at: http://www.professionaldreamers.net/_prowp/wp-content/uploads/978-88-904295-3-8-ch1.pdf. Last access May 31, 2017.

Stavrides, Stavros 2011: *Communities of Crisis, Square in Movement.* Working paper no. 6. Trento: professionaldreamers. Available at: http://www.professionaldreamers. net/_prowp/wp-content/uploads/Stavrides-Communities-of-crisis-fld.pdf. Last access May 31, 2017.

Taddio, Luca 2012: *Global Revolution.* Milan: Mimesis.

UN Human Rights Council 2013: *Report of the Independent Expert on the Effects of Foreign Debt and Other Related International Financial Obligations of States on the Full Enjoyment of All Human Rights, Particularly Economic, Social and Cultural Rights, on His Mission to Greece.* Geneva.

Vradis, Antonis 2012: Wri(o)ting Cities: Some Candid Questions on Researching and Writing about Urban Riots. In: Katherine Robinson, Adam Kaasa & Gunter Gassner (eds.), *Writing Cities II.* London: LSE, pp. 88–93.

Vradis, Antonis & Dimitris Dalakoglou (eds.) 2011: *Revolt and Crisis in Greece: Between a Present yet to Pass and a Future still to Come.* Oakland CA: AK Press and Occupied London.

Monia Cappuccini, urban anthropologist, is interested in youth culture, urban movements and social conflict. Apart from a Ph.D. in engineering-based architecture and urban planning from University La Sapienza of Rome, she earned the additional title of Doctor Europeaus as a result of a scientific partnership developed with the National Centre of Social Research (EKKE) in Athens. Her latest monograph is titled *Austerity and Democracy in Athens, Crisis and Community in Exarchia* (Cham: Palgrave Macmillam). (monia.cappuccini@gmail.com)

"NEW" GREEK FOOD SOLIDARITIES (*ALLILEGGIÍ*)
Communalism vis-à-vis Food in Crisis Greece

James Verinis, Roger Williams University, Bristol (USA)

In this paper I extend the anthropological analyses of "new" solidarity (*allileggii*) networks or movements in Greece to rural regions and agricultural life as well as new groups of people. Food networks such as the "potato movement", which facilitates the direct sales of agricultural produce, reveals rural aspects of networks that are thought to be simply urban phenomena. "Social kitchens" are revealed to be humanistic as well as nationalistic, bringing refugees, economic migrants, and Greeks together in arguably unprecedented ways. Through a review of such food solidarity movements – their rural or urban boundaries as well as their egalitarian or multicultural tenets – I consider whether they are thus more than mere extensions of earlier patterns of social solidarity identified in the anthropological record.

Keywords: solidarity, rural–urban dichotomy, ethno-national identity, globalization, food

"New" Greek Solidarity Movements

When I first began to reflect on the work I had conducted for my Ph.D. dissertation between 2008 and 2010[1] in the southern Peloponnesian prefecture of Laconia (which was primarily about Greek/non-Greek farmer relationships [Verinis 2015]), I sought to account for some statistical evidence that many non-Greeks had left Greece since the onset of the financial crisis.[2] Mainstream media has focused heavily on the rise of support for the Greek far right, particularly the now infamous neofascist party *Chryssí Avgí*, or Golden Dawn, whose members have been responsible for all sorts of brutal and illegal acts against individuals they deem unworthy of Greek identity. This data and media focus has somewhat overshadowed interest in solidarity movements as well as the seemingly paradoxical evidence I had collected during my dissertation fieldwork – that many bonds between Greeks and non-Greeks in rural areas had strengthened since the early 1990s.[3] What is more, to say that economic migrants are not simply exploited by neoliberalism is generally anathema to anthropology, despite its interest in data niches vis-à-vis qualitative approaches such as my focus on a certain relatively small group of economic immigrants. Nonetheless, inspired by the unprecedented achievements and future visions of certain Albanians, Moldovans, Ukrainians, Romanians, Bulgarians as well as farmers of other South-Eastern/Eastern European/Balkan ethno-nationalities whom I have had experiences working with in Greece, I remained convinced that certain forms of co-ethnic

James Verinis 2018: "New" Greek Food Solidarities (Allileggií).
Communalism vis-à-vis Food in Crisis Greece.
Ethnologia Europaea 48:1, 99–115. © Museum Tusculanum Press.

rapprochement continue to grow roots in the country despite or perhaps because of the phenomena we call the financial crisis and austerity. I visited former fieldwork sites and interlocutors in 2016 in order to determine if this was true.

I had not yet begun to consider whether this rapprochement was a new form of solidarity per se. Yet one increasingly interesting line of inquiry in recent scholarship on Greece is in fact concerned with new forms of sociality and communalism emerging there, often between supposedly disparate groups of people in their joint attempt to survive socio-economic tumult. Consequently I have begun to see much of my former work in this light.

This special issue on resistance and change in Mediterranean Europe has asked contributors to consider the roles that persistent cultural patterns (Schönberger 2015) – such as those involving informal networks, family relationships and friendship-based coalitions – play in the formation of new collaborative communities. Works by John Campbell (1964), Evthymios Papataxiarchis (1991), Juliet du Boulay (1991), Michael Herzfeld (1992) and others who created the first ethnographic record of Greece highlight the historical particulars of friendship, sociality, and communalism in the country as basic processes we often still refer to when we speak of Greek national or cultural identity. Recent solidarity movements, or *kínisi allilegíí*, certainly build upon persistent cultural patterns or past relationships between the state and its citizenry. Yet, most contemporary Greek solidarity movements are forms of resistance to current, dominant, neoliberal political and economic structures in Europe and thus novel in this sense at least.

Kínisi allilegíí may not seem ideologically familiar either. Greek "solidarians" are a mix of anarchists, communists, supporters of the current coalition led by center left Syriza, urban globalists, the apolitical, and conservative ruralites as well. Scholars debate whether solidarity initiatives are the offspring of previous leftist political movements or whether they are wholly new (Cabot 2015). Some confusion is due to the fact that contemporary kínisi allilegíí are largely unofficial, as opposed to conventional

institutions and thus, to varying degrees, unobservable. As Castells, Caraça and Cardoso (2012) have pointed out, these "networked movements" lack an organizational structure and are characterized by a lesser degree of identification and fluid membership.

Right-wing affiliations are typically not represented in these movements; however, one can certainly find solidarity initiatives of other kinds, such as those less inclusive networks supported by Golden Dawn or the Greek Orthodox Church. Members of Golden Dawn set up their own "Greek only" soup kitchens, for example. Yet the solidarity movements in Greece I refer to provide an array of people with such essentials as medicine, health care, legal aid, food products and prepared meals. The "no middleman movement" or "potato movement" (*kínima tis patátes*), which facilitates the direct sales of agricultural produce, and solidarity health clinics are two such prominent movements or networks (Arampatzi 2016; Cabot 2015, 2016; Rakopoulos 2014, 2016a, 2016b). Heath Cabot's account (2016) is noteworthy for her discussion of the involvement of non-Greeks in certain health clinics. In chronicling their active participation, Cabot describes non-Greeks as "deeply marginalized". Presumably she means that this is the case outside of solidarity economies, as these older South-Eastern/Eastern European/Balkan migrants, as well as more recent migrants from Africa, South Asia, and the Middle East are arguably in more horizontal relationships with fellow care seekers, if not also with care workers, within new solidarity health clinic contexts (2016: 153). Notable also is the fact that one of the two clinics Cabot worked with had an even distribution of care seekers – half of Greek and half of non-Greek origin. Petros, an Albanian care seeker in this clinic, stands outside of neighborhood supermarkets every weekend collecting food for others in need. In this capacity Petros is arguably also a care provider. In all, this somewhat upended hierarchy or orientation to conventional understandings of marginalization and mutual aid is a crucial point that the study of food exchange (as well as new exchanges of other necessities of life) can make as part of an evaluation of "new" solidarities. Food in particular engenders certain behavioral transgressions as well as holistic scholarly analysis, drawing together exclusive spaces such as the "urban" and "rural", discrete ethnic groups, as well as the Global South and the Global North, as refugee food aid initiatives in Greece (a developed country with its own food crisis) have begun to show us.

I have found these, as well as other scholarly accounts of emerging solidarity networks or movements essential to my reevaluation of co-ethnic rapprochement in rural areas. I suggest that rural co-ethnic cooperation and these movements have more than a few things to do with one another. Small-scale agriculture, family farms, the communalism of the Greek village, or *horió,* and the quality of rural life have become quite symbolic in light of the financial crisis. Largely unprecedented collaborations in urban areas such as Patras, Athens, and Thessaloniki aimed at safeguarding the most existential components of life rely quite heavily on these rural, traditional, historical, and ideological foundations. Novel networks that produce food and save and exchange seeds in traditional manners or with alternative ideological foundations have formed as resistant responses to neoliberal campaigns that intensify and commodify agriculture. They resist global agribusiness and financial austerity measures that have threatened family farms with extinction. Food networks – those interested in safeguarding biodiversity and small-scale production as well as direct channels of distribution and affordable access to meals – can be considered a certain category of networks or collaborations. While Greece has only recently become a country of immigration, the involvement of non-Greeks makes these collaborations arguably more egalitarian than their comparable predecessors as well. They certainly are more egalitarian than those political and economic forces they claim to resist.

In my research on Greek ethno-national identity and the incorporation of post-socialist immigrants into various components of Greek life in the early 2000s, I was led to study immigrant incorporation into olive economies in particular. As happens in countries with relatively poor neighbors, a reliance on labor-intensive industries (such as olive culti-

vation on sloping land), and an aging population, amongst other pushing and pulling variables, cheap and flexible labor finds its place. Yet immigrant incorporation develops in certain instances and not always in the same manner as elsewhere. Non-Greeks were in the process of becoming far more integral to rural Laconian communities in the early 2000s than as sources of cheap labor, as I will continue to describe. In crisis Greece, food and agriculture have regained significance and it is little wonder that in becoming integral to the survival of small-scale agricultural practices and traditional rural values, non-Greeks should be found at the heart of a variety of new Greek solidarity movements as well. It is also unsurprising that scholars have been led to consider *kínisi allilegíí* that place food at the core of their ideological stances. It is for these reasons that I sought to revisit old topics and interlocutors, as well as new food sites such as those I have begun to describe here – so as to continue to illuminate the myriad socioeconomic roles immigrants play in Greece and draw a portrait of some new roles food is now playing in Greek society.

Solidarity food markets, solidarity food grower networks, social kitchens (*koinonikés kouzínes*), seed banks and exchange networks, food rescue movements, along with what I term "rural solidarity networks", make up this current reflection on Greek ethno-national identity. Identity, resistance, and change vis-à-vis food is surely not a new idea, as articles such as Sutton et al. (2013) attest – regarding the relationships between food and contemporary protest movements during Egypt's Arab Spring, New York's Occupy Wall Street, and in Greece at the outset of the current financial crisis for example. Yet what, specifically, it is that food movements and networks provide residents with in order so that they now transgress conventional or traditional social and spatial divides in Greece remains largely unaccounted for.

Rurality, Cities, and Solidarity

To begin linking these movements or networks, I will briefly reiterate the current state of shifting affairs between urban and rural in Greece. Of course, urban Greece (Athens and Thessaloniki primarily) has been the hardest hit by austerity and the consequent loss of wages and pensions. The rate of unemployment is markedly worse there. The degradation of the traditional safety nets of the family and the ancestral farm compounded by new medical, legal, and educational needs in the contemporary "developed" urban world makes surviving the crisis in these cities more difficult than in rural Greek areas. Consequently, Athina Arampatzi (2016) rightly speaks of specifically "urban" solidarity spaces where the exchange of essential goods takes place. Yet Chaia Heller's work on the *Confédération Paysanne* (2013), one of France's largest farmers' unions, for example, encourages us to focus on solidarity food movements from the perspective of rural producers as well. In doing so we might look to evidence in support of a new "back to the land" movement in Greece (Al Jazeera 2012; Cockburn 2011; Donadio 2012; Kasimis & Zografakis 2012; Verinis 2015). We should consider the fact that the crisis benefits *laikés* – traditional open-air food markets – as opposed to comparably more expensive supermarkets or more generally encourages people to reinvest in rural Greek agriculture. We should consider reversions to traditional rural Greek menus in Athenian restaurants (Kochilas 2010) and on traditional Greek cooking television shows (Sutton 2014), and the ethical ramifications such a turn implies. In doing so, we become more interdisciplinary and nuanced in our approach to contemporary Greek ethnic identities or moral economies (Scott 1977; Thompson 1971). More specifically, we comprehend how the rural experiences crisis itself as well as how it is symbolized in more urban areas (Angelopoulos 2016). Nikos, one of the Greek olive farmers I worked with in Laconia, insisted in 2009 that his son Spiros, then nine years old, would do anything except farm olives as he grew older. Now seventeen and subject to new employment constraints as well as certain other reevaluations of the rural, Spiros plans to attend university to study agronomy and farm the olive fields that he has inherited from his grandparents. Repeasantization is now seen as a way through – if not also out of – the crisis.

As with the ecology of urban neighborhoods as proposed by the Chicago School (Park & Miller 1921, in Glick-Schiller 2008), life in now global Greek countrysides involves certain new ecological and migratory patterns that solidarity networks are enabling people to create. These new patterns between rural and urban places as well as between Greeks and new immigrants take symbolic as well as material form. As Cabot says (2016: 161), "There is more to explore here in terms of urban and rural aspects of memory and the question of what generates 'political' consciousness." We were tactfully reminded of the complementarity of rural and urban aspects of Greek solidarity in 2011 when communist party MP Liana Kaneli brought a loaf of bread and a bottle of milk into a parliament meeting to decry the austerity-driven food insecurity that Greeks were suffering from. The ethics and values now espoused by "new" food movements thought to primarily exist in urban areas are increasingly echoed by ruralites (both Greek and non-Greek) in response to patents on genes and seeds, bureaucratic and corporate hurdles surrounding organic certification, international corruption, and global price competition.

There is state and EU support for a small percentage of traditional small-scale farms, yet the vast majority of Greek farming families are struggling to survive.[4] Dutch rural sociologist Jan van der Ploeg is one rather clear voice on this; "[Food] empires proceed as a brutal ecological and socio-economic exploitation, if not degradation of nature, farmers, food and culture" (2008: 14). This kind of reaction to global agribusiness also emerges amongst what we might call a global Greek peasantry in new food solidarity patterns. As Greek residents weigh new shared threats, to food security perhaps notably, new social movements now inspire rural and urban Greeks to cut across spatial and other domains of their lives. Social kitchens are one such manifestation of the inspiration to do so.

Social Kitchens

Koinonikés or *syllogikés kouzínes*, 'social' or 'collective kitchens', have only recently emerged in Greece. They have developed in response to the contemporary financial crisis as well as to the more hierarchical models of "soup kitchens" (Papataxiarchis 2016: 208). Immigrants, the homeless, the unemployed, the poor, and most recently refugees share food with one another in these places. The slogan for *El Chef* collective kitchen in Athens is "we cook collectively, we serve solidarity." Interestingly, the inspiration for El Chef, one of the first social kitchens, begun in 2007, was to enact solidarity with migrants before the economic recession truly set in, which then encouraged them to extend their network to include Greeks as well.

Konstantinos Polychronopoulos, the founder of another prominent kitchen, *O Állos Anthrópos*, 'the other person' or 'fellow man', describes what distinguishes social kitchens from soup kitchens; "They took [the sandwiches] only when they saw that I also ate one. There was mistrust in the beginning. And I got into their shoes… I wouldn't receive food if I hadn't seen how it was made, too. So I started preparing food on the street" (Wanshel 2016).

As their slogans attest, social kitchens are indeed "open to all". I was free to eat and socialize with whomever I chose whenever I had the opportunity to attend social kitchen meals. As I observed the goings on around the social kitchen O Állos Anthrópos in Monastiraki Square in central Athens one afternoon in the summer of 2016, I realized that part of what social kitchens signify is a lack of boundaries. For much of the time, I could not tell whether I was in the social kitchen or not. On that day, a homeless Greek man sitting next to me, presumably there to partake of the social kitchen, began to beg for some beer from a well-dressed Pakistani man sitting across from him who was there on a work break. A second Greek man, also well-dressed and also drinking beer then asked where the Pakistani man was from. At the close of a short exchange, the second Greek man contributed his own beer to the mix as the three toasted to each other's good health – "*stin yiá mas*". Where is the "real" social kitchen? In any case, there is something postmodern, if not entirely novel, in relation to the anthropological record about certain phenomena emerging in as well as around social kitchens.

Food Rescue and Laikés

Variations of "to whom" or "for whom" were responses I often heard from vendors at neighborhood food markets or laikés when, as a volunteer for *Boroúme* ("We Can", a non-profit organization working to reduce food waste and combat malnutrition in Greece), I would ask if they had any portions of their produce to offer as a donation – *kamía merítha fagytó xaméni*. Some vendors are indeed concerned that no refugees should receive food while Greeks remain hungry. While Boroúme does not discriminate, they do selectively reveal information so as to maintain relationships with participating vendors. While much of the produce Boroúme collects does go to church soup kitchens and boarding houses for the primarily Greek mentally ill, surplus often goes to refugee charities now as well. Of course, when social scientists like myself or the film crew from the Austrian organization Wastecooking, who filmed Boroúme at markets in June 2016, inquire in private about the different groups of people who might benefit from such food rescue endeavors, Boroúme is quick to point to all of them.

Resentment of EU austerity packages and the political presentation of them as "generous" has only furthered Greek distrust of any formal policy measures and emboldened ideological beliefs that preface solidarity activities as modes of sharing as opposed to giving, especially systematized giving. One afternoon, while the Wastecooking film crew was filming, a vendor asked me what they were doing. He protested against my explanation that they were documenting the need to combat hunger and malnutrition in Greece, insisting rather that he and his Indian co-worker were not hungry; "We're not hungry here in Greece. We are *mánges!*" (*Then pí-name ethó stin Ellátha, eímaste mánges!*). A *mángas* is a "player", someone with swagger, ego, and particular Greek pride in working-class values. The vendor then asked his Indian co-worker if he was hungry and, with the same obstinate and traditional Greek thrust of the chin to indicate no, the Indian man confirmed that he was indeed not.[5] In this exchange the vendor drew a line around himself and his Indian co-worker, setting Greek residents apart from those who need charity as well as apart from the Austrian filmmakers, seen by him as representative of Northern/Central Europe and the *Troika* (the International Monetary Fund, the European Financial Stability Facility, and the European Commission) or the *Troikanoi* (Troikians) – the "real" foreigners.

Another vendor performed a similarly defiant reaction to the film crew's presence on another occasion, insisting that food rescue volunteers (including me) "take more bags," shouting "Take it! Everything's free in Greece!" As we struggled to carry all of the food he was so "graciously" offering us, he tactfully shamed us into looking like thieves – just another group of people taking advantage of Greece's excellent and cheap agricultural produce as well as its image of a nation that has so poorly managed its own resources and finances that it is up to the European Union, bankers, and charitable organizations to solve hunger there.[6]

Of course Boroúme is not so simplistic an organization as such reactions to their activities might lead us to believe. Along with a host of other initiatives, their "Gleaning Program" or *Sto Xoráfi* ('In the Field') brings volunteers to rural/agricultural areas serving Athens in order to help reduce food waste at the level of the farms and allow these urbanites to better understand food production regimes. Advocates of Spain's own rising gleaning movement say that it not only feeds the hungry but also improves diets, reduces pressure on land use, restores lost aesthetic abilities to evaluate food, and provides work for the socially excluded (Nelson 2016). Boroúme has also begun a program called "The Field of Boroúme" in which they take advantage of underutilized public farms owned by state municipalities (in Spata outside of Athens for example) to cultivate produce to distribute to residents there. They engage local schoolchildren in this program, planting potatoes, broccoli, and cabbages so as to restore interest in agricultural pursuits and donated close to one ton of produce in 2016. In so doing, as part of a larger solidarity movement which brings people together to meet each other's needs, Boroúme programs become, as Boroúme co-founder Alexander Theodo-

ridis told me, a "meeting ground" between the urban and the rural.

As ideological lines become drawn out and contemplated in the process of sharing food, in certain "seams of empire" (Tsing 2012) such as Greece, relatively unprecedented alliances form. Existential crises have certainly helped social kitchens, food rescue operations, and solidarity food markets (to which I now move) emerge quite suddenly in Greece. What new thinking or discourses about food and solidarity, in light of the various tears in traditional Greek safety nets, have enabled these charitable organizations as well as others more focused on sharing economies – various new manifestations of civil society – to operate?

Solidarity Food Markets

Solidarity food market initiatives in Greece, also known collectively as "the potato movement" or "no middleman movement", make direct attempts to exclude middlemen (*mesázontes*) and merchants (*hondrempóroi*) who buy wholesale and then sell to individual food stores and chains in urban areas. They preface direct sales of agricultural produce to benefit small-scale, socio-economically threatened farmers as well as financially impotent urban and peri-urban consumers.

These initiatives originated primarily in and around the northern Greek cities of Thessaloniki, Preveza, and Drama, but have been spreading throughout the country, and countryside, as I argue. Despite the fact that solidarity food markets are much less visible in relatively conservative areas of Greece, such as Laconia prefecture (the south-eastern corner of the Peloponnese where I lived between 2008 and 2010), many farmers who participate in solidarity Athenian markets do in fact come from as far away as Laconia. They come for economic purposes but also because of new structural and ideological connections they now share with urban Greeks, from new roads to new alignments based on shared political opponents.[7] *Agronaftes*, or Agronauts, a collective of small producers or solidarity growers from the Peloponnese primarily serving consumers in Athens, is similar in structure to Community Supported Agriculture (CSA) programs that have been operating in the United States since the 1990s – members buy seasonal shares up front and thus absorb some of the farmer's risk. However, solidarity growers are more overtly ideological. They share the perspective of care farming initiatives, such as Litsis Ecological Farms in Thessaloniki, for example, which reorients farms toward the inclusion of therapeutic care of vulnerable groups of people as a supplemental goal to food production. Agronauts is an example of "socially supported agriculture" in Greece, or "*koinoniká ypostirízomei georgía*" which incorporates goals that lie outside the context of conventional global agribusiness.

Agronauts was founded by a small group of farmers led by Vangelis Vlachakis, who left Athens when he became unemployed in the early years of the current economic crisis and returned to Laconia to cultivate his grandfather's fields. The Agronauts' network also includes other prominent members from Laconia, such as the food company Diamond House in Glykovrisi which produces pasta and biscuits for Agronauts as well as e-blocko.gr shops online and in e-blocko stores, specializing in traditional and local food products from all over Greece at producer prices. Agronauts work toward the maintenance of the social economy, or third economic system as members call it, which prefaces reciprocity as opposed to the first economic system (that which is private, oriented toward economic gain) and the second economic system (that of the state, oriented toward social planning). Agronauts also acts as a platform for small and organic farmers to meet and exchange information on sustainable cultivation, the expansion of smallholder activities, and particularly the cultivation of traditional varieties vis-à-vis Peliti, Greece's most prominent seed exchange network, in response to the commercialization of diets, the intensification of agriculture, and environmental degradation.[8]

As one of many solidarity food market networks currently operating in the country, Agronauts is a specific new link between Athens and the rural Peloponnese as well as a general representation of new solidarity economies now emerging across the country and amongst new sectors of the population.

Food and Refugees

As with austerity, there has been almost no way for any scholar interested in any aspect of Greek society today to avoid thinking critically about the most recent global refugee phenomenon. As Papataxiarchis explains, "'solidarity' responses to the financial crisis have been extended into new fields of application – solidarity has replaced hospitality as the dominant mode of engagement with refugees" (2016: 208). Katerina Rozakou explains in some more depth:

> The "needy" refugee, this classical figure of humanitarianism (Fassin 2007; Redfield 2005), has entered the sphere of solidarity. Despite the fact that, perhaps, only a minority of local people actively got involved in organised voluntary work with refugees, the accumulation and circulation of goods was massive. Even people who were sceptical of the newcomers and fearful of contagious diseases, contributed offerings. "Everybody gives," solidarians noted, and added that the specificities of the Syrian refugee population mobilised these donations. "They are families, children and women," they explained; thus, groups who are not only vulnerable in humanitarian terms and fuel typical portrayals of refugeeness (Malkki 1996), but also culturally significant social categories (cf. Green 2012; Voutira 2003). Thus, in a context where kinship is highly valued, the view of families en route generated vast and, sometimes, unexpected local responses. (Rozakou 2016: 196)

Refugees were quickly thrown into solidary networks vis-à-vis their immediate needs for such things as food and clothing, things that had only recently become exchanged amongst Greeks and non-refugee migrant groups through social networks. A special issue of *Social Anthropology,* the journal of the *European Association of Social Anthropologists* in the spring of 2016, from which I quote Papataxiarchis and Rozakou, was organized to address this almost unbelievably coincidental need that many Greeks and the growing spectrum of non-Greeks now have for essential goods.

It is not the first time that people from Middle

Eastern or South Asian countries have made their way to Greece looking to move on to "Europe". American-led invasions of Afghanistan and Iraq in the early 2000s brought young men escaping violence to Greece, searching for money to send to their families back home, even to remote villages in the Peloponnese like Goritsa where I lived at the time. Small in numbers as they were, some of the first non-Western people many rural Greeks had ever seen, these small groups of young men were rather feared in contrast to the refugee families described by Rozakou above. Despite the fact that Greek families typically made donations of old clothing and food to "their" Afghans in Goritsa, I was scolded by my Greek friends and family for associating with *Afghanoí* outside of work in the fields, especially when I was accompanied by my wife or would eat with them in the derelict village houses they occupied at the time.

Perhaps ironically, despite the influx of refugees in Greece, according to all of the residents of Goritsa I spoke with and based on my own observations in 2016, there are now fewer immigrants in Greek villages. There never has been any hard or reliable data on Afghans in mountain villages and the economic downturn has made them some of the first to lose employment there, as many Greeks return to farms and all seek to cut superfluous costs, such as for unskilled labor picking olives. Perhaps sentiments have indeed changed – as Rozakou's interlocutors suggest, "everybody gives." Perhaps that is a result of the demographic and other related changes in the refugee crisis; while South Asian and Middle Eastern refugees were once small groups of wandering young, primarily Afghan, men, there are now massive concentrations of refugee families in refugee camps, controlled areas on islands in the eastern Aegean Sea, and specific urban neighborhoods. In any case, the sharing of resources such as food and clothing, as well as medical care seems to have increased.

As borders with the rest of Europe have become less and less permeable, many migrants and refugees have taken up residence in what are referred to as *domés allilegíes* or "solidarity structures" in cities. Having no name other than their addresses – a re-flection of the absence of national histories and social hierarchies one feels within them – Notara 26 and Axarnon 78 are two such structures amongst the huge proportion of abandoned Athenian real estate resulting from the financial crisis.[9] Through the settlement of derelict urban spaces by migrants and even the emplacement of refugees within them, these "refugee squats" become icons of the solidarity movement, spatially chastising what the financial crisis and fears of migrant "hordes" in other European countries with more closed borders have done to Greeks and refugees alike.[10]

As might be expected, the basic and essential issues of fundraising and food and clothing stocks are typically discussed in squat meetings co-organized by refugees and solidarian workers. Giorgos, one solidarity worker I occasionally spoke with in 2016, coordinated a covert donation to refugees by the baby food manufacturer he worked for. Obtaining food supplies in such ways, cooking and eating together has become a prominent way for relationships between diverse groups to develop. It has also become a way to advertise these relationships between refugees and Greeks in solidarity campaigns, on the internet as well as in other discursive formations. Notara 26 often displayed images of people cooking and eating together on their website at the time.[11]

In such sites I began to see new coordinations, arguably novel or postmodern, between the survival strategies of the Global North and those of the Global South (Heller 2013: 2). My inclusion in weekly meetings at Notara 26 was through entirely horizontal channels; from Giorgos I was handed off to another solidarian, who brought me to my first meeting. No one sought to identify my role then, nor at subsequent meetings. At first I had little idea as to who was Greek and who was not. I spoke with solidarians and refugees often without knowing who was who, except for their proficiency in Greek or their accent in English. And as I departed from the field, there was no expectation as to what I would do with the information I had gathered. In this sense too, perhaps, some of us gazing in were also given somewhat unprecedented roles, as Papataxiarchis says of international solidarian participants in refugee camps on Lesbos (2016).

Rural Solidarity Movements

I now double back to the rural settings I first encountered in the early 2000s. I propose that there too, "new" solidarity movements exist, often revolving around the beliefs and behaviors of solidarity growers such as Agronauts who are partly responsible for the emergence of the solidarity markets described above. They are focused particularly on safeguarding small-scale agriculture, other values inherent to traditional agricultural communities, and agricultural biodiversity. Yet there are specific links between rural solidarity movements or networks and social kitchens, solidarity food markets, and food rescue movements identified primarily in urban areas. These include a focus on such things as the amelioration of social conflicts between groups in everyday practices and strategies, sustainability, and the consideration of the marginal position of Greece in relation to the northern European core. Somewhat without formal networks, largely unobservable, and at risk of co-optation by conventional politics though they may be, the rural socio-ecological movements I describe in this section are future visions of food, agriculture, and communal life by a new collection of rural residents.

Adding rural solidarity movements to these other movements is perhaps somewhat arbitrary. That people need to collectively produce food and eat to survive wherever they are or share occupational practices whoever they are is arguably intellectually empty. Yet *paréa*, 'company', in the sense of people being together with other people – to share subsistence goods– is born in Greek meals. Many Greek cultural values, such as paréa have emerged from agricultural life. The contemporary socio-economic crisis in Greece has reinforced the family character of farms and inspired new cooperative strategies in the light of this particular cultural value (Ragkos et al. 2016). Greek masculinities and femininities are similarly engaged as women have begun to take places on farms again in response to joblessness (Petrou 2012). More to the point, the external environment of the EU and globalized agriculture is largely seen as unfriendly in comparison to the internal environment or actors. Ethno-national and rural-urban hierarchies are being reconfigured as a result, in conjunction with such cultural values as paréa. Alternatives to EU bureaucracy as well as incentives to consolidate and scale up agriculture are sought from within the confines of local rural villages which now include many non-Greek residents.

Along with paréa, *allilovoíthia*, 'mutual aid' or 'other helping', certainly part of a segmentary logic of traditional Greek life, remains a core component of rural commensality. This village or horió logic has been transplanted onto the frameworks of solidarity economies today, in urban as well as rural locations (Loizos 1975; Rakopoulos 2016b: 143; Vernier 1984). As Theodoros Rakopoulos points out, "the overall tendency [of solidarity work], including claims to the *horio*, temporarily tackles difference, and suggests similarity or assimilation" (2016b: 148). Whether these strategies be considered more specifically in the spirit of collaboration (Terkessidis 2015), *convivéncia* (Suárez-Navaz 2005), endogenous development (Ray 2000), or some other theoretical proposition, agriculturalists in Greece of various ethno-national backgrounds have now long been taking advantage of new opportunities to establish solidarity with one another. Beyond the affordable labor that non-Greeks have provided Greeks with since the beginning of the post-socialist migrations in the early 1990s, they also provide the means for rural Greeks in an extremely expensive and bureaucratic EU to continue living in a manner consistent with the history of rural Greek livelihoods – by harvesting and selling animal manure (a cheaper alternative fertilizer), wild hyacinth bulbs (a traditional food Greeks seldom harvest themselves any longer), or producing homemade *tsípouro* (a grape pomace liquor as a means to reach *kéfi*, 'good humor' or 'good life', with others) for example (Papataxiarchis 1991).

The post-socialist emigration to Greece, primarily from Albania beginning in 1991, is now a key component of modern Greek history. The integration of Greek-speaking or Orthodox Christians from the region of Albania Greeks refer to as North Epirus, people collectively known as *Vóreioépirótes* or North Epirots, along with many who were lumped in with this controversial group of people, has become manifest largely in terms of the traditional capabilities in stone construction and agriculture that they possessed. As global agribusiness trends continue to threaten the viability of relatively small-scale Greek agriculture, the costs of maintaining these sometimes ancient villages and agricultural spaces have become increasingly insurmountable.[12] Because of the lack of institutional support frameworks, local farmers have sought collaboration with new migrants on their own terms. These terms have of course been somewhat exploitative from the perspective of much work in political economy (Lawrence 2007; Petrou 2005). Numerous scholars have convincingly argued that Europeans have exploited migrants living in various states of precarity by excluding them from paths to citizenship and fair wages so as to safeguard their own diminishing shares of European economic wealth. Some, such as Cheliotis and Xenakis (2016) insist that Greek state policies that create arduous asylum procedures (or no procedures at all) for the regularization of illegal migration and migrant employment are part of a larger movement to provide the country with affordable labor. This is another form of resistance to the marginalization resulting from European neoliberalism, perhaps. However, given Greece's weak scalar positioning with regard to Europe and the absence of policy support for small-scale agriculture, it is hardly surprising that rural Greeks remain largely disinterested in policy reforms that have seldom benefitted them in any substantial way and would prefer to seek to ameliorate their situations in traditional terms they have some control over.[13]

In their indifference to EU bureaucracy or in keeping with the segmentary logic of traditional Greek reciprocal relationships with "others", Greek farmers have indeed sought to take whatever advantage they can from positions that are superior to those of non-Greeks. Nonetheless, from the outset, and increasingly as Greece's relationship within the EU has become more tenuous and subsequent

migration waves from Africa, South Asia, and the Middle East inform reactions to the earlier migrations (Papadapoulos & Fratsea 2013), we see ethnic rapprochement that I now consider part of a rural solidarity movement, one that puts local residents of multiple ethnicities in more horizontal relationships with one another. Solidarity networks in small cities like Sparta and the surrounding countryside in Laconia, as opposed to [global] cities that have a critical mass of migrants or more absolute breaks in socio-economic safety nets (such as that between urban Greeks and their agricultural pasts), exhibit diverse hierarchies and forms of identification with and incorporation of immigrants. A shared familiarity with certain aspects of the Mediterranean landscape, climate, fruits, and soils is being discovered, for example. Rural Greek villages and landscapes are being reterritorialized or reappropriated by this quasi-coalition to reestablish *convivéncia*. In other words, rural solidarity movements, while never so egalitarian, contest the simplistic view of migrant exploitation. The case of Lurka D. related by Vassilis Nitsiakos (2003), a portrayal of an Albanian man who has become "like a son" to a man whose own son has emigrated abroad, or the many accounts that I have made of non-Greeks who have become farmers in their own rights (Verinis 2015), some of whom I revisit below, are testimonies to this.

One of the ways that I came to realize this coalition or movement, albeit inherently quasi or informal (not easily identified as Castells, Caraça and Cardoso put it, 2012), was through the process of evaluating the potential during fieldwork in 2016 for official state rural development policy to address the incorporation of immigrants in rural development programs as has happened in the USA for example. All local Greek farmers, non-Greek farmers, Laconian municipal agronomists, and officials from rural development programs such as the Greek Young Farmer Program I spoke with, along with the secretary general at the Greek Ministry of Rural Development and Food in Athens himself (a well-known rural sociologist), deflected, seemed bewildered by, or just plain ignored my queries about the potential for such policy initiatives. My exasperation eventually gave way to a realization that, for all parties, the point is to avoid official policy. In light of the fact that EU or state politics are not seen as capable of addressing the difficulties small-scale farmers face or the plight of immigrants, let alone simultaneously, it is better to simply avoid policy approaches altogether. This resistance is hardly a neat opposition, in *medias res* perhaps, but it is ubiquitous.

As with the seemingly arbitrary nature of food movements or rural networks, to label this significant resistance might seem like somewhat of an academic stretch. Papataxiarchis (2016) asks us to consider the irony of identifying a set of "solidarity" movements in a place traditionally segmentary, its people in generally agonistic if not altogether antagonistic relations with one another. Agricultural cooperatives that dominated the social, political, and economic landscapes of rural Greece between the Ottoman period and the 1990s have become largely ineffectual except for a few cases such as the fruit cooperative of Naoussa in northern Greece or the cooperative of olive oil producers in Kritsa, Crete. Similarly, successful small anonymous corporations (S.A.s) such as Kefalas Sparti and Bläuel Greek Organic Food Products, both of which produce primarily olives and olive oil in Laconia prefecture, are relatively few. In the absence of any formal or even traditional way to align horizontally with anyone in particular so as to withstand global economic forces that threaten the survival of small and cooperative endeavors (threats in the form of rural stigma and depopulation as well as cheap Argentine lemons or high quality olive oil from California), alternative relationships develop between Greeks and long-standing non-Greek residents, as they become kin through marriage and baptism, engage in reciprocal relations, and share community life in general. As Greeks and non-Greeks participate alongside each other in these agricultural endeavors, in the *agonía* or struggle of contemporary rural Greek life, they share and exchange sensual relationships which enculturate, reevaluate, and reposition them as participants in the production of new memories.[14]

Visiting with some of my most evocative non-Greek farmer interlocutors in Laconia in 2016 strengthened my convictions that food and agriculture continue to bring Greek residents into such significant relations with one another. Of course immigrant residents in Greece have certainly fallen on hard times. Stefanos and Fotini, Bulgarians who have lived in Skoura – a village less than ten kilometers southeast of Sparta – for decades, have given up running the *kafeneío* they had run during the years of my dissertation fieldwork, that which had placed them at the center of village life. Their two children have also since moved back to Bulgaria despite having spent most of their lives in Greece. Yet Stefanos and Fotini refuse to leave their adopted home and have consequently put all of their energies into their beekeeping and olive farming endeavors. In these hard times, they have reinvested in traditional small-scale agriculture much like their Greek neighbors.

Albanian Lefteris is in a comparable position. Noteworthy are the ways he now conspires with local Greeks in order to frighten neighboring Roma away from his fields, in the Laconian village of Asteri, by allowing the Roma to think, as the police suggested to him, that he is a "dangerous Albanian".[15] While this tool is a by-product of an exploitive relationship in which Lefteris would normally suffer, Albanians such as Lefteris now wield some of these conspiratorial tools along with Greeks for their own benefit. What is more, the conspiracy is arguably reminiscent of traditional Greek agonistic relations between segmented groups. All of this complicates a standard political economy approach to Pierre Bourdieu's "flexploitation" (1998: 85).[16]

Mitsos continues to farm olives in nearby Zoupena with the same fervor since first arriving from Albania more than twenty-five years ago. As with Lefteris and other "non-Greeks" I farmed with between 2008 and 2010, Mitsos' children were born in Greece. Despite the fact that Mitsos is not generally considered to be Vóreioépirótis, his exceptional charm and extended family ties (through baptisms in the Greek Orthodox church necessitating Greek godfathers and godmothers, school friends of his children, and so on) have helped him to participate in all sorts of collaborations with local Greek families. He continues to sell his olives directly to merchants at the Greek supermarket chain Promithefitkí. In a somewhat uncanny way, Mitsos displays the kind of Greek hospitality or *philoxenía* that ethnographers of Greece have long written of, showering other members of his *paréa* with copious amounts of coffee and cigarettes (as always, he insisted I take *tenakéthes* – 17 liter tins – of his olive oil home with me after my last visit in 2016). While this can be seen as mere mimicry of Greek mannerism, it disrupts as much as it reinforces traditional segmentary reciprocal relations.

Mitsos admitted that some Albanians have left as the economic downturn has become a true crisis over the last few years. Yet, as he told me, not one of the dozen or so Albanians that I had worked with and whom Mitsos knew well have left their respective homes in Laconia. And while Mitsos did agree that it has become harder to buy land from Greek landowners, he had recently bought more in order to reinvest in his farm operations.

As had been the case in previous years, Greeks would often go out of their way to explain to me how they knew Mitsos in 2016. One morning an older Greek man from Zoupena named Pandelis proudly pointed out that he has known Mitsos since the day he arrived from Albania. Pandelis made sure to explain to me in a *kafetéria* one afternoon what an exceptional "Albanian" Mitsos is. Critical analysis may normally interpret this descriptor as divisive. Using the phrase *o Alvanós mou* ('my Albanian') has been a common exclusionary strategy for decades now, but it also sets a kinship boundary line between one family's "Albanian" (worker or *koumbáros* [relative through baptism or marriage]) from the "hordes" of Albanians that "poured" through the borders in the early 1990s. Pandelis' description is hardly inclusive of Albanians in one sense. And yet, in keeping with traditional Greek agonistic relations between family farms, it is quite inclusive indeed.[17]

Another window deeper into the relationship Mitsos and Pandelis share opened during a discussion that followed. In response to Mitsos' questions about the old man's overall wellbeing, Pandelis began to describe recent problems he had had in passing a kidney stone. Mitsos instructed him, in some detail, how to make a tea from the stomach of a chicken so as to facilitate relief. As Albanians have long had less access to Western biomedicine, Greeks now rely on Albanians for alternative therapies during these desperate financial times. Beyond the obvious depth of their relationship, the exchange of this traditional rural remedy is indicative of a larger set of responsibilities to share essential goods that rural Greek residents of various ethno-nationalities now feel toward each other. Pandelis complained about how long it would take to get an appointment to see his doctor as well as the "useless" pills that he had already been given and listened intently to the young Albanian's prescription.

Individual rural families and business-owners are incorporating non-Greeks of myriad ethnonational backgrounds into their personal and professional lives in the abovementioned ways. They become godparents of immigrant children and sell local non-Greeks portions of their farms, as opposed to Athenians whom they essentially see as absentee landlords, so as to establish sustainable face-to-face socio-economic safety nets in local terms. These Greeks and non-Greeks are in a somewhat novel relationship, to the extent that they conspire to benefit each other for the first time in modern Greek history. And yet the ways that they conspire are historically particular and local. At times now it can be a non-Greek who facilitates or conjures the Greek senses of philoxenía, paréa, allilegíi, and even *philótimo* – the dominant Greek value of experiencing and valuing oneself as part of a system of group relatedness. Whether it is considered a solidarity network or movement, these new rural relations have much to do with other communitarian coalitions that have garnered the attention of social scientists in the past few years. They revolve around many of the same ethical dilemmas that urban solidarians have concerned themselves with and are predicated upon many of the same beliefs and practices that food solidarity movements are predicated upon – mutual subsistence, the sharing of responsibilities, a reformulation of social hierarchies, and resistance to neoliberal Europe.

Conclusion

New solidarities are inherent to capitalist procedures in difficult financial periods. Of course the new solidarities I discuss in this paper – forms of reliance on kin networks, neighbors, neighborhood, or village – are reminiscent of many forms of reciprocal relations in the Greek past. Yet a culture of indifference and cynicism with regard to the bureaucracy of EU technocracy has grown since the state's incorporation in 1981 into the EU federation (Herzfeld 1992). Reliance on each other has taken on sometimes uncanny forms in order to fulfill social as well as somatic needs. The financial crisis has encouraged this reliance on historical, cultural patterns as well as a new collection of participants.

The relationship I describe between various kinds of food movements is also a proper Greek *topos*. Yoghurting, a form of public critique born in the 1950s – throwing sheep's milk yoghurt on people, typically politicians in order to shame them for being corrupt and the antithesis of the "honorable" Greek peasant – has again become a form of critique of urban (read non-Greek) values (Sutton et al. 2013). An academic consideration of yoghurting, or the networks and movements described in this paper, not only draws together the Greek urban and rural in ideological as well as materialistic ways. It brings to light the expanded significance food now enjoys vis-à-vis EU austerity, global migration patterns, the refugee crisis, technocracy, concerns about bioengineering, and other "trouble spots" particular to the twenty-first century.

In these different solidarity food movements we see networks emerge around one group, be they migrant non-Greeks or disenfranchised Greeks or refugees, and inevitably they have come to include others, as in the case of the social kitchen El Chef (initially focused on Greek relationships with migrants) and O Állos Anthrópos (which has recently extended itself to the island of Lesbos or Mytilene to commune with refugees there). Instances of rapprochement, between Greeks and non-Greeks, rich and poor, and producers and consumers crystallize as people share food and drink at social kitchens, conspire together to support each other's traditional rural ways of life, or share pride in being able to provide each other with food and thus without the need for charity in traditional food markets.

Historical as well as present-day ethnic entrepreneurism should certainly be considered (Dimen-Schein 1975; Glick-Schiller 2008). Mark Granovetter (1973) argues that communities that continue to rely upon strong ties of kinship and ethnicity will lock themselves in economically stagnant enclaves. This prognosis, in the light of a crisis of capitalism as well as a global migration crisis, invites scholars to investigate supposed "weak" ties of friendship and trust – how and when they might become extended or "strong", even transcending social hierarchies and expectations of reciprocation. As we speak of flexploitation but also begin to think about the myriad other opportunities that also emerge in the form of new social flexibilities to recapture social capital, we should consider whether or not this is "our father's" ethnic entrepreneurism. Ethnic entrepreneurism includes the exploitation of others but can also include significant co-ethnic rapprochement. Kin and ethnic boundaries reveal themselves as having quite a few permutations in some cases. Possibilities for social development that focuses on this "new" Greek social capital as opposed to financial capital may become more visible if ethnic entrepreneurism is considered for all that it is. Otherwise we not only reify ethnicity as something beyond the tool that it is, as Dimen-Schein warns, but we lose opportunities to use it in order to socially organize in a diversity of ways.

These are the potentialities in Anna Tsing's "seams" or "patches" of empire. People seek to survive certain unprecedented and destructive forms of modernity. Alliances that may seem incidental to larger forces must be investigated. As Anastasia Karakasidou has written: "In the new millennium, it is certain that cancer strikes Greeks and Slavs, Vlachs and Gypsies, Christians and Muslims indiscriminately" (2011: 396). Fertilizers, mono-cropping, and pesticides have made whole swaths of enemies, regardless of their ethno-national identities, religions, and political statuses. Resilience, in ecological, social, economic, cultural, and even in evolutionary terms, is now sought in emergent solidarities – sites of new belonging and ethical concerns (Bourdieu, in Vidali 2015: 195). Though hardly utopic, these are ubiquitous beginnings in the amelioration of socioeconomic problems that all kinds of people currently face.

One set of destructive forms of modernity is made up of contemporary problems many Greek people face in growing, distributing, obtaining, cooking, and eating food. I believe that identifying a set of food solidarity movements or networks has the potential to address these problems and contribute to broad theories of Greek "solidarity" as part of a postmodern or post-colonial Greek history as well as anthropological theories of the European Mediterranean, which is increasingly affected by global migrations. In the case of my fieldwork amongst Greek and non-Greek farmers begun in 2008 as well as in this more recent fieldwork period, a motley crew of Greeks increasingly seem to share kéfi with one

Ill. 1: A contemporary collection of Greek residents conspire to subsist in central Athens. (Photo: James Verinis, 2016)

another. Kéfi, which again is 'good humor' or 'good life', is premised on a disregard for social hierarchies and actions that might be in any way construed as gifts (Rozakou 2016). Kéfi evolves outside of official political policies and capitalist markets. The world of obligations in traditionally agonistic Greek life also gives way in kéfi to other forms of sociality, expanding other culturally specific notions such as philoxenía or paréa. As Greek residents, including even some relatively recently arrived economic migrants and political refugees, attempt to reconstruct the village or horió or some other form of community, in urban as well as rural places, the transcendent kéfi is at play. Non-Greeks such as Mitsos have done a great deal to reinvigorate this specific form of solidarity. He and other non-Greek farmers I have worked with have now also become key to my thinking about new exchanges of essential goods taking place in new food solidarity movements that complicate the rural–urban and Greek–non-Greek dichotomies. Is kéfi a way for scholars to comprehend relationships in Greece that do not technically exist? That question is perhaps best discussed over a meal.

Notes

1 Fieldwork in 2016 was funded by an Engaged Anthropology Grant from the Wenner-Gren Foundation.

2 The Greek Statistical Service (ELSTAT) reported that 133,787 Albanian nationals left Greece in 2011–2012. Similarly, the Greek Social Security Fund (IKA) reported that the number of Albanian nationals insured in 2009 reached 121,902, while at the end of 2013 the number decreased to 85,893.

3 The post-socialist 1990s ushered in the first pronounced immigration to Greece in nearly seventy years, since over one million Greeks from Asia Minor had been repatriated in the 1923 Treaty of Lausanne.

4 A 1991 Commission of the European Communities (CEC) paper entitled "The development and future of the Common Agricultural Policy," insists that despite abandonment, agriculture remains highly significant in a number of ways; "Sufficient numbers of farmers must be kept on the land. There is no other way to preserve the natural environment, traditional landscapes, and a model of agriculture based on the family farm as favored by society generally." Yet things have not borne out in ways reflective of this policy. A study conducted by the Technical College of Agricultural Engineers in Madrid found that the smallest olive plantations in the

southern EU member states, those which were the most favorable to the health of local ecosystems, suffered a net annual loss of 402.50 euro per hectare while the farms that had the most negative impact had an annual profit of 1,378 per hectare (Euromed 2008).

5 Daniel Knight has written that Greeks now flock to cafés and restaurants in a defiant refusal to play the role of the downtrodden poor (2015: 121–131, in Herzfeld 2016: 202).

6 Dimitris Theodossopoulos (2016) explores ideological dispositions toward such charitable organizations in the contemporary Greek context, particularly amongst members of the communist party – the KKE – in Patras.

7 While it takes only 2.5 hours to get from Athens to Sparta today, it was close to double less than ten years ago.

8 Peliti, Greece's most well-known exchange network of landrace, indigenous, and unmodified seed, launched its first "Solidarity Caravan for Seed" across Europe in the Spring of 2016 to help establish an association between cultural and seed diversity.

9 Axarnon 78 is also sometimes referred to as the Athens City Plaza Hotel. As a former hotel, it is remarkable that it is now a refugee squat, but also remarkable is the fact that it is not dilapidated like other squats in the city. This contributes to the fact that it has retained its former identity to an extent.

10 A social geographer named Thomas Maloutas at Harokopeio University in Athens has developed a new social atlas that, amongst other things, overlays homelessness with vacant buildings scattered all over the city in keeping with solidarian ideals.

11 On August 24, 2016, Notara 26 was burned beyond repair by arsonists with incendiary devices.

12 Greek agriculture, along with other Mediterranean countries, does not fair relatively well in comparison to the intensive production regimes of more central and northern European countries such as the Netherlands (Van der Ploeg 2003, 2008).

13 Laconia is a particularly peripheral Greek prefecture, one of the least favored areas (LFAs) in Greece. It consistently has some of the lowest national rankings in such terms as unemployment, savings, and income (Verinis 2015: 187). Its relationship to other Greek prefectures is reflective of Greece's relationship to other EU member countries.

14 Nadia Seremetakis (1994: 144) describes such sensorial relationships as "exchanges of feeling", which are more than merely secondary to Raymond Williams' "structures of feeling".

15 See Bakalaki (2003) on the origins of an "Albanophobia", which emerged as the borders between Albania and Greece opened in 1991.

16 That Lefteris and his wife Dora have become Greek citizens since I last saw them in 2012 is beside the point perhaps, yet this does also complicate simplistic understandings of ethnic marginalization in recent social science literature on Greece.

17 That [rural] Greece does not subscribe to the exact kinds of political correctness typically found in the [urban] United States with regard to talk about race or ethnicity is certainly an important point to consider. In reminding me how to get to his house, Stefanos suggested with no hint of sarcasm that I simply ask where Stefanos "the Bulgarian" lives. In fact, like all the non-Greeks I knew, I referred to people's ethno-nationalities after their first names beside their phone numbers in my mobile phone.

References

Al Jazeera 2012: People and Power: Greece – the Odyssey. *Al Jazeera*, December 27.

Angelopoulos, Georgios 2016: Ex Nihilo Fit: On the Greek Crisis. In: *Greece is Burning*. Cultural Anthropology Series. April 21.

Arampatzi, Athina 2016: The Spatiality of Counter-Austerity Politics in Athens, Greece: Emergent "Urban Solidarity Spaces". *Urban Studies* 54:9, 2155–2171.

Bakalaki, Alexandra 2003: Locked into Security, Keyed into Modernity: The Selection of Burglaries as Source of Risk in Greece. *Ethnos* 68:2, 209–229.

Du Boulay, Juliet 1991: Strangers and Gifts: Hostility and Hospitality in Rural Greece. *Journal of Mediterranean Studies* 1:1, 37–53.

Bourdieu, Pierre 1998: *On Television*. New York: The New Press.

Cabot, Heath 2015: The Banality of Solidarity. *Occasional Papers, Modern Greek Studies Association, Journal of Modern Greek Studies* 7.

Cabot, Heath 2016: "Contagious" Solidarity: Reconfiguring Care and Citizenship in Greece's Social Clinics. *Social Anthropology* 24:2, 152–166.

Campbell, John 1964: *Honour, Family and Patronage: A Study of Institutions and Moral Values in a Greek Mountain Community*. Oxford: Clarendon Press.

Castells, Manuel, João Caraça & Gustavo Cardoso 2012: *Aftermath: The Cultures of the Economic Crisis*. Oxford: University Press.

Cheliotis, Leonidas K. & Sappho Xenakis 2016: Punishment and Political Systems: State Punitiveness in Post-dictatorial Greece. *Punishment & Society* 18:3, 268–300.

Cockburn, Patrick 2011: How Greeks were Driven Back to the Land: Naxos Hangs on by its Fingernails. Counter Punch, http://www.unz.com/pcockburn/how-greeks-were-driven-back-to-the-land/.

Dimen-Schein, Muriel 1975: When is an Ethnic Group? Ecology and Class Structure in Northern Greece. *Ethnology* 14, 83–97.

Donadio, Rachel 2012: With Work Scarce in Athens, Greeks Go Back to the Land. *New York Times*, January 8.

Euromed Sustainable Connections 2008: Anna Lindh Foundation. Food Security and Sustainability. *Institute for Global and Community Resilience*. Huxley College of the Environment. August 7.

Glick-Schiller, Nina 2008: *Beyond Methodological Ethnicity: Local and Transnational Pathways of Immigrant Incorporation*. Willy Brandt Series of Working Papers in International Migration and Ethnic Relations 2:08.

Granovetter, Mark S. 1973: The Strength of Weak Ties. *American Journal of Sociology* 78:6, 1360–1380.

Heller, Chaia 2013: *Food, Farms, and Solidarity: French Farmers Challenge Industrial Agriculture and Genetically Modified Crops*. Durham: Duke University Press.

Herzfeld, Michael 1992: *The Social Production of Indifference: The Symbolic Roots of Bureaucracy in Western Europe*. Chicago: University of Chicago Press.

Herzfeld, Michael 2016: Critical Reactions: The Ethnographic Genealogy of Response. *Social Anthropology* 24:2, 200–204.

Karakasidou, Anastasia 2011: National Purities and Ecological Disasters: Greek Modernity and the War on Nature. *Dialectical Anthropology* 35:4, 387–401.

Kasimis, Charalambros & Stavros Zografakis 2012: "Return to the Land": Rural Greece as Refuge to Crisis. Paper presented at the XIII World Congress of Rural Sociology, Lisbon, Portugal, July 29 to August 4.

Kochilas, Diane 2010: As Goes Greek Cuisine, So Goes the Greek Economy. *Washington Post*, June 12.

Lawrence, Christopher 2007: *Blood and Oranges: Immigrant Labor and European Markets in Rural Greece*. New York & Oxford: Berghahn Books.

Loizos, Peter 1975: *The Greek Gift: Politics in a Cypriot Village*. Oxford: Blackwell.

Nelson, Arthur 2016: *The Guardian*, July 15.

Nitsiakos, Vassilis 2003: *Testimonies of Albanian Immigrants*. Athens: Odysseas [in Greek].

Notara 26 2016: Accessed July 21, http://www.notara26.info.

Papadapoulos, Apostolos G. & Loukia Maria Fratsea 2013: Between Insecurity and Integration: Sub-Saharan African Migrants in Crisis-Stricken Greece. *Regions Magazine* 289:1, 5–9.

Papataxiarchis, Evthymios 1991: Friends of the Heart: Male Commensal Solidarity, Gender, and Kinship in Aegean Greece. In: Peter Loizos & Evthymios Papataxiarchis (eds.), *Contested Identities: Gender and Kinship in Modern Greece*. Princeton: Princeton University Press.

Papataxiarchis, Evthymios 2016: Unwrapping Solidarity? Society Reborn in Austerity. *Social Anthropology* 24:2, 205–210.

Petridou, Evangelia 2001: Milk Ties: A Commodity Chain Approach to Greek Culture. Ph.D. diss., University College London.

Petrou, Michalis 2005: Immigrants, Agricultural Work, and Producers: Cultural Particularities and the Journey of Symbiotic Relations in a Rural Community [Μεταναστες, Γεωργικη Εργασια, και Παραγωγοι: Πολιτισμικες Ιδιαιτεροτητες και το οδιπορικο των Συμβιωτικων Σχεσεων σε μια Κοινοτιτα]. In: Αγροτικη Κοινωνια και Λαικος Πολιτισμος: Επιστημονικο Συνεδριο στην Μνημη το Σταθη Δαμιανακου. Athens, May 25–27.

Petrou, Michalis 2012: Rural Immigration, Family Farm Modernisation and Reactivation of Traditional Women's Farming Tasks in Greece: Masculinities and Femininities Reconsidered. *South European Society and Politics* 17:4, 553–571.

van der Ploeg, Jan Douwe 2003: *The Virtual Farmer: Past, Present and Future of the Dutch Peasantry*. The Netherlands: Royal Van Gorcum B.V.

van der Ploeg, Jan Douwe 2008: *The New Peasantries: Struggles for Autonomy and Sustainability in an Era of Empire and Globalization*. London: Earthscan.

Ragkos, Athanasios, Stavriani Koutsou & Theodoros Manousidis 2016: In Search of Strategies to Face the Economic Crisis: Evidence from Greek Farms. *South European Society and Politics* 21:3, 319–337.

Rakopoulos, Theodoros 2014: The Crisis Seen from Below, Within, and Against: From Solidarity Economy to Food Distribution Cooperatives in Greece. *Dialectical Anthropology* 38:2, 189–207.

Rakopoulos, Theodoros 2016a: Solidarity, Ethnography, and the De-instituting of Dissent. *Occasional Papers. Modern Greek Studies Association, Journal of Modern Greek Studies* 7.

Rakopoulos, Theodoros 2016b: Solidarity: The Egalitarian Tensions of a Bridge-concept. *Social Anthropology* 24:2, 142–151.

Ray, Christopher 2000: Editorial. The EU LEADER Programme: Rural Development Laboratory. *Sociologia Ruralis* 40:2, 163–171.

Rozakou, Katerina 2016: Socialities of Solidarity: Revisiting the Gift Taboo in Times of Crises. *Social Anthropology* 24:2, 185–199.

Schönberger, Klaus 2015: Digitale Kommunikation: Persistenz und Rekombination als Modus des soziokulturellen Wandels. Theoretische Begriffsarbeit in empirischer Absicht. In: Thomas Hengartner (ed.), *Kulturwissenschaftliche Technikforschung III*. Zürich.

Scott, David 1977: *The Moral Economy of the Peasant: Rebellion and Subsistence in Southeast Asia*. New Haven: Yale University Press.

Seremetakis, Nadia (ed.) 1994: *The Senses Still: Perception and Memory as Material Culture in Modernity*. Boulder: Westview Press.

Suárez-Navaz, Liliana 2005: *Rebordering the Mediterranean: Boundaries of Citizenship in Southern Europe*. New York: Berghahn Books.

Sutton, David 2014: *Secrets from the Greek Kitchen: Cooking,*

Skill, and Everyday Life on an Aegean Island. Oakland: University of California Press.

Sutton, David, Nefissa Naguib, Leonidas Vournelis & Maggie Dickinson 2013: Food and Contemporary Protest Movements. *Food, Culture & Society* 16:3, 345–366.

Terkessidis, Mark 2015: *Kollaboration.* Berlin: Suhrkamp.

Theodossopoulos, Dimitris 2016: Philanthropy or Solidarity? Ethical Dilemmas about Humanitarianism in Crisis-afflicted Greece. *Social Anthropology* 24:2, 167–184.

Thompson, E.P. 1971: The Moral Economy of the English Crowd in the Eighteenth Century. *Past and Present* 50, 76–136.

Tsing, Anna Lowenhaupt 2012: Unruly Edges: Mushrooms as Companion Species for Donna Haraway. *Environmental Humanities* 1:1, 141–154.

Verinis, James P. 2015: The Black Swans of Greece's Global Countrysides: Post-socialist Immigrant Farmers, Small Greek Farms, Integration, and [under] Development. Ph.D. diss., State University of New York at Binghamton.

Vernier, Bernard 1984: Putting Kinship to Good Use: The Circulation of Goods, Labour, and Names on Karpathos. In: Hans Medick & David Warren Sabean (eds.), *Interest and Emotion: Essays on the Study of Family and Kinship.* Cambridge & New York: Cambridge University Press.

Vidali, Maria 2015: Sustainable Landscape and Community on the Greek Island of Tinos. *European Journal of Sustainable Development* 4:2, 195.

Wanshel, Elyse 2016: *Huffington Post*, May 10.

James P. Verinis, Ph.D., is a cultural anthropologist whose research, conducted primarily in Greece and surrounding parts of South-Eastern Europe, has focused on ethno-national identity, the revival of the modern Olympic Games, immigration, agriculture, food, and the environment. He is currently adjunct professor of anthropology at Roger Williams University and Salve Regina University in Rhode Island, USA.

(jverinis@gmail.com)

JEECA

Journal for European Ethnology and Cultural Analysis

edited by Alexa Färber,
Irene Götz, Ina Merkel,
Johannes Moser and
Friedemann Schmoll
on behalf of the
**Deutsche Gesellschaft
für Volkskunde**

ISSN 2511-2473

MORE INFORMATION ON
waxmann.com/jeeca

JEECA
2017/1

Journal for European Ethnology
and Cultural Analysis

Ove Sutter
"Welcome!"
The emotional politics of voluntary work
with refugees

**Martina Klausner, Milena D. Bister,
Jörg Niewöhner, Stefan Beck (†)**
Choreographies of clinical and urban everyday
life. Results of a co-laborative ethnography
with social psychiatry

Konrad J. Kuhn
Networks, identity politics, and a narrative
of distinction. On the knowledge-historical
relations between "völkisch" and Swiss
Folklore Studies (Volkskunde)

Sebastian Mohr, Rolf Lindner
Learning to get involved with people:
a conversation with Rolf Lindner about the
ethnographer's fear of the field

WAXMANN

Issue 1/2017

Ove Sutter

"Welcome!"
The emotional politics of voluntary work with refugees

Martina Klausner, Milena D. Bister, Jörg Niewöhner, Stefan Beck (†)

Choreographies of clinical and urban everyday life.
Results of a co-laborative ethnography with social psychiatry

Konrad J. Kuhn

Networks, identity politics, and a narrative of distinction.
On the knowledge-historical relations between "völkisch" and
Swiss Folklore Studies (Volkskunde)

Sebastian Mohr, Rolf Lindner

Learning to get involved with people: a conversation with Rolf Lindner
about the ethnographer's fear of the field

WAXMANN

Steinfurter Str. 555   Fon +49 (0)2 51 – 2 65 04-0   info@waxmann.com
48159 Münster   Fax +49 (0)2 51 – 2 65 04-26   www.waxmann.com
Germany